THE UNITED STATES NAVY
IN WORLD WAR II

OSPREY
PUBLISHING

THE UNITED STATES NAVY
IN WORLD WAR II

FROM PEARL HARBOR TO OKINAWA

MARK E. STILLE

OSPREY PUBLISHING
Bloomsbury Publishing Plc
Kemp House, Chawley Park, Cumnor Hill, Oxford
OX2 9PH, UK
29 Earlsfort Terrace, Dublin 2, Ireland
1385 Broadway, 5th Floor, New York, NY 10018,
USA
E-mail: info@ospreypublishing.com
www.ospreypublishing.com

OSPREY is a trademark of Osprey Publishing Ltd

First published in Great Britain in 2021

In the compilation of this volume we relied on the
following previously published Osprey titles: NVG
114: *US Navy Aircraft Carriers 1922–45*, NVG 118:
US Submarines 1939–45, NVG 130: *US Navy
Aircraft Carriers 1942–45*, NVG 162: *US Destroyers
1934–45*, NVG 165: *US Destroyers 1942–45*, NVG
169: *US Fast Battleships 1936–47*, NVG 172: *US Fast
Battleships 1938–9*, NVG 208: *US Navy Dreadnoughts
1914–45*, NVG 210: *US Heavy Cruisers 1941–45*,
NVG 214: *US Heavy Cruisers 1943–75*, NVG 220:
US Standard-type Battleships 1941–45 (1), NVG 229:
US Standard-type Battleships 1941–45 (2), NVG 236:
US Navy Light Cruisers 1941–45, NVG 251:
US Navy Escort Carriers 1942–45, and NVG 259:
US Flush-Deck Destroyers 1916–45.

Artwork previously published in NVG 114 (pp. 69,
70, 75, and 79), NVG 118 (pp. 259, 265, 268, and
272), NVG 130 (pp. 90, 92, 93, and 99), NVG 162
(pp. 231, 234, and 238), NVG 165 (pp. 243, 246,
249, and 253), NVG 169 (pp. 147 and 150), NVG
172 (p. 156), NVG 208 (p. 121), NVG 210 (pp.
169, 173, 176, and 181), NVG 214 (pp. 191 and
195), NVG 220 (pp. 125, 130, 133, and 135),
NVG 229 (136, 139, and 141), NVG 236 (pp. 205,
209, 214, and 219), NVG 251 (pp. 105, 107, and
110), NVG 259 (p. 229), and RAID 26: Tora! Tora!
Tora! (p. 31).

Maps by Bounford.com, previously published in
CAM 214: *The Coral Sea 1942* (pp. 16 and 36),
CAM 226: *Midway 1942* (p. 38), CAM 255: *The
naval battles for Guadalcanal 1942* (p. 42), CAM
313: *The Philippine Sea 1944* (p. 50).

Contents page image: *Bon Homme Richard*, the last
Essex-class carrier completed in time to see wartime
service. (Naval History and Heritage Command)

A catalog record for this book is available from the
British Library.

ISBN: HB 978 1 4728 4804 8;
eBook 978 1 4728 4803 1;
ePDF 978 1 4728 4806 2;
XML 978 1 4728 4805 5

21 22 23 24 25   10 9 8 7 6 5 4 3 2 1

Index by Zoe Ross
Printed and bound in India by Replika Press Private
Ltd.

Osprey Publishing supports the Woodland Trust,
the UK's leading woodland conservation charity.

To find out more about our authors and books visit
www.ospreypublishing.com. Here you will find
extracts, author interviews, details of forthcoming
events and the option to sign up for our newsletter.

CONTENTS

INTRODUCTION

Even before the first Japanese bomb fell on Pearl Harbor, the United States Navy (USN) was at war. On September 4, 1939, President Roosevelt instituted a security zone in the western Atlantic and ordered the USN to conduct the so-called Neutrality Patrol within it. This was anything but neutral since its primary purpose was to report the presence of German units so that the Royal Navy (RN) could take appropriate actions. Invariably, this led to friction and finally combat between German and American naval forces. On April 10, 1941, destroyer *Niblack* reported attacking a submarine contact with depth charges off Iceland. Though this attack was mounted on a false contact, it demonstrated that American naval units were prepared to engage German forces. In July, the USN dispatched a 25-ship task force to occupy Iceland. This was the first USN task force to see foreign service during the war.

The undeclared naval war with Germany heated up on September 4, 1941 when destroyer *Greer* gained contact on a German submarine and dropped depth charges. The U-boat retaliated by firing two torpedoes, but both missed. From this point, USN units were given permission to shoot first at Axis units operating in the security zone. Since the USN was now escorting convoys across the Atlantic to a point south of Iceland, another clash was inevitable. The Germans drew first blood on October 17 when destroyer *Kearny* was hit by a submarine-launched torpedo. Eleven sailors were killed and 22 wounded. Only days later, on October 23, destroyer *Reuben James* was torpedoed and sunk by a German U-boat with 100 men lost.

Despite these incidents, the American public had no appetite for entering the war. Events in Europe had also failed to stir the American public into the realization that America could not remain neutral forever. In June 1940, France surrendered to Germany, leaving the United

The Washington Naval Conference and Five-Power Treaty, 1921–22

Between 1921 and 1922, the world's largest naval powers gathered in Washington DC to negotiate naval disarmament. Nine separate nations took part in the conference. Great Britain, Japan, France, and Italy were invited to take part in talks on reducing naval capacity, while Belgium, China, Portugal, and the Netherlands were invited to join in discussions on the situation in the Far East. Three major treaties emerged out of the Washington Naval Conference: the Five-Power Treaty (regarding warship tonnage), the Four-Power Treaty (focusing on future crises in East Asia), and the Nine-Power Treaty (acknowledging the territorial integrity of China).

The Five-Power Treaty, signed by the United States, Great Britain, Japan, France, and Italy, called for each of the countries involved to maintain a set ratio of warship tonnage.

The United States and Great Britain were restricted to 500,000 tons of capital ships, Japan 300,000 tons, and France and Italy each 175,000 tons. The United States and Great Britain were allowed an increased tonnage because they maintained navies in both the Pacific and Atlantic oceans to support their colonial territories. The treaty also called on all five signatories to stop building capital ships and reduce the size of their navies by scrapping older ships. Tonnage limits were also set for aircraft carriers.

Some classes of ships were left unrestricted. As a result, a new race to build cruisers emerged after 1922, leading the five nations to return to the negotiating table in Geneva in 1927 and London in 1930 in an effort to close the remaining loopholes in the Treaty.

Kingdom alone. The potential danger was evident to Congress which on July 19 passed the Two-Ocean Navy Act to provide for the defense of the United States and the Western Hemisphere. This was the largest naval appropriation in US history. It authorized the building of a fleet almost equal in size to the entire Imperial Japanese Navy (IJN) – 18 aircraft carriers, 7 battleships, 33 cruisers, 115 destroyers, 43 submarines, and 15,000 aircraft. This constituted a 70 percent increase in the size of the USN and it provided the bedrock for the USN's eventual victory in the war.

From the USN's very uncertain beginning conducting the Neutrality Patrol, entry into World War II came in an unexpected and what seemed a disastrous manner. The Roosevelt Administration had reacted to Japan's continued and brutal aggression in the Far East with a series of economic reprisals. Feeling the pressure, and with European possessions in Asia ripe for the taking after the surrender of France and the Netherlands and the United Kingdom unable to properly defend its possessions while fighting a war in Europe against Germany and Italy, Japan decided to fight its way out of the developing economic stranglehold. The only force capable of defeating Japan's expanded vision of aggression was the USN's Pacific Fleet based at Pearl Harbor in the Hawaiian Islands. Since the USN had to defend American interests in two oceans, the IJN possessed an edge in the Pacific, particularly in naval air power, both land and carrier based. This window of opportunity was small since construction of the Two-Ocean Navy was already under way. The table below illustrates the strength of the two principal Pacific naval powers at the dawn of war on December 7, 1941.

USN and IJN Naval Forces December 7, 1941					
	IJN	USN			
		Pacific Fleet	Asiatic Fleet	Atlantic Fleet	Total
SHIP TYPE					
Carriers					
Fleet	6	3	0	4	7
Light	3	0	0	0	0
Escort	1	1	0	1	2
Battleships					
Modernized	10	9	0	6	15
New	0	0	0	2	2
Heavy Cruisers	18	12	1	5	18
Light Cruisers	17	9	2	8	19
Destroyers					
Old	33	21	13	36	70
New	69	45	0	52	97
Submarines					
Old	31	6	6	43	55
New	32	21	23	5	49

The table also shows the considerable proportion of the USN's strength that was deployed in the Atlantic at the start of the war. This was due in large part to the transfer of significant portions of the Pacific Fleet earlier in 1941 to reinforce the Neutrality Patrol.

The USN expected the war to begin when it did, but it failed to anticipate the way that it began. When the Japanese struck Pearl Harbor on December 7, 1941 with all six of its fleet carriers, it caught all but one of the Pacific Fleet's battleships in port. In only a few minutes, five USN battleships were sunk or placed out of action for a prolonged period. Since all three USN carriers were absent, along with most of the modern cruisers, the Pacific Fleet's capability to conduct operations was not as severely reduced as is usually portrayed. The basic problem inhibiting USN early war operations in the Pacific was an overall numerical inferiority. The lack of battleships was not a serious impediment, since the attack on Pearl Harbor had demonstrated their limited capabilities in the new type of warfare about to rage across the Pacific.

The small Asiatic Fleet was unable to defend the Philippines and by early March 1942 was routed. This was expected, but what was not expected was the IJN's ability to conduct concurrent offensives across the Pacific. In this defensive phase of the war, which only lasted from December 1941 until

June 1942, the USN used its available strength to aggressively challenge major IJN operations. At Coral Sea in May 1942 and at Midway the following month, American naval forces stopped the Japanese advance and blunted its offensive power.

Further evidence of the aggressive mindset of the USN's senior leadership was provided in August 1942 when the USN launched its first offensive in the Pacific. The first offensive was directed at the obscure island of Guadalcanal located in the Southern Solomons where the Japanese were building an airfield. The fact that the USN was still outnumbered in every major ship category did not deter it from initiating offensive operations, nor did a very uncertain logistical support situation for such an operation. Guadalcanal was the most prolonged campaign of the war, lasting until February 1943, and it included two carrier battles and five major surface engagements. In the end, the USN emerged victorious, but it lost more major combatants during the campaign than the IJN.

The USN had been roughly handled in the night surface actions off Guadalcanal. It continued to have the same difficulties as the Allied offensive moved up the Solomons. It took until November 1943 after another six clashes for the USN to master the art of night fighting. It was also at this point that USN task forces began to be comprised of ships built entirely during the war. The IJN had fought the USN's prewar fleet to a standstill, but now it had to take on a second fleet of the USN's wartime construction.

In Europe, the USN played a larger role than is generally realized. On several occasions, the USN sent its latest warships to augment the RN's Home Fleet or to release it for other duties. The USN played the leading role in defeating the U-boat threat in the western and central Atlantic. The largest American naval contribution to Allied victory was the construction of amphibious forces capable of mounting landings around the periphery of Africa and Europe. The USN played a major role in six major amphibious operations – North Africa in November 1942, Sicily in July 1943, Salerno in

The Geneva Naval Conference, 1927

This conference saw the United States, Great Britain, and Japan discussing more expansive naval limitations. It ended in failure, however, as the parties did not reach agreement, allowing the naval arms race to continue unchecked in its wake.

The 1927 conference discussed extending the 1922 Washington Five-Power Treaty to include other classes of vessels not included in the original treaty, such as cruisers, destroyers, and submarines. France and Italy refused to participate in the conference. The United States, Great Britain, and Japan did meet in Geneva and began negotiations on the extension of naval limitations.

The United States proposed that the existing 5:5:3 ratios between the three powers be extended to include auxiliary vessels; that the maximum size of cruisers remain at less than 10,000 tons with 8-inch guns; and that the total tonnage of cruisers be limited to 400,000 for the United States and Great Britain (240,000 tons for Japan). Great Britain proposed dividing the classes of cruisers into "heavy" and "light," so that heavy cruisers did not exceed 10,000 tons, but light cruisers did not exceed 7,000. They also proposed an overall cruiser limit of 70 ships and 600,000 tons. Japan proved to be the most flexible party with regard to the cruiser limitations, but preferred that a 10:10:7 ratio be applied to auxiliary vessels, rather than the Washington Conference ratio of 5:5:3.

The talks broke down over whether "parity" should be measured based on tonnage or number of vessels. The United States preferred tonnage, while the British preferred to count the fleet. In addition, Great Britain set forth a "doctrine of requirements," which attempted to assert that the size of a nation's naval fleet should be based on what it required to defend its territory. The stalemate over the cruiser question in particular led to the conference ending without agreement.

September 1943, Anzio in January 1944, northern France in June 1944, and lastly southern France in August 1944.

Just as the Allies were landing in France, another immense operation was unfolding across the world in the Marianas. The invasion of the Marianas in June 1944 prompted the largest carrier battle in history. The result was the destruction of the IJN's carrier force as the USN displayed its mastery of carrier warfare. The other major naval battle of 1944 was also the largest one in naval history. At the Battle of Leyte Gulf, the IJN committed the entirety of its remaining strength to defeat the US invasion of the Philippines and preserve Japan's access to the resources of Southeast Asia. The result was the final destruction of Japanese sea power. The USN's proficiency of surface and carrier warfare, supported by a logistical system of unparalleled size, was on full display.

The final stage of the war offered new challenges for the USN. Foremost of these was the Japanese kamikaze threat which began in October 1944 and grew in ferocity through the Okinawa campaign from April to June 1945.

The London Naval Conferences, 1930 and 1935

After an unsuccessful conference in Geneva in 1927, Great Britain, the United States, Japan, France, and Italy gathered in London in 1930 to revise and extend the terms of the Washington Five-Power Treaty of 1922.

By 1930 both Great Britain and the United States were anxious to reach a deal to avoid an all-out arms race and forced their naval officers to take a back seat to their diplomats in the negotiations.

The restrictions on tonnage on Great Britain, the United States, and Japan relative to one another remained an important area for discussion. Japan insisted that the ratio for non-capital ships ships be increased to a proportion of 10:10:7, rather than maintaining the 5:5:3 ratio in effect for capital ships. The United States opposed this, but ultimately conceded the point; the official terms of the treaty granted the 10:7 ratio on light cruisers and destroyers and maintained the 10:6 ratio on heavy cruisers.

The maximum tonnage for light cruisers was also a key area of discussion. The United States was strongly opposed to any maximum lower than 10,000 tons, given its requirement to conduct far-ranging operations in the Pacific. It refused to yield on this issue.

The tonnage of non-capital ships was limited by the resultant London treaty, as well as the size and gun power of submarines and destroyers. The treaty also set maximum tonnage for cruisers at 339,000 tons for Great Britain, 323,500 tons for the United States, and 208,850 tons for Japan. The maximum numbers of heavy cruisers were set at 18 for America, 15 for Great Britain, and 12 for Japan. Tonnage limits were also established for destroyers and submarines and limits set for their size and armament.

In 1935, the powers met again in Londonto renegotiate the Washington and London treaties before their expiration the following year. The Japanese walked out of this conference, but Great Britain, France, and the United States signed an agreement declaring a six-year hiatus on building large light cruisers in the 8,000- to 10,000-ton range.

In the final few months of the war, the USN had mastered the kamikaze threat, at least to the point where it never curtailed or halted planned operations. With the Japanese merchant marine destroyed by the USN's submarine force, Japan was reduced to hoping it could defeat the planned Allied invasion of Japan before it was starved into submission.

Besides briefly tracing the strategy, tactics, and operations of the USN during the war, this book focuses on the ships of the USN during the war. As will be seen, the quality of American ships was generally outstanding, as were the weapons aboard them. Overall, the technical excellence of the USN's fighting platforms was unsurpassed by any foreign navy. This was undoubtedly true regarding wartime production. The USN produced the best submarine of the war in the Gato/Balao class, the best destroyers in the war in the Fletcher class, the best light cruisers in the war in the Cleveland class, and the best heavy cruisers of the war in the Baltimore class. The Essex-class carriers were the most powerful carriers of the war, and thus the most powerful ships of the war, and were the spearhead of the American advance across the Pacific. The Iowa-class battleships were the most advanced battleships ever built and, though not as heavily armed or protected as the IJN's Yamato class, were superior fighting platforms due to their superior speed and better fire-control systems, which would have likely provided them with the edge in any imaginary duel between the two most capable classes of battleship ever built. Besides producing excellent fighting ships, the USN produced them in overwhelming numbers. This combination led to final victory and placed the USN in an unassailable position as the most powerful navy in the world.

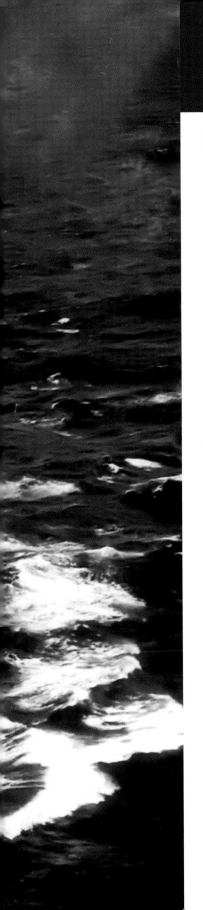

CHAPTER 1

UNITED STATES NAVAL STRATEGY AND TACTICS IN WORLD WAR II

STRATEGY IN THE WAR AGAINST JAPAN

To say the USN had a strategy and executed it to defeat Japan would be an exaggeration. The USN did have War Plan Orange (later incorporated into the Rainbow War Plans before the US entry into the war) that it used for decades as the planning basis for a war against Japan, but in the event of actual war the USN was not free to execute its strategy without reference to several other influences. The most important of these, and no doubt the most irritating to almost every USN officer who met him, was Army General Douglas MacArthur. Having survived the fall of the Philippines, he was placed in command of a large chunk of the Pacific Theater and was determined to avenge his defeat and make good his

Oklahoma leads two other battleships in a line ahead formation in this photograph from March 1930. The ships have their main batteries trained to starboard in preparation for a gunnery exercise. This was the epitome of naval power during the period and USN strategy and tactics revolved around the battleship. (Naval History and Heritage Command)

promise to return to the islands. This required an advance through the South Pacific, which was virtually the antithesis to War Plan Orange. Second in importance was the requirement to gain the acceptance of the Combined Chiefs of Staff (the military leaders of the United States and the United Kingdom) since any offensive operation in the Pacific had to comport with the agreed "Germany first" strategy. Despite the interference of MacArthur and the oversight of the British, the USN generally succeeded in fighting the war it wanted in the Pacific. In fact, after the war, several admirals remarked that the war had unfolded generally as they had practiced at the Naval War College.

War Plan Orange was the bedrock of USN planning for almost 30 years. The USN had contingency plans for several different conflicts, and each had a color that was code for a potential enemy. Orange represented Japan, which was the most likely future enemy. War Plan Orange, first drawn up in 1911, unfolded in this manner. The Japanese would attack the Philippines (then an American possession) and the American and Filipino garrison would fall back to the Bataan Peninsula where they were expected to hold out for six months. This would give the USN time to execute an advance across the Central Pacific to relieve the garrison. Such an advance required the seizure of islands along the way to provide logistical bases. The latest versions of the plan solved the logistics problem by taking Eniwetok in the Marshall Islands and Truk Atoll in the Caroline Islands. Once the proper support had been secured, the battle fleet would advance into the Philippine Sea and fight a climactic battle with the IJN. The outcome of this decisive battle would decide the war.

War Plan Orange was not just a strategic outline of how a war against Japan would be executed, it was also the touchstone for budgeting and ship design purposes. The battle fleet had to be able to execute the three phases of War Plan Orange. The entire plan was underwritten by the strength of the USN's battle fleet that would have to operate at unprecedented distances from its main base in Hawaii. As the USN's battle fleet moved into the central and western Pacific, it would have to contend with Japanese submarine and air attack before eventually gaining the opportunity to engage the IJN's battle fleet. This required that screening units be able to neutralize the submarine threat and that all fleet units possess antiaircraft capabilities to handle what was expected to be a severe air threat. To prevail in the decisive clash, USN battleships had to have superior protection and the ability to hit at long ranges. All other fleet components had a role to play in this decisive clash, as will be outlined later.

As agreed with the British as early as January 1941, overall Allied strategy focused on the defeat of Germany – the "Germany first" strategy. It was

USN Senior Leadership

The USN possessed an impressive collection of command figures at the start of the war. President Roosevelt styled himself as a Navy man and had served as Assistant Undersecretary of the Navy during World War I. The civilians who ran the Navy reported directly to him. The Secretary of the Navy oversaw a complex system of nine bureaus (later eight) which were responsible for all the aspects of running a navy. The three Secretaries of the Navy during this period, Charles Edison, Frank Knox, and James Forrestal, were extremely effective. Testimony of this was the fact the USN grew many times over from 1940 until the end of the war, becoming the world's most powerful naval force in the process.

The efficient bureaucracy was matched by an equally effective command structure. When war came, the USN was broken down into three operational entities – the Atlantic, Pacific, and Asiatic Fleets. Admiral Husband Kimmel, Commander in Chief of the Pacific Fleet, was also designated as Commander in Chief, US Fleet. Following the Pearl Harbor attack, Kimmel was relieved of his command. On December 18, 1941, the USN's command structure was altered to create a new authority based in Washington, DC to direct the Navy's global war. Admiral Ernest King was selected for this role, which also gave him a seat on the Joint Chiefs of Staff. In March 1942, he was also appointed as the Chief of Naval Operations. This gave him absolute power over the course of the USN's global operations. King immediately put his stamp on the job and demonstrated his intent to take the war to the Japanese as aggressively as possible.

Though tempted to meddle early in the war, King developed a cadre of highly competent leaders. Admiral Chester Nimitz was selected to lead the Pacific Fleet and proved an excellent choice. Nimitz shared King's innate aggressiveness and combined it with meticulous planning and execution. The Atlantic Fleet was given to Rear Admiral Royal Ingersoll who played an important, if unknown, role in fighting the German submarine threat until this was taken over by the new Tenth Fleet in May 1943. The Asiatic Fleet was under the command of Admiral Thomas Hart. This command was a backwater and was never given enough assets to carry out its main mission of defending the Philippines. After the collapse of the Allied position in Southeast Asia, the fleet was dissolved.

Admiral Nimitz (left) receiving the Distinguished Service Medal from Admiral King aboard battleship *Pennsylvania* on June 30, 1942. The award was for Nimitz's leadership of the Pacific Fleet during the battles of Coral Sea and Midway. These two men dominated USN strategy during the Pacific War. (Naval History and Heritage Command)

essential to keep the United Kingdom and the Soviet Union in the war since this was the quickest way to defeat Germany. US war plans were supposed to comply with this vision, but Admiral Ernest King did not take this to mean that he could not conduct an aggressive defense in the Pacific. Japan had to be prevented from expanding in the South Pacific to protect the sea lanes of communications (SLOC) to Australia. As far as King was concerned, the only defense was an active defense.

Strategic situation in May 1942

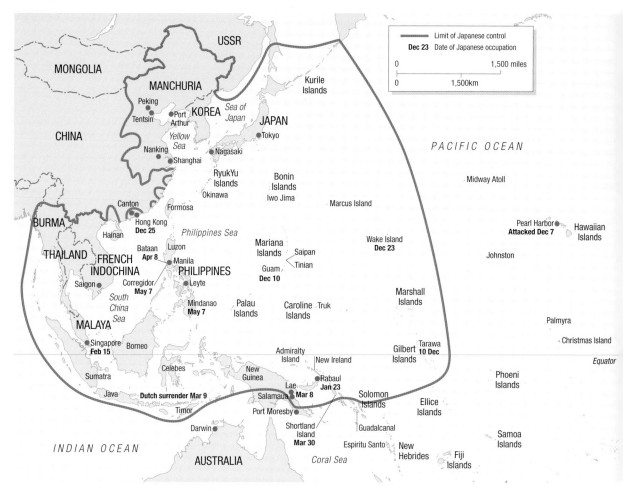

In the aftermath of Pearl Harbor, King decided to ignore the USN's sacrosanct War Plan Orange. The reasons for this were two-fold. First, the fleet built to execute it had just been decimated at Pearl Harbor. Second, events drove King in a new direction. The Japanese seizure of Rabaul on the island of New Britain in January 1942 suggested a Japanese thrust into the South Pacific. King's initial instructions to Nimitz were to hold Hawaii and Midway in the Central Pacific, but also to protect the SLOCs running from the United States to Australia. Protecting the SLOCs required that a line of fortified bases in the South Pacific be created as quickly as possible. These bases included Canton and Christmas Islands, Fiji, Samoa, Bora Bora, and

New Caledonia. These not only secured the SLOCs but created a foundation from which offensive operations could be launched.

Given the "Germany first" strategy, it seemed that King's vision of even limited offensive action in the Pacific had little chance of being implemented. He faced opposition from the Army, and this raised inter-service rivalry to new levels. King got his way because he understood that the United States was going to be able to produce enough military and naval strength to fight simultaneous offensive wars in both the Europe and the Pacific Theaters. He also played up fears that Australia was under threat and had to be protected; of course, securing the SLOCs was a vital prerequisite. Most of all, events furthered his strategic vision.

Following their seizure of Rabaul on January 23, the Japanese turned it into a major base and planned to use it as a springboard for further advances into the South Pacific. The Japanese landed troops on eastern New Guinea in March. In May, the Japanese mounted a major operation in the South Pacific with the primary goal of seizing Port Moresby on southeastern New Guinea from which they could bring northeastern Australia into air attack range. This move resulted in the Battle of the Coral Sea and was the first major Japanese setback of the war. Though the attempt to take Port Moresby failed, the Japanese did succeed in adding Tulagi in the Southern Solomon Islands to their list of conquests. They built a seaplane base there and soon began work on an airfield on the island of Guadalcanal just across the channel from Tulagi.

As the Japanese eyed major advances in the South Pacific, they also made a move to threaten the American position in the Central Pacific. This was the operation to take Midway Atoll and to draw the remainder of the Pacific Fleet into a decisive battle so the IJN could complete the job of crushing it. This attempt failed completely at the cost of four of the IJN's six fleet carriers. Nimitz's decision to defend the Central Pacific aggressively with virtually all his remaining fleet assets paid off handsomely.

With the Japanese threat in the Central Pacific removed, King could again focus on the South Pacific. To grab the initiative in the aftermath of Midway, he ordered Nimitz to initiate offensive operations in the South Pacific. The first target was Tulagi and Guadalcanal, but the ultimate objective was to take back Rabaul and end the Japanese threat in the region. Since Guadalcanal was within the Southwest Pacific Area under MacArthur, King had to work with Army Chief of Staff George Marshall to administratively place Guadalcanal within the Pacific Ocean Area command under Nimitz. The price for this was to agree that the subsequent advance up the Solomons and the effort to isolate and capture Rabaul would be under MacArthur's overall direction. With this agreement in place, the main effort of US forces in the Pacific Theater moved to the South Pacific and remained there for the next 15 months.

King's decision to begin offensive operations in the South Pacific, and specifically in the Solomons, led to a grinding six-month battle of attrition. The initial landing on Guadalcanal and Tulagi, and two other nearby islands, went well. But the IJN quickly regained its balance and prepared to reverse the American gains. Even after Midway, the IJN outnumbered the USN in most ship categories, so the success of the Guadalcanal gambit was anything but assured. Had the Japanese treated this as the opportunity to inflict a decisive defeat on the USN that they had missed at Pearl Harbor and Midway, they could have massed sufficient forces to defeat the first American offensive in the Pacific War. Instead, they committed increasing force, but never enough to fully neutralize the American-held airfield on Guadalcanal that provided the decisive edge in the campaign. Nimitz threw in everything he had to hold the island and inflict an increasing level of pain on the Japanese.

Victory at Guadalcanal, achieved in February 1943 when the Japanese evacuated the island, was just the first phase of the campaign to seize Rabaul. The original vision from July 1942 divided the campaign into three phases. The initial phase was to seize Tulagi and Guadalcanal Islands. The second phase called for the capture of the remainder of the Solomons and the northeastern part of New Guinea. The final phase was the capture of Rabaul itself.

By the end of the Guadalcanal campaign, the situation in the South Pacific had been significantly altered. The growing power of the USN was fully on display. Attrition to the IJN during the Guadalcanal campaign had been significant; these losses drove the IJN to disengage from the Guadalcanal campaign to save itself for a future decisive battle against the USN under better conditions. The Japanese ability to contest a renewed American advance into the Central and Northern Solomons had been severely degraded.

The Solomons campaign was the first opportunity for the Americans to use an island-hopping strategy. This offered the potential to disrupt the Japanese defensive strategy of making the Americans fight for every island on the long road to Japan. The basic premise of American planning for the campaign was the requirement to advance up the Solomons to seize airfields. Once airpower was in place in the Northern Solomons, Rabaul could be isolated and then eventually captured. It was necessary to seize Bougainville Island in the Northern Solomons to strike Rabaul with sufficient weight of air power to neutralize it. Seizing an airfield in the Central Solomons was a pre-requisite to a landing on Bougainville. The obvious choice was to seize the airfield on Munda Point on New Georgia in the Central Solomons. This airfield became the focus of the battle for the Central Solomons.

In March 1943 a series of meetings commenced in Washington, DC that guided the course of the Pacific War for the remainder of 1943. Representatives from both MacArthur's and Nimitz's commands were present. MacArthur's representative presented a five-phase plan to recapture Rabaul that was essentially the same from July 1942. Timing of the operations was flexible, but it was assumed that Rabaul could be seized in 1943. The forces for such an operation were not available, which forced a significant modification to MacArthur's plans. A more realistic plan was adopted that included the seizure of only the southeastern part of Bougainville to capture the necessary airfields and a landing on Cape Gloucester in western New Britain. The big change was that the capture of Rabaul would be deferred to 1944. In the event, the capture of Rabaul never took place since Japanese naval and air forces based there were withdrawn in early 1944. The neutralization of Rabaul left the large Japanese garrison to wither on the vine.

From a strategic perspective, the entire campaign to neutralize Rabaul was not the best investment of American resources. It took from February until December 1943 to advance up the roughly 400 nautical miles (nm) up the Solomons from Guadalcanal to Bougainville. This advance tied up the bulk of the USN's forces in the Pacific. Any offensive in the Central Pacific could only be mounted by taking forces from the South Pacific. The Central Pacific was always the USN's preferred route on the road to Tokyo.

By mid-1943, it was clear that the USN's increased strength could sustain offensives on two fronts. One was already under way, running up the Solomon Islands and then through New Guinea toward the Philippines. The other was from Hawaii through the Central Pacific. This basic outline for a two-front offensive against the Japanese for 1943–44 was approved at the Trident Conference held in Washington, DC on May 12–17, 1943 by the Combined Chiefs of Staff from the United States and Great Britain.

The Central Pacific axis of advance was predominantly a naval show under the command of Nimitz. However, lack of resources and command rivalry in the Pacific forced an alteration of the plans for a Central Pacific offensive. The original plan coming out of the Trident Conference called for the seizure of the Marshall Islands and the Caroline Islands. By July 1943, it was obvious that an attack on the Marshalls was logistically unfeasible without drawing forces from the Southwest Pacific Area command under the control of MacArthur, so the Joint Chiefs ordered Nimitz to attack the Gilbert Islands instead with a target date of November 15, 1943.

This modified scheme was approved at the Quebec Conference held in Canada on August 17–24, 1943. Future Central Pacific operations were confirmed as sequential invasions of the Gilberts, Marshalls, Carolines, and then the Palau Islands. King inserted the Marianas as a possible substitute for the Palaus. After the conference, King was supported by General Henry H. Arnold, commander of the Army Air Forces, who wanted to use the Marianas as a base for mounting B-29 bomber attacks against Japan. The new B-29 had the range to fly from the Marianas to the Japanese home islands. By the Cairo Conference in December 1943, the Allied leaders clearly saw the advantages of the Central Pacific drive and the benefits of seizing the Marianas in particular. The attack on the Marianas was scheduled for October 1944, following the seizure of the Marshalls in January and Truk in July. A Central Pacific campaign plan was issued by Nimitz's staff in December 1943 and revised in January 1944 with a projected November 1 invasion of the Marianas.

As the pace of operations quickened, the debate between Nimitz and MacArthur became more heated. At a planning conference in Washington, DC in February and March, the schedule for Central Pacific operations was examined again and altered significantly. MacArthur's staff fought for an advance along northern New Guinea into Mindanao in the Philippines. King was determined to keep his Central Pacific drive as the primary focus. When Nimitz joined the conference, he proposed two possible schedules for the remainder of the year. One called for Truk to be bypassed, Saipan in the Marianas to be attacked by June 15, and landings on the Palaus on October 1.

The Joint Chiefs of Staff agreed on a hybrid approach. They embraced Nimitz's short-term schedule mixed with MacArthur's longer-term goal of invading Mindanao. The final sequence of operations was set as the occupation of Hollandia on the coast of northern New Guinea by MacArthur's forces with support from Nimitz's carriers on April 15, the bypassing of Truk, followed by the initial landings on the Marianas on June 15. The next targets were the Palaus in mid-September and Mindanao in mid-November.

The outline of operations for late 1943 and the first half of 1944 proceeded as planned. Saipan in the Marianas was attacked on schedule on June 15. The invasion prompted an attempt by the IJN to fight yet another decisive battle; the result was decisive, but not in the way the Japanese planned. The Battle of the Philippine Sea fought on June 19–20 resulted in the destruction of the IJN's carrier force and severely jeopardized its ability to contest any further USN advance.

With the Marianas secured, the southern and central Pacific advances were ready to merge. King's preferred option was to invade Formosa with the purpose of cutting Japan off from the resource areas in Southeast Asia. The Philippines would be cut off and left to wither just as Rabaul and Truk had been. As expected, MacArthur had a visceral dislike for anything but invading the Philippines and returning them to American control. Given the choice of invading Formosa or the Philippines, the Joint Chiefs decided to ignore King's advice and attack the Philippines. Even Nimitz said after the fact that the decision to attack the Philippines was the right one. The invasion of Leyte in the central Philippines in October 1944 was followed by several other invasions in the Philippines, culminating in MacArthur's return to Luzon in January 1945. Though the major part of Luzon was recaptured by February, mopping up operations in the Philippines continued until the end of the war.

With the Philippines recaptured, planning began for the final approach to Japan. For this phase, the USN planned to advance from two directions. One was through the Bonin Islands, which were composed of mostly volcanic islets too small for an airfield. The only exceptions were Chichi and Iwo Jima. The second line of advance was in the Ryukyus stretching from the Japanese home islands down to Formosa. The largest island in this chain was Okinawa. King saw the advantages in Nimitz's proposal to occupy both Iwo Jima and Okinawa and quickly endorsed it. Iwo Jima was selected because an airfield could be built on it more quickly than on rocky Chichi Jima. The Army Air Force supported the operation since fighters based on Iwo Jima had the range to support B-29 operations over Japan. The operation to take Iwo Jima was scheduled first because it was expected that taking the small volcanic island would be easier than taking the much larger Okinawa. The directive for these operations was issued from the Joint Chiefs of Staff in October 1944 and within four days Nimitz's staff had prepared a study that became the basis for the final plan.

The landing on Iwo Jima, beginning on February 19, was one of the toughest fights of the Pacific War. For the only time during the war, dug-in Japanese defenders exacted more casualties on the invading Americans than they suffered themselves. Severe fighting raged until March 26. Fighting on Okinawa was no less bitter and raged from April 1 until June 21 when American troops reached the southern end of the island and ended organized resistance. In addition to the fierce resistance on the ground, the Japanese unleashed a storm of suicide aircraft to attack the invasion fleet. The last kamikaze attack off Okinawa occurred on July 30, bringing the four-month suicide onslaught against the USN to an end.

For the final drive on Japan, War Plan Orange and its successor Rainbow Plans foresaw a naval blockade of Japan supported by continuing bombardment, and no need for a land invasion. The Japanese home islands were also subjected to an increasing aerial assault from USN carrier aircraft and Army Air Force B-29s. Despite misgivings from USN planners, as early as April 1944 momentum began to grow for a full-fledged invasion of Japan. By May 1945, MacArthur's staff had created a preliminary plan for a two-stage invasion. Employment of nuclear weapons made such a bloody operation unnecessary.

USN TACTICS
Fleet Action Tactics

The USN planned extensively for a decisive clash with the IJN's battle fleets. In this fight, battleships would play a central role. The USN was counting on the fact that it could bring a larger number of battleships to the fight, but to bring this advantage to bear considerable thought and practice was devoted to the pre-gunnery phases of a fleet action. Determining the enemy's exact location was crucial for the proper employment of the battle line. Up until 1939, scouting was the primary responsibility for cruisers. After that point, it was recognized that aircraft could perform this function better while reducing the vulnerability of cruisers to enemy action.

Once the enemy was located, the approach phase was initiated. This could take several days and came to be dominated by naval airpower. In a series of annual fleet exercises, called Fleet Problems, aircraft carriers demonstrated that they were essential for scouting and gaining air superiority. The same exercises seemed to demonstrate that carriers were vulnerable and were unable to stop the advance of the main battle fleet. This placed the battleship in the role of being the only ship which could successfully engage another battleship.

Following the approach phase, the engagement phase began. The focus here was on the destruction of the IJN's battle line. USN battleships were trained to

The bitterness of the fighting during the last months of the war was epitomized by the advent of suicide aircraft attacks on American naval units. Here, carrier *Essex* is struck by a kamikaze on November 24, 1944, off Luzon. (NARA)

conduct long-range fire and to concentrate fire on their Japanese counterparts as quickly as possible. Even with the best fire-control systems available, the USN found that conducting accurate long-range gunnery was extremely difficult. A well-trained crew could direct fire on a target at over 30,000 yards range. During Fleet Problems, opening engagement ranges gradually increased to 35,000 yards. Once a fire-control solution was gained, the USN emphasized full 8- or 12-gun salvos. Spotters on the tops of the battleship masts were challenged to spot fire since at 30,000 yards only the superstructure of an enemy battleship was visible because of the curvature of the earth at that range. Even well-trained gun crews and observers saw their accuracy significantly decrease at long range. This tendency could be mitigated by using aircraft for spotting if air superiority had been gained. A Naval War College estimate stated that spotting with aircraft would result in six times more hits.

Such a fleet action never occurred during the Pacific War and little of these tactics or the training behind them proved relevant for actual wartime conditions. It is nevertheless interesting to consider the outcome of such a clash had it occurred. The biggest factor potentially affecting the outcome of a fleet engagement was carrier air power. Even before the start of the war, both the IJN and USN were operating their carriers as independent strike formations. Their strike operations would have been focused on each other; after the probable neutralization of both carrier forces, it remains unclear what impact any surviving carriers would have had against the opposing battle fleet. The IJN would have had a probable advantage since it possessed more carriers and these carried a much better torpedo bomber. Only torpedoes could seriously damage or sink heavily armored battleships. In an actual battleship duel, neither side possessed a marked advantage in gunnery accuracy. A hypothetical large-scale gunnery duel would have been more heavily influenced by the greater numbers of USN battleships and their generally higher level of side and horizontal protection. Another potential factor was the superiority of the IJN's torpedoes which possessed a range comparable to USN battleship guns. The Americans were entirely ignorant of this development which could have had devastating consequences.

Night-fighting Tactics

During the war, IJN and USN battleships fought only two actions, and both were at night. To avoid airpower, all but one major surface action between the two navies was fought at night. The IJN had a clear superiority in night-fighting tactics since these were central to its vision of how to win a major fleet action. The USN also trained for night combat, but this training focused on what was called "Major Tactics" associated with the decisive engagement between battle lines. Essentially, it called for American cruisers and destroyers to locate and attack Japanese battleships at close range with torpedoes. The training to attack a slow-moving and usually illuminated battleship came at the expense of "Minor Tactics" which dealt with combat between light units.

The USN entered the war with inadequate night-fighting tactics and capabilities. This was marked by an emphasis on gunnery and a flawed torpedo doctrine. USN cruisers and destroyers were expected to conduct attacks on Japanese formations. The tactic for this was called "Night Search and Attack" in which cruisers and destroyers located and then attacked enemy battleships with torpedoes. Three phases were identified for the Night Search and Attack. In the first, destroyers would form a line abreast scouting formation to locate the enemy. Once found, cruiser and destroyer gunfire would force a gap in the enemy screen allowing the destroyers to penetrate the enemy formation. In the next phase, the destroyers located the battleships and transmitted contact reports to other friendly units. In the final phase, large numbers of destroyers would attack the enemy battleships at close range with torpedoes. Gunfire was to be used against the battleship's bridge and superstructure to diminish the effectiveness of the enemy's defensive fire. This was continually practiced, and it reinforced the concept that only battleships were worthy of torpedo attack and that the targets would be slow and well illuminated and thus easy to hit. This had little resemblance to the type of night combat experienced during the war.

Going into the Guadalcanal campaign during which five major night actions were fought, the conviction that gunnery was the key to victory remained firm. From battleships on down, gunnery was viewed as the dominant factor. At night, battleships were rarely committed, so this left cruisers to provide the firepower needed for victory. Early in the Guadalcanal campaign, the firepower of the heavy cruiser was preferred as its heavier 8in shell possessed the penetrative power to defeat its Japanese counterparts. The heavy cruisers took severe losses at Guadalcanal, and in the later phases of the campaign when Japanese destroyers were the primary adversaries, the fast-firing 6in guns on the light cruisers were preferred in night combat.

The light cruisers could blanket a target with an enormous barrage of 6in shells. Combined with radar, American admirals were convinced that they could engage a target at 10,000 yards and destroy it before it could fire torpedoes. This was totally ignorant of the true capabilities of the Japanese Type 93, which had an effective range comparable to cruiser gunnery.

As USN tactics changed due to the lessons of war, the role of the destroyer remained secondary. American night-fighting tactics were totally ignorant of the potential of American torpedoes, which had proven largely ineffective during the battle for Guadalcanal. This was a result of both bad tactics and faulty technology. Destroyer tactics were totally subservient to the cruiser; destroyers were only used to finish off cripples from cruiser gunfire or to screen the cruisers from destroyer attack. Destroyers were tied to the cruisers and not allowed to operate independently. If these bad tactics were not recognized by the American admirals fighting in the Solomons, they were noticed by both Nimitz and King. Both recognized the unhealthy focus on gunnery and the ignorance of the potential of American torpedoes and the dangers presented by Japanese torpedoes. Nimitz went as far as to comment on February 15, 1943: "In no night action has our destroyers' major offensive strength, the torpedo, been used effectively."

USN destroyers practice a massed torpedo attack in September 1936. The ships are advancing through a smokescreen laid by aircraft. Actual wartime conditions bore no resemblance to this exercise. (Naval History and Heritage Command)

In answer to the prodding from Nimitz and King, and in response to the unquestioned success of Japanese destroyers, going into 1943 the USN began to question its torpedo tactics. On February 20, the commander of the Pacific Fleet's destroyers issued a new tactical bulletin. All Japanese ships, destroyer and above, were now seen to be suitable torpedo targets. He also ordered that the speed setting of the Mark 15 torpedo be lowered from 45 to 32 knots to extend the range of the weapons to 10,000 yards. This allowed the destroyers to exploit their radars and attack targets beyond visual range at night. By July 1943 all the technical faults of the Mark 15 torpedo were recognized and corrected. Once the torpedo was rendered effective, the combination of radar, an effective torpedo, and new tactics made American destroyers a potent weapon.

Going into 1944, the USN had proven its ability to adapt to the changing nature of naval warfare. After an uncertain start, the USN had revamped its night-fighting doctrine which was now built around the incorporation of radar. The key difference was the utilization of the full offensive potential of destroyers. They were now unleashed to execute independent torpedo attacks on Japanese ships. This tactic proved deadly during the latter part of the Solomons campaign in 1943 when the Americans eclipsed the night-fighting superiority of the Japanese. Another major enhancement was the employment of cruiser guns at night controlled by radar.

Carrier Tactics

Going into the war and throughout 1942, American carrier tactics were less mature than those practiced by the IJN. In a combat scenario, American carriers launched a morning and afternoon search by dive-bombers. If a target was located, a strike was launched as soon as possible with every available dive-bomber and torpedo plane. Available fighters were usually divided with half providing strike escort and the other half assigned to defend the ship. American strike tactics were focused on the operations of a single carrier air group. When launching a strike, the entire air group could not be accommodated in a single deck load, so a large strike required two separate deck loads. This created a potentially long launch cycle as the first deck load waited overhead for the second deck load to be spotted and launched. Once launched, different aircraft speeds and altitudes precluded a joint formation. The separate squadrons would usually proceed in loose order to the target, hopefully not losing contact with each other along the way. There was no attempt to coordinate multiple air groups from different carriers even if they were going after the same target.

Further complicating the task of American strike planners was the short ranges of their aircraft. The dive-bomber squadrons assigned to scout missions flew out as far as 325nm. They carried a 500lb bomb to strike anything they found. Strike missions were more limited in range. In the strike role, the dive-bombers had a doctrinal strike radius of up to 275nm with a 500lb bomb and some 200nm with a 1,000lb bomb load. Torpedo bombers were limited to a range of 175nm with a torpedo loaded. The strike range of early war fighters was also about 175nm.

Dive-bombing was the most effective strike tactic available to a USN air group at the start of the war. On a strike mission, escorting fighters were tasked to clear the way for the dive-bombers. A standard dive-bombing profile began with a shallow dive from 20,000ft followed by a steep dive from 15,000–12,000ft. The dive was made at the angle of 65–70 degrees and would be pressed to 1,500–2,000ft above the target before the bomb was dropped. A dive-bombing squadron was divided up into several six-aircraft divisions so that they could attack a target from different directions to overwhelm its defenses. The best direction to attack a target was along its longitudinal axis since this presented the largest possible target.

Since torpedo bombers were so vulnerable, the ideal tactic was to conduct a coordinated attack with the dive-bombers to split the target's defenses. Early-war USN torpedo bombers were forced to conduct an attack at very low speed because of the limitations of the Mark 13 torpedo.

The preferred tactic was an anvil attack with aircraft attacking from both bows simultaneously so that whatever direction the target maneuvered it would be exposed. If the pilot judged his approach correctly, the torpedo would enter the water 1,400 yards from the target. With the introduction of the TBF/TBM Avenger torpedo bomber and modifications to the Mark 13, torpedo attacks in 1944 were made from 800ft at a speed of 260 knots. By 1944 American torpedo bombers were proven ship-killers but in 1942 this was not the case.

Strike cohesion was a real problem for American carrier air groups in 1942. In 1944 strikes were still conducted separately by individual carriers, but rigorous pre-deployment air group training meant squadrons were better able to stick together on the way to their targets. Even in 1944 the principal weakness of USN carrier air groups was the short strike range of their aircraft. Depending on tactical circumstances, maximum strike range was limited to about 200nm, with the typical search range remaining at 325nm.

USN tactics for fleet air defense provided uneven results in 1942. The best way to defend a task force was with a Combat Air Patrol (CAP) launched from carriers. Conducting radar-directed interceptions of incoming enemy aircraft had the potential to disrupt enemy air attacks. However, during the four carrier battles of 1942, CAP tactics were still embryonic, and the results differed wildly. The Grumman F6F Hellcat fighter, introduced in late 1943, had the performance to make CAP more effective, but the real key remained effective fighter direction. USN fighter direction tactics improved by trial and error, but by mid-1944 a solid doctrine was in place to maximize the chances of intercept. In the climactic carrier battle of 1944, the Fast Carrier Task Force was able to operate a centralized fighter direction scheme under the control of a fast force fighter direction officer (FDO). Working with the FDOs in the other task groups and on each carrier, it was possible to shift available fighters from the control of one task group to the other while keeping a central reserve to handle future raids. Some Japanese raids were intercepted by fighters as far as 60nm from the carriers, and almost always the defending Hellcats were positioned with an altitude advantage. As successful as these efforts generally were, it was impossible to defeat a large Japanese raid with CAP alone. Antiaircraft fire remained an important element of fleet air defense. The proliferation of 40mm guns in twin and quadruple mounts aboard ships from destroyers up through carriers, and the provision of proximity-fuzed shells for the ubiquitous 5in/38-caliber (5in/38cal) gun, made American antiaircraft fire even more effective than it had been in 1942, when it was able to decimate attacking Japanese aircraft formations.

CHAPTER 2
OPERATIONS

THE PEARL HARBOR RAID

As mentioned in the introduction, the IJN refused to open the Pacific War according to script. This was surprising because the IJN had its own version of War Plan Orange that also called for a climactic fleet action in the western Pacific. However, the commander of the IJN's Combined Fleet, Admiral Yamamoto Isoruku, refused to be so passive and instead opted for a more aggressive opening move with the design of crippling the USN's battle fleet at its base at Pearl Harbor and thereby damaging American morale at the onset of the war. The USN failed to comprehend that the IJN possessed the capabilities to conduct such an ambitious opening attack and instead stuck to its own script that any opening Japanese moves would be limited to hostilities in Southeast Asia. The result was total strategic and tactical surprise by the Japanese carrier task force at Pearl Harbor on the morning of December 7, 1941.

The Pacific Fleet under Admiral Kimmel was not ready for battle. Kimmel had assumed responsibility for patrols around Pearl Harbor and possessed adequate numbers of long-range scout aircraft to conduct a full 360-degree search, but he decided that it was wiser to maintain the overall readiness of his force to support the movement of the fleet once war began rather than to wear the aircraft down on constant patrol duties. This meant that north of Oahu, the direction from which the Japanese strike force approached, was unwatched.

Even though the Japanese were undetected by search aircraft, there were other opportunities for the Americans to gain warning of the approaching attack. This included the detection of a Japanese midget submarine in the channel leading to Pearl Harbor as early as 0342hrs and a report from a destroyer of attacking the same target at 0720hrs. In addition, radar on Oahu detected a pre-strike Japanese reconnaissance aircraft at 0613hrs and the strike

Lindsey, a Sumner-class destroyer converted to a minelayer, was extensively damaged by two kamikazes on April 12, 1945. The second hit set off the forward magazine. The ship was later towed to safety and repaired, but not before 57 of its crew was killed and another 57 wounded. (NARA)

Pearl Harbor ship locations, 0755hrs, December 7, 1941

KEY

No. = ship's number
c. = date commissioned
conv. = date converted
BB = battleship
DD = destroyer
CA = heavy cruiser
CL = light cruiser
SS = submarine
CM = minelayer
DM = light minelayer
DMS = fast minesweeper

YMS = minesweeper
PT = motor torpedo boat
AD = destroyer tender
AV = seaplane tender
AH = hospital ship
AK = cargo ship
AO = oil tanker
AR = repair ship
AX = auxiliary ship
PG = patrol gunboat

KEY TO SHIPS

1. *Phoenix* (Brooklyn class, No.46: CL, c.1938)
2. *Blue* (Craven class, No.387: DD, c.1937)
3. *Whitney* (AD, No.4: c.1919)
4. *Conyngham* (Mahan class, No.371: DD, c.1936)
5. *Reid* (Mahan class, No.369: DD, c.1937)
6. *Tucker* (Mahan class, No.374: DD, c.1936)
7. *Case* (Mahan class, No.370: DD, c.1935)
8. *Selfridge* (Porter class, No.357: DD, c.1937)
9. *Ralph Talbot* (Craven class, No.390: DD, c.1938)
10. *Patterson* (Craven class, No.392: DD, c.1938)
11. *Henley* (Craven class, No.391: DD, c.1937)
12. *Aylwin* (Farragut class, No.355: DD, c.1935)
13. *Farragut* (DD, No.348: c.1934)
14. *Dale* (Farragut class, No.353: DD, c.1935)
15. *Monaghan* (Farragut class, No.354: DD, c.1933)
16. *Ramsay* (DM, No.16: conv.1930)
17. *Gamble* (DM, No.15: conv.1931)
18. *Montgomery* (DM, No.17: conv.1931)
19. *Trever* (DMS, No.16: conv.1940)
20. *Breese* (DM, No.18: conv.1931)
21. *Zane* (DMS, No.14: conv.1940)
22. *Perry* (DMS, No.17: conv.1940)
23. *Wasmuth* (DMS, No.15: conv.1940)
24. *Medusa* (AR, No.1: c.1924)
25. *Curtiss* (AV, No.4: c.1940)
26. *Tangier* (AV, No.8: c.1940)
27. *Utah* (Ex-BB, No.31: c.1911)
28. *Raleigh* (Omaha class, No.7: CL, c.1922)
29. *Detroit* (Omaha class, No.8: CL, c.1922)
30. *Phelps* (Porter class, No.360: DD, c.1936)
31. *MacDonough* (Farragut class, No.351: DD, c.1935)
32. *Worden* (Farragut class, No.352: DD, c.1934)
33. *Dewey* (Farragut class, No.349: DD, c.1934)
34. *Hull* (Farragut class, No.350: DD, c.1935)
35. *Dobbin* (AD, No.3: c.1924)
36. *Solace* (AH, No.5: c.1941)
37. *Allen* (DD, No.66: c.1916)
38. *Chew* (DD, No.106: c.1918)
39. *Nevada* (Oklahoma class, No.36: BB, c.1914)
40. *Vestal* (AR, No.4: c.1909)
41. *Arizona* (Pennsylvania class, No.39: BB, c.1916)
42. *Tennessee* (California class, No.43: BB, c.1919)
43. *West Virginia* (Maryland class, No.48: BB, c.1921)
44. *Maryland* (BB, No.46: c.1920)
45. *Oklahoma* (BB, No.37: c.1914)
46. *Neosho* (No.23: AO)
47. *California* (BB, No.44: c.1919)
48. *Avocet* (AV, c.1918)
49. *Helm* (Craven class, No.388: DD, c.1937)
50. *Bobolink* (YMS, No.20: c.1919)
51. *Vireo* (YMS, No.52: c.1919)
52. *Rail* (YMS, No.26: c.1918)
53. *Tern* (YMS, No.31: c.1919)
54. *Shaw* (Mahan class, No.373: DD, c.1935)
55. *Cassin* (Mahan class, No.372: DD, c.1933)
56. *Downes* (Mahan class, No.375: DD, c.1933)
57. *Pennsylvania* (BB, No.38: c.1915)
58. *Oglala* (CM, No.4: c.1917)
59. *Cachalot* (SS, No.170: c.1933)
60. *Helena* (St. Louis class, No.50: CL, c.1938)
61. *Jarvis* (Craven class, No.393: DD, c.1934)
62. *Argonne* (AX, No.31: c.1921)
63. *Sacramento* (PG, No.19: c.1914)
64. *Mugford* (Craven class, No.389: DD, c.1934)
65. *Rigel* (AD, No.13: c.1921)
66. *Cummings* (Mahan class, No.365: DD, c.1937)
67. *Honolulu* (Brooklyn class, No.48: CL, c.1937)
68. *Schley* (No.103: DD, c.1918)
69. *Ramapo* (No.12: AO)
70. *San Francisco* (Astoria class, No.38: CA, c.1934)
71. *New Orleans* (Astoria class, No.32: CA, c.1932)
72. *Preble* (DM, No.20: conv.1937)
73. *Swan* (AV, No.7: c.1919)
74. *St. Louis* (CL, No.49: c.1938)
75. *Bagley* (Craven class, No.386: DD, c.1938)
76. *Tracy* (DM, No.19: conv.1937)
77. *Pruitt* (DM, No.22: conv.1937)
78. *Grebe* (YMS, No.43: c.1919)
79. *Sicard* (DM, No.21: conv.1937)
80. *Thornton* (AV, No.11: conv.1939)
81. *Hulbert* (AV, No.6: conv.1939)
82. *Tautog* (SS, No.199: T class, c.1940)
83. *Dolphin* (SS, No.169: D type, c.1932)
84. *Narwhal* (SS, No.167: N type, c.1930)
85. *Pelias* (SS tender, No.14: c.1941)
86. *Sumner* (AX, No.32: c.1913)
87. *Castor* (AK, No.1: c.1940)

itself at 0645hrs. None of these contacts roused the American leadership, which collectively refused to accept the possibility of a Japanese attack.

The fleet lying in Pearl Harbor that morning did not comprise the majority of the Pacific Fleet's combat units, but it did include eight of the fleet's nine battleships. Also present were two heavy cruisers, six light cruisers, 30 destroyers, and five submarines. In an extremely fortuitous turn of events for the USN, none of the fleet's three carriers was present. *Enterprise* was at sea with three cruisers and nine destroyers on a ferry mission to Wake Island and *Lexington* had departed Pearl Harbor on December 5, with three cruisers and five destroyers to ferry aircraft to Midway. The third carrier, *Saratoga*, was at Puget Sound Navy Yard undergoing repairs.

The first wave of Japanese aircraft, totaling 183 planes, arrived over its targets just before 0800hrs. Its focus was the battleships arrayed in the harbor. Seven of the eight battleships were moored in "Battleship Row" and the eighth was in a dry dock in the navy yard. The first Japanese aircraft to attack were 40 torpedo bombers. Sixteen targeted where the carriers were usually moored. Despite the absence of the carriers, most of the Japanese pilots attacked the ships moored in their place. Target ship *Utah* was hit by two torpedoes and sunk; cruiser *Raleigh* was hit by a torpedo but survived. Other pilots went looking for other targets. Several found cruiser *Helena* moored nearby and hit it with a torpedo. Five pilots joined the attack on Battleship Row.

Of the eight battleships on Battleship Row, five were vulnerable to torpedo attack. Since the battleships were usually moored in pairs, three ships were moored inboard and could only be attacked with bombs. The main attack force of 24 torpedo bombers, joined by the five mentioned above, laid waste to Battleship Row. Battleships *Oklahoma* and *West Virginia* were moored directly in front of the approaching torpedo bombers and therefore suffered the most damage. *Oklahoma* took five torpedo hits and capsized with the loss of 415 men. It was never brought back into service. *West Virginia* was hit by seven torpedoes, but its crew took immediate steps to prevent it from capsizing. The ship sank to the bottom of the harbor but was raised and returned to service in July 1944. *California* took two torpedo hits, and these were sufficient to cause it to settle on the harbor floor. It was raised and returned to service in January 1944. *Nevada* was hit by a single torpedo that caused severe flooding.

Concurrently with the torpedo bombers, another 49 aircraft carrying large 1,760lb bombs conducted a horizontal bombing attack on Battleship Row. Two bombs hit *Arizona* and one of these penetrated its horizontal armor and caused its forward magazine to detonate. The forward half of the ship was shattered; it sank with the loss of 1,103 men. *Arizona* was never

returned to service. Other bomb hits were scored on *Maryland*, *Tennessee*, and *West Virginia*, but due to their location or because the bombs failed to fully detonate, damage to these ships was light.

The second wave included 78 dive-bombers targeted against ships in the harbor. Even though these highly trained pilots were attacking stationary targets (except for *Nevada*), the results were very disappointing. Only about 15 of the dive-bombers hit their target for the loss of 14 dive-bombers. *Nevada* was hit by six bombs and forced to beach. It was repaired and returned to service in June 1943. *California* took another hit, but damage was not severe. Two destroyers in the same dry dock as *Pennsylvania* were heavily damaged and not rebuilt until 1944. Another two light cruisers, a destroyer, and a seaplane tender took varying degrees of damage.

The remaining Japanese strike aircraft were devoted to attacking airfields around the island. This crippled American airpower and resulted in the destruction of 97 USN aircraft. Total USN personnel losses were 2,008 killed and 710 wounded. As bad as this was, it could have been worse. Of the 18 ships sunk or damaged, only three failed to see service again. Most of the damage was focused on the battleships, but of these two were operational within weeks, one in February 1942, one in June 1943, and the final two in 1944. The Pacific Fleet was not crippled at Pearl Harbor, but it would quickly have to learn how to fight a new kind of war.

This is a view of Battleship Row taken by a Japanese aircraft in the early stages of the attack. The time is about 0800hrs as the torpedo planes are in the process of doing their work, but the level bombers have not yet made their appearance. Seen from lower left to right are *Nevada*, *Arizona* with repair ship *Vestal* outboard, *Tennessee* with *West Virginia* outboard, *Maryland* with *Oklahoma* outboard, oiler *Neosho* and finally *California*. *West Virginia*, *Oklahoma*, and *California* have already been torpedoed, marked by ripples and spreading oil, and the first two are listing to port. Splashes from torpedo drops and torpedo tracks are visible at left and center. The smoke in the center is from the torpedoed light cruiser *Helena*. The heavier smoke in the distance is from Hickam Field which has already been attacked by dive-bombers. (Naval History and Heritage Command)

THE FORGOTTEN FIGHT OF THE ASIATIC FLEET

The small Asiatic Fleet was comprised of heavy cruiser *Houston*, light cruisers *Boise* and *Marblehead*, 13 four-stacker destroyers, and 29 submarines. The most powerful ship among these was *Boise*, but it went aground on January 21 on an uncharted reef and was forced to return to the United States for repairs. This inadequate force was tasked to defend the Philippines, a mission clearly beyond its capabilities, and then to assist Allied navies in defending British and Dutch possessions in Southeast Asia.

When war came, Admiral Hart's fleet was out of position. All but two of the submarines, five destroyers, and the fleet's support ships were at their home base at Cavite Navy Base near Manila. This facility was within range of Japanese air attack. This became a problem on December 10 when Japanese bombers laid waste to Cavite, destroying a submarine and damaging several other ships in the process. From that point, the fleet operated out of northwest Australia with the main mission of defending the Netherlands East Indies (NEI). This was almost equally futile as defending the Philippines given the size of available Dutch, British, and Australian naval forces in the region. In fact, the NEI was virtually undefended by ground forces and Allied air power was outclassed by Japanese air forces. Nevertheless, if well handled, the Asiatic Fleet and other Allied naval forces could strike blows at the Japanese invasion forces spread all over the NEI and hope to delay the Japanese advance.

The Japanese invasion of Borneo led to the first surface battle of the war involving USN surface forces. On the morning of January 24, four USN destroyers arrived undetected at the anchorage of the Japanese invasion force off Balikpapan. The American destroyers swept into the anchorage at 27 knots and using torpedoes and 4in gunfire sank four transports and a patrol boat. The destroyers departed without being damaged before the IJN covering force could react. This was clearly a tactical victory and the best performance of an American destroyer force until 1943. However, it did nothing to slow down the Japanese advance.

More lasting results were hoped for the Combined Striking Force (CSF), formed on February 1 and comprised of *Houston*, *Marblehead*, seven USN destroyers, and several Dutch cruisers and destroyers. When a Japanese invasion force was headed for Makassar on the Southern Celebes, the CSF was committed to stop it. This mission was aborted by Japanese air power that struck the CSF on February 4. Both USN cruisers were hit by bombs; poorly protected *Marblehead* almost sank and was forced to leave the theater for repairs. *Houston* had its aft 8in turret knocked out, but it remained in action. Another sortie by the CSF to defend Sumatra from a Japanese invasion met a similar fate. On February 15, the CSF (which now included six USN destroyers) was heavily bombed. Though no ships were hit, the force was again forced to abort its mission.

As the Japanese advanced on the main NEI island of Java, the units of the Asiatic Fleet fought its last desperate battles. On the night of February 19–20, six USN destroyers were among the Allied units that attacked a Japanese invasion force off Bali. In the Battle of Badoeng Strait, the outnumbered Japanese escort fought well and was able to fend off three Allied attack forces. One USN destroyer was damaged and was sent to a port in Java for repairs. After the dry dock it was in collapsed, and following the fall of Java, the ship was captured by the Japanese and put back into service as a patrol boat.

In a final effort to save Java from invasion, the CSF sortied on February 26 to intercept a Japanese invasion force approaching the island. The USN contribution to the CSF on this occasion was *Houston* and four destroyers. The Dutch admiral leading the CSF doggedly attempted to get at the invasion convoy, which led to the Battle of the Java Sea. With a total of 32 ships on both sides, it was one of the largest surface battles of the Pacific War. The battle began as a long-range gunnery duel in the afternoon between cruisers and lasted well into the night. Japanese gunnery crippled a RN heavy cruiser and a destroyer, but the real damage was done by long-range Japanese torpedoes that sank one Dutch destroyer and two Dutch cruisers. During the battle, the USN destroyers launched 41 torpedoes with no success. *Houston* survived the battle but ran into a large Japanese invasion force in the Sunda Strait on the night of February 28–March 1. After a running action, it was sunk with the accompanying Australian light cruiser *Perth*. Of *Houston's* crew of 1,061, only 368 survived the sinking, and of these, 102 died in Japanese captivity. The Asiatic Fleet had fought to extinction. All of its cruisers were sunk or damaged. Only seven of its 13 destroyers survived. Its large submarine force proved largely ineffective, as will be explained later.

STOPPING THE JAPANESE ADVANCE AT CORAL SEA AND MIDWAY

The Japanese advance into the South Pacific forced a USN response. Two carrier task forces, centered on *Yorktown* and *Lexington*, were dispatched to the South Pacific. Aircraft from these carriers struck a Japanese invasion

The South Pacific before the Battle of the Coral Sea

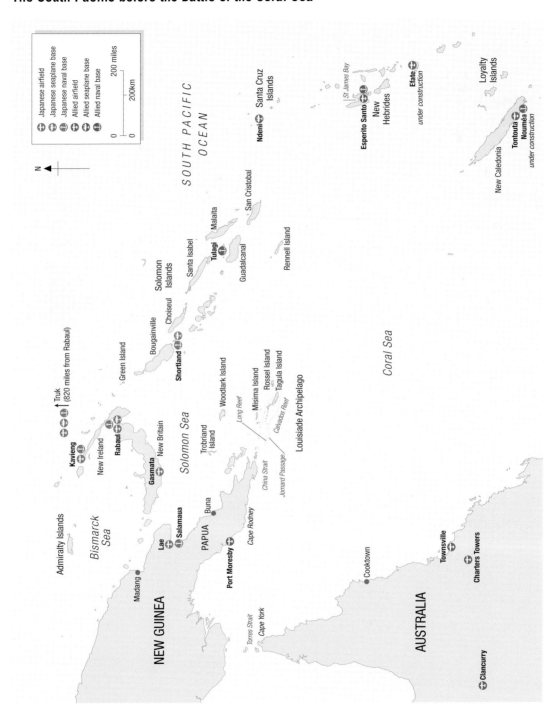

force off Lae-Salamaua on New Guinea on March 10. This raid had strategic implications since it forced the IJN to send carriers to the region in order to resume its advance. This set up the first carrier battle of the war.

USN intelligence warned Nimitz of a large-scale Japanese offensive in the South Pacific scheduled for May with cover provided by three carriers. Nimitz wanted to send carriers *Enterprise* and *Hornet* to reinforce the two carriers already there, but the two additional carriers were unavailable since they had just conducted a raid on Tokyo on April 18 and could not reach the Coral Sea in time. Nimitz was still confident that his force of two carriers, eight cruisers (two Australian), and 13 destroyers could stop the Japanese invasion force bound for Port Moresby on New Guinea. The Allied force faced a Japanese force of similar size centered on the fleet carriers *Shokaku* and *Zuikaku* and light carrier *Shoho*.

Since this was the first carrier battle in history, it turned out to be a messy affair. The Japanese landed on Tulagi Island on May 3. The next day, the surprised Japanese invasion force was subjected to a series of air attacks from *Yorktown*, accounting for one destroyer. During May 5–6, both carrier forces sparred inconclusively, with both sides missing opportunities to strike first. The same happened on May 7, but this time both sides launched full strikes against secondary targets. The Japanese strike came across and sank

This remarkable photo shows the moment of impact of the first torpedo to hit *Yorktown*. Another would hit seconds later. Every time a USN carrier was hit by a torpedo in the carrier battles of 1942, the carrier ended up being sunk. (Naval History and Heritage Command)

Duel of the carriers, June 4, 1942

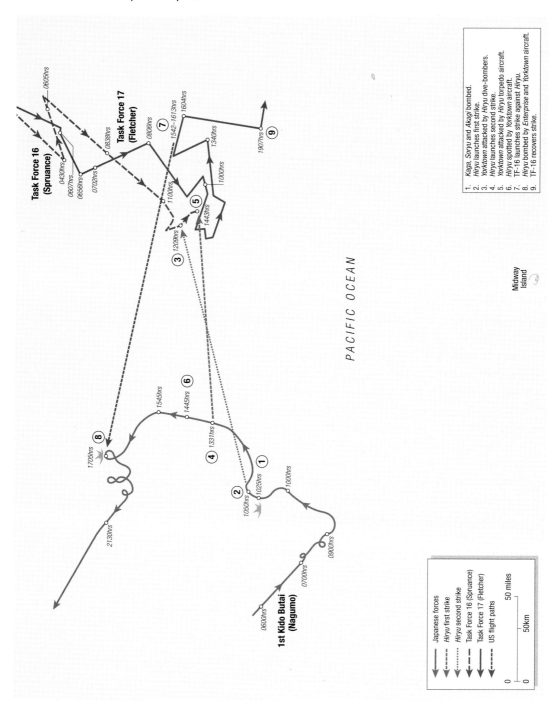

Task Force 16 (Spruance)

Task Force 17 (Fletcher)

0605hrs
0430hrs
0607hrs
0656hrs
0702hrs
0838hrs
0806hrs
0800hrs
1100hrs
1542–1613hrs
1604hrs
1340hrs
1000hrs
1209hrs
1443hrs

PACIFIC OCEAN

Midway Island

1545hrs
1445hrs
1331hrs
1025hrs
1000hrs
1050hrs
1705hrs
2130hrs
0900hrs
0700hrs
0600hrs

1st Kido Butai (Nagumo)

1. *Kaga, Soryu* and *Akagi* bombed.
2. *Hiryu* launches first strike.
3. *Yorktown* attacked by *Hiryu* dive-bombers.
4. *Hiryu* launches second strike.
5. *Yorktown* attacked by *Hiryu* torpedo aircraft.
6. *Hiryu* spotted by *Yorktown* aircraft.
7. TF-16 launches strike against *Hiryu*.
8. *Hiryu* bombed by *Enterprise* and *Yorktown* aircraft.
9. TF-16 recovers strike.

Japanese forces
Hiryu first strike
Hiryu second strike
Task Force 16 (Spruance)
Task Force 17 (Fletcher)
US flight paths

50 miles
50km

an oiler and a destroyer; the USN strike of 93 aircraft was more profitable since it was able to locate and destroy *Shoho*. Finally, on May 8, the main carrier action took place. Both sides located the other and again launched full strikes that found their intended targets.

The Americans were the first to get their strikes into the air. *Yorktown* launched 39 aircraft and *Lexington* another 36. Reaching the target area, they found only *Shokaku* since *Zuikaku* was hidden in a squall. Three dive-bombers placed their 1,000lb weapons on *Shokaku*, but all the torpedo bombers missed. Damage to *Shokaku* was severe; forced to leave the battle, the big carrier was out of action until August 1942.

The Japanese strike consisted of 69 aircraft. Both USN carriers were operating together with an escort of five cruisers and seven destroyers. The CAP was largely ineffective and both carriers were subjected to severe attack. *Lexington* faced the heavier attack by 14 torpedo bombers and 19 dive-bombers. The carrier was deluged by bombs, but only two hit and these caused minor damage. The real threat was posed by the torpedo bombers. Two of these succeeded in hitting the huge carrier. Later in the afternoon, fumes from a cracked aviation fuel tank exploded and led to the loss of the ship. *Yorktown* was hit by a single bomb and was in no danger of sinking. Rear Admiral Frank Fletcher believed he had saved Port Moresby from invasion and decided to withdraw to preserve *Yorktown*.

The Battle of the Coral Sea was the first Japanese defeat of the war. Port Moresby was not subjected to invasion. Japanese losses were heavy and had a severe impact on the clash of Midway the following month. Of the three Japanese carriers committed to the Coral Sea operation, one was sunk, another damaged, and the third was rendered combat ineffective because of heavy losses to its air group.

Coral Sea was just the prelude to Yamamoto's decisive battle at Midway. By committing his entire strength and assuming the USN would fight according to the Japanese script, Yamamoto believed he would finish off the Pacific Fleet. But as he had made his Midway battle somewhat dependent on the outcome of the subsidiary Coral Sea battle where all three IJN carriers had been placed out of action for various reasons, the IJN's carrier force faced evens odds at Midway. Yamamoto made the situation worse by spreading his forces all over a huge chunk of the Pacific. This lack of concentration proved fatal.

Nimitz was again aware of the impending Japanese move and was again determined to commit all his available forces to defeat it. *Yorktown* was hurried back from Coral Sea and repaired within days to allow it to join *Enterprise* and *Hornet* off Midway. In total, Nimitz's forces included three carriers, eight cruisers, 17 destroyers, and 19 submarines. Combined with the 125 aircraft based on Midway, the Americans had another 233 aircraft available on the three carriers. This meant that at the point of contact the IJN was actually outnumbered since only its carrier force was brought into action. The IJN carrier force consisted of carriers *Akagi*, *Kaga*, *Soryu*, and *Hiryu*, two battleships, three cruisers, and 12 destroyers. Aircraft onboard the four carriers totaled 225.

Midway was the only carrier battle during the war in which one side successfully ambushed the other. Given excellent intelligence and having keen insight into Japanese operational intentions, Nimitz placed his three carriers in the flank of the Japanese carriers' launch point to attack Midway. On the morning of June 4, flying boats from Midway spotted the Japanese carriers. Fletcher, the senior officer present, ordered a full strike from *Enterprise* and *Hornet*, but kept some of *Yorktown*'s aircraft in reserve. The strikes from *Enterprise* and *Hornet* suffered from extreme dispersion, as was often the case during 1942. The outline of the battle can be described briefly. American strike aircraft from Midway were directed at the Japanese carrier force. They suffered heavy losses at the hands of defending Japanese fighters and were ineffective. The next series of attacks was mounted by the slow torpedo bombers from the American carriers. These suffered even greater losses and were equally ineffective. The battle was decided when *Enterprise*'s dive-bombers found the Japanese carriers and were joined by a squadron of dive-bombers from *Yorktown*. Because of faulty IJN CAP doctrine, the dive-bombers arrived over the Japanese carriers undetected and free from fighter opposition.

In only a few minutes, *Enterprise*'s dive-bombers struck *Akagi* and *Kaga*, while *Yorktown*'s dive-bombers hit *Soryu*. The eight bombs that struck the three Japanese carriers decided the battle. Heavily damaged, all three later sank. The Japanese struck back with the air group from the undamaged *Hiryu*. In two attacks, both directed at *Yorktown*, the Japanese were able to press home their attacks through a marginally effective American CAP, and place two bombs and two torpedoes on *Yorktown*. This damage eventually proved fatal. *Yorktown* was left dead in the water and suffered two more torpedo hits from a Japanese submarine; the battered carrier sank on the morning of June 7. Retribution against *Hiryu* was rendered on the afternoon of June 4 when dive-bombers from *Enterprise* hit it with four bombs and left it crippled.

The loss of four IJN fleet carriers decided the battle. In the pursuit phase of the battle, the USN sank a heavy cruiser and badly damaged another. Rear Admiral Raymond Spruance, in charge of the USN carrier battle at this point, was rightly too cautious to advance too far to the west to be caught by the superior surface forces that Yamamoto had finally concentrated. Midway was an epic victory, but it was not decisive. The offensive punch of the IJN had been blunted, but the USN was still outnumbered in the Pacific. The cost to the Americans was small – carrier *Yorktown*, one destroyer, 144 aircraft, and 362 sailors, Marines, and airmen killed.

TURNING POINT AT GUADALCANAL

If one event in the Pacific War can be said to be decisive, then that would best apply to the Guadalcanal campaign. This campaign included five major surface battles and two carrier battles. It was the kind of campaign the IJN preferred not to fight and exactly the type of campaign the USN could fight. Following six months of grinding attrition around Guadalcanal, the IJN was demonstrably weaker, but the USN had grown stronger with the benefit of the first of the Two-Ocean Navy ships reaching the Pacific.

Heavy cruiser *San Francisco* at Pearl Harbor on December 4, 1942, on its way to the United States for repairs after being damaged in the First Naval Battle of Guadalcanal. The ship was hit by an estimated 45 shells, some "friendly," causing extensive topside damage. (Naval History and Heritage Command)

The Second Naval Battle of Guadalcanal

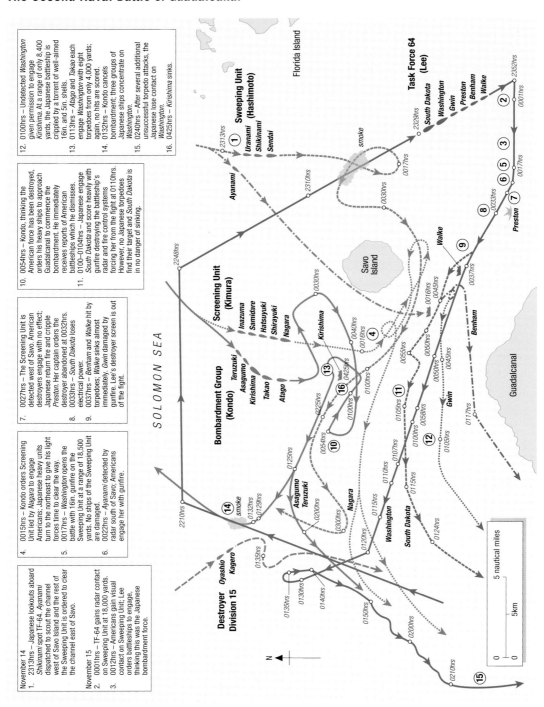

November 14
1. 2313hrs – Japanese lookouts aboard *Shikinami* spot TF-64. *Ayanami* dispatched to scout the channel west of Savo Island and the rest of the Sweeping Unit is ordered to clear the channel east of Savo.

November 15
2. 0001hrs – TF-64 gains radar contact on Sweeping Unit at 18,000 yards.
3. 0012hrs – Americans gain visual contact on Sweeping Unit; Lee orders battleships to engage, thinking this was the Japanese bombardment force.

4. 0015hrs – Kondo orders Screening Unit led by *Nagara* to engage Americans; Japanese heavy units turn to the northeast to give his light forces time to clear the way.
5. 0017hrs – *Washington* opens the battle with 16in. gunfire on the Sweeping Unit at a range of 18,500 yards. No ships of the Sweeping Unit are damaged.
6. 0022hrs – *Ayanami* detected by radar south of Savo; Americans engage her with gunfire.

7. 0027hrs – The Screening Unit is detected west of Savo. American destroyers engage with no effect; Japanese return fire and cripple *Preston*. Her captain orders the destroyer abandoned at 0032hrs.
8. 0033hrs – *South Dakota* loses electrical power.
9. 0037hrs – *Benham* and *Walke* hit by torpedoes; *Walke* sinks almost immediately; *Gwin* damaged by gunfire. Lee's destroyer screen is out of the fight.

10. 0054hrs – Kondo, thinking the American force has been destroyed, orders his heavy ships to approach Guadalcanal to commence the bombardment. He immediately receives reports of American battleships which he dismisses.
11. 0100–0104hrs – Japanese engage *South Dakota* and score heavily with gunfire destroying the battleship's radar and fire control systems forcing her from the fight at 0110hrs. However, no Japanese torpedoes find their target and *South Dakota* is in no danger of sinking.

12. 0100hrs – Undetected *Washington* given permission to engage *Kirishima*. At a range of only 8,400 yards, the Japanese battleship is crippled by a torrent of well-aimed 16in. and 5in. shells.
13. 0113hrs – *Atago* and *Takao* each engage *Washington* with eight torpedoes from only 4,000 yards; again, no hits are scored.
14. 0132hrs – Kondo cancels bombardment; three groups of Japanese ships concentrate on *Washington*.
15. 0240hrs – After several additional unsuccessful torpedo attacks, the Japanese lose contact on *Washington*.
16. 0425hrs – *Kirishima* sinks.

The campaign did not start auspiciously for the USN. After the landing on Guadalcanal and three smaller islands on August 7, the IJN gathered a scratch force of five heavy cruisers, two light cruisers, and one destroyer to attack the invasion fleet. Leaving Rabaul on the afternoon of August 7, the Japanese force headed toward Guadalcanal. Despite being spotted on the way by Allied aircraft, when the Japanese arrived off Guadalcanal in the early morning hours of August 9, they gained complete surprise against the Allied surface deployed to protect the invasion transports. The Allied force was deployed in three non-supporting groups and proved itself totally unready for night combat. In the first phase of the Battle of Savo Island, the Japanese cruisers pummeled Australian heavy cruiser *Canberra* with 24 hits (it later sank), and damaged heavy cruiser *Chicago* with a torpedo. Inexplicably, none of the Allied ships in this group reported what had just happened. In the next phase, the Japanese cruisers came across a USN force built around heavy cruisers *Astoria*, *Quincy*, and *Vincennes*. Once again, the Americans were surprised. The Japanese cruisers fired torpedoes first and then closed to finish off their targets with 8in shells. All three cruisers were sunk. After defeating the Allied escort force, the Japanese commander decided to break off the action and return to Rabaul, squandering the best chance the Japanese had of stopping the American invasion in its tracks.

Savo Island remains the worst USN defeat at sea. Four heavy cruisers (one Australian) were sunk and one damaged, along with two destroyers damaged. Personnel losses were heavy with 1,077 sailors killed and 709 wounded. The USN clearly had a lot to learn about night fighting.

The USN did not contest the night waters around Guadalcanal until October 11–12. On this occasion, a force of two heavy and two light cruisers and five destroyers faced a Japanese force of approximately equal size. At the Battle of Cape Esperance, the USN gained the element of surprise using radar. Now it was the turn of the Japanese to fight a confused battle and react poorly. USN gunfire sank a heavy cruiser, heavily damaged another, and sank a destroyer. Once it regained its composure, the IJN struck back and sank an American destroyer, as well as inflicting heavy damage on light cruiser *Boise*, and moderate damage on heavy cruiser *Salt Lake City*. American gunfire contributed to the damage that sank the one destroyer and damaged another one. Nevertheless, it was still an American victory.

The struggle for Guadalcanal was decided by control of the airfield on the island. The Americans were able to keep the airfield operational and stocked with enough aircraft to make any large-scale Japanese reinforcement of the island impossible. Unable to suppress the airfield with air attacks, the IJN tried to do it with a naval bombardment. This tactic worked in October, and in November, with the campaign moving to a climax, the IJN sought to bombard the airfield again before the arrival of a large reinforcement convoy. This set the stage for the most vicious night battle of the entire war with 27 ships engaged. The IJN sent two battleships, with an escort of one light cruiser and 11 destroyers, to neutralize the airfield. The USN scraped up two heavy cruisers, three light cruisers, and eight destroyers to contest the planned bombardment. The clash, known as the First Naval Battle of Guadalcanal, occurred on the night of November 12–13. The American commander failed to use the radar warning of the approaching Japanese with the result that the battle turned into a close-quarters brawl. The American ships concentrated much of their fire on battleship *Hiei*. At close range, the American shells did serious damage to the battleship. *Hiei* was crippled and in the morning was discovered steaming helplessly in circles. It was finished off by air attack on November 13. Two IJN destroyers were also sunk and two more damaged. Of the 13 USN ships, only two destroyers emerged from the battle undamaged. Heavy cruisers *San Francisco* and *Portland* were heavily damaged; light cruisers *Atlanta* and *Juneau* were sunk, and light cruiser *Helena* moderately damaged. Four destroyers were sunk, and two were heavily damaged. Despite this carnage, the Americans achieved their mission when the shattered Japanese force broke off the engagement.

The Japanese did not accept defeat on the morning of November 13. On the night of November 13–14, they conducted a bombardment with two heavy cruisers, but this failed to knock out the airfield. They prepared to conduct a major bombardment the next night. The force ordered to execute this mission consisted of battleship *Kirishima*, two heavy cruisers, two light cruisers, and 12 destroyers. At this decisive moment, Vice Admiral William Halsey had no choice but to commit a scratch force of battleships *Washington* and *South Dakota*, and four destroyers. The battleships were possibly the most powerful ships in the entire world but were not designed to fight at night in closed waters where they faced a high torpedo threat. As outlined in the accompanying map, Halsey's gamble paid off. Early in the battle the cohesion of the USN force was destroyed, with all four destroyers and *South Dakota* being knocked out, but *Washington* was able to engage *Kirishima* at close range and blow it apart with 16in gunfire. The Japanese were again forced to cancel their bombardment. *Kirishima* and a destroyer were sunk. *Washington*'s virtuoso performance stopped the last major IJN operation to recapture Guadalcanal.

In the last engagement of the Guadalcanal campaign, the Battle of Tassafaronga on November 30, a USN force of four heavy cruisers, one light cruiser, and six destroyers was smashed by an outnumbered and surprised Japanese force of eight destroyers. The four heavy cruisers were all hit by torpedoes, with *Northampton* sinking. The IJN lost a single destroyer in an exhibition of its continuing mastery of night fighting.

Though the surface forces of both navies were most active during the campaign, their carrier forces also saw action when the Japanese conducted major operations to recapture the island. The first IJN operation to knock the Marines off the island was conducted in August. This was the first example of the IJN not understanding the kind of battle they were fighting. The IJN carrier force was rebuilt after Midway and in August 1942 it included *Shokaku*, *Zuikaku*, and light carrier *Ryujo*. Yamamoto ordered the Combined Fleet, led by its carriers, to destroy USN forces around the island and get a reinforcement convoy with 1,500 troops to the island. The operation was unlikely to succeed since USN forces protecting the 10,000 Marines on Guadalcanal included three fleet carriers.

The first carrier battle of the campaign, the Battle of the Eastern Solomons fought on August 24, was the most indecisive carrier battle of the war. The IJN did strike the American carriers and damaged *Enterprise*. A second strike received faulty target data and missed an opportunity to finish off the damaged *Enterprise*. The USN failed to attack the main Japanese carrier force but did find *Ryujo* and sent it to the bottom. The next day, the Japanese troop convoy was mauled and forced to retreat. The battle was a clear tactical victory for the Americans.

The final carrier battle of 1942 was the only Japanese victory in the five carrier battles fought during the war. By October, the USN's carrier strength in the Pacific had been reduced to *Enterprise* and *Hornet*. *Wasp* was sunk by a Japanese submarine attack on September 15, and *Saratoga* was still under repairs from a submarine torpedo attack suffered on August 31. To support the Marines on the island, Halsey decided to risk his only two operational carriers in an operation beyond the range of friendly aircraft operating from Guadalcanal against a Japanese force of four carriers. After days of shadow boxing, the two carrier forces clashed on October 26. Once again, the American strikes were scattered. Of the 75 strike aircraft launched, only ten actually located and attacked a Japanese fleet carrier. USN dive-bombers heavily damaged *Shokaku*, but it again survived to fight another day. Light carrier *Zuiho* was also forced out of action with bomb damage. Most importantly, Japanese aircraft losses were extremely heavy. USN CAP and antiaircraft fire were equally effective and accounted for a total of 99 aircraft destroyed. Japanese aircrew losses were also heavy. The scale of these losses affected the future viability of the IJN's carrier force.

Despite the cost to the Japanese, they inflicted a defeat on the USN's carrier force. In a brilliantly coordinated attack, carrier *Hornet* was crippled early in the battle and was later sunk. *Enterprise* was also subjected to a well-executed attack. On this occasion, the deadly Japanese torpedo bombers failed to score a hit, allowing the carrier to escape and play a major role in the decisive battles in November.

The six-month campaign exacted a high toll from both navies. USN losses totaled 25 major surface units, with the IJN losing 18. On top of this, the IJN lost over 800 aircrew. Most importantly, the Japanese effort to defeat the first American offensive of the war had failed. The flood of new USN units gave it the means to continue, and accelerate, the advance.

SLOGGING UP THE SOLOMONS

As already outlined, the capture of Guadalcanal was only the first phase in the Allied plan to recapture Rabaul. Following the February 1943 Japanese withdrawal from Guadalcanal, the second phase of MacArthur's plan began to unfold. On June 30, the Americans landed on Rendova Island. From there, they prepared to leapfrog to New Georgia and the key airfield at Munda.

The American landing in the Central Solomons was the impetus for a series of night surface battles as the Japanese reinforced their garrisons on various islands in the region and the USN tried to stop them. The IJN still held the advantage in these night battles since its destroyers were well trained for this type of combat and because the USN still failed to comprehend the range advantage possessed by IJN torpedoes over cruiser guns. The USN had already decided that chasing destroyers with heavy cruisers was ill advised and decided to put light cruisers with their faster-firing guns in the forefront. The USN's night-fighting doctrine and use of radar was immature, but it gradually overcame these challenges and erased the IJN's advantage at night.

The first night encounter occurred on March 6, 1943, when light cruisers *Cleveland*, *Montpelier*, and *Denver* encountered two Japanese destroyers off Kolombangara Island in the Central Solomons. Using radar, the cruisers were able to detect the Japanese first and then smother them in 6in shellfire. Both destroyers were sunk with no loss to the Americans. This small-scale encounter seemed to validate the USN's new night-fighting doctrine and the role of the light cruiser. In reality, it demonstrated that the side that gained surprise usually translated it into victory. In the next engagement, the Battle of Kula Gulf on the night of July 5–6, a USN task force led by light cruisers *Helena*, *Honolulu*, and *St. Louis* again gained surprise with radar, but concentrated its fire on the lead Japanese destroyer. The Japanese recovered quickly and unleashed a torpedo barrage which turned the battle. *Helena* was struck by three torpedoes and sank. The Americans claimed to have sunk three IJN destroyers and damaged five more with radar-controlled gunfire, but the true toll was a single destroyer sunk. Only days later, at the Battle of Kolombangara on July 12–13, the superiority of IJN torpedoes over USN gunfire was again demonstrated. This time, neither side gained the surprise. *Honolulu* and *St. Louis* were both hit by torpedoes and had their bows blown off; a New Zealand light cruiser was hit and heavily damaged; and an American destroyer was also sunk by a torpedo. The cost to the IJN was a light cruiser sunk by 6in gunfire.

This brought an end to USN attempts to chase Japanese destroyers in the restricted waters of the Solomons with light cruisers. Destroyers were now given this mission. The next action did not occur until the night of August 6–7 when six USN destroyers engaged four IJN destroyers at the Battle of Vella Gulf. The Japanese courted disaster by using the same route from several previous runs. The new American tactic of giving destroyers the lead was immediately vindicated. Using radar, the Americans let the Japanese close to 6,300 yards and then fired 22 torpedoes. At least five hit, accounting for three destroyers.

Another action was fought on August 18 between four USN destroyers and four IJN destroyers off Vella Lavella Island. Both sides exchanged torpedo and gunnery barrages, but no ships suffered any serious damage. The Japanese decision to abandon the Central Solomons put the next destroyer clash off until October 6. At the Battle of Vella Lavella, three USN destroyers fought outnumbered against five IJN destroyers. The Americans launched their torpedoes first, but the barrage was ineffective. The ensuing gunnery barrage damaged a destroyer and brought it to a halt. It was later sunk. The Japanese counterattack hit two destroyers with torpedoes. One could not be saved and was later scuttled.

There was one more Solomons encounter in which USN light cruisers played a prominent role. This was the Battle of Empress Augusta Bay on November 2 when an American task force of light cruisers *Cleveland*, *Columbia*, *Montpelier*, and *Denver*, escorted by eight Fletcher-class destroyers, took on an IJN force of two heavy and two light cruisers and six destroyers that was attempting to attack an American invasion force. The battle did not go according to plan for either side, but the USN had finally learned to minimize the IJN's torpedo threat with radical high-speed maneuvering. The cruisers pumped out an incredible volume of fire – 4,591 6in and 705 5in shells, but scored only about a dozen hits, several of which were duds. Nevertheless, this was sufficient to sink a light cruiser and damage several other ships. Another Japanese destroyer was sunk by USN destroyers. *Denver* and *Columbia* were both hit by dud 8in shells which caused minor damage. This clear victory in a night battle was the finest moment of the war for a USN light cruiser force.

The final destroyer action of the campaign witnessed one of the best performances by USN destroyers during the entire war. At the Battle of Cape St George on November 25, five USN destroyers faced an equal number of IJN destroyers making an evacuation run from Bougainville. Firing torpedoes guided by radar, the American destroyers first sank the two Japanese destroyers providing cover. Then they chased down and sank one of the destroyers carrying troops. In this text book action, the American force suffered no damage.

The Solomons campaign from March to November 1943 inflicted additional attrition on the IJN. In particular, losses to its destroyer force were heavy, with 25 being lost in the Solomons or off nearby New Guinea. Such losses were irreplaceable for the IJN. With new tactics, new aggressive leadership, and the proven ability to harness the advantage of radar, the USN gained night-fighting dominance over the IJN.

THE FAST CARRIER TASK FORCE ON THE RAMPAGE

The USN's drive across the Central Pacific was led by the Fast Carrier Task Force. In the second half of 1943, Essex-class fleet carriers and Independence-class light carriers reached the Pacific. First used in raids against Japanese-held islands, the fast carriers were covering major amphibious operations by late 1943. The large aircraft capacities of the fleet carriers, their excellent aircraft piloted by well-trained aircrews, and a much improved capability to defend themselves against conventional air attack transformed the war in the Pacific. After its beating in the Guadalcanal and Solomons campaign, the IJN's carrier force was in no position to challenge the American advance.

In August 1943, the new carriers made their combat debut when *Essex*, *Yorktown* and light carrier *Independence* conducted a raid against Marcus Island. The next month, fleet carrier *Lexington*, joined by light carriers *Princeton* and *Belleau Wood*, hit Tarawa Atoll in the Gilbert Islands. In November, all six of the carriers struck Wake Island. None of the raids encountered heavy resistance, but they were useful for honing the skills of the new ships.

An IJN build-up at Rabaul in November forced the diversion of several carriers to the South Pacific. A series of raids on Rabaul by *Saratoga*, *Essex*,

Bunker Hill, Princeton, and *Independence* crippled an IJN cruiser force caught in harbor. Japanese attempts to hit the carriers with land-based aircraft were unsuccessful, with heavy losses.

By November there were enough carriers to create four separate carrier task forces to cover the invasion of the Gilbert Islands. The Fast Carrier Task Force consisted of 11 carriers – prewar ships *Saratoga* and *Enterprise*, four Essex-class carriers, and five light carriers. Makin and Tarawa Atolls were seized, the latter after a tough fight. The IJN made no major attempt to intervene but did succeed in sinking an escort carrier with a submarine attack and damaging *Independence* with a torpedo during a dusk air attack.

The Marshall Islands were next. Nimitz's bold plan called for the seizure of undefended Majuro in January 1944, and then landings on Kwajalein Atoll to take its huge, enclosed anchorage and airfields. After seizing Eniwetok Atoll in the western Marshalls the following month, the other atolls were bypassed. The operations were covered by 12 carriers of the Fast Carrier Task Force.

February 1944 also marked the largest display of USN naval air power to date and was a portent of things to come. Beginning on February 17 and lasting for two days, nine carriers pounded the IJN's Central Pacific bastion at Truk Atoll with a total of 1,250 offensive sorties. After this two-day battering, Truk had been neutralized as a major IJN base. In the process, 250 Japanese aircraft were destroyed and 39 warships and merchants sunk. The IJN's response was feeble, but *Intrepid* was torpedoed and damaged in a night air attack. Later in the month, six fast carriers struck targets in the Marianas for the first time.

The rampage continued on March 30–April 1 when ten carriers struck the IJN naval base at Palau. Just like at Truk, the warships of the Combined Fleet were pulled out in time, but losses to defending Japanese aircraft were heavy and another 36 merchants and auxiliaries were sunk. In April, the Fast Carrier Task Force supported MacArthur's landing at Hollandia on New Guinea. At the end of the month, the fast carriers made a return strike on Truk, this time with 2,200 sorties.

THE CARRIERS CLASH

The largest USN operation of the war to date was targeted on the Marianas. On June 15, Marines successfully landed on Saipan. The IJN planned yet another decisive battle to protect the Marianas since they were within Japan's inner defense zone. The result was the largest carrier battle in history.

Tactical disposition of Task Force 58

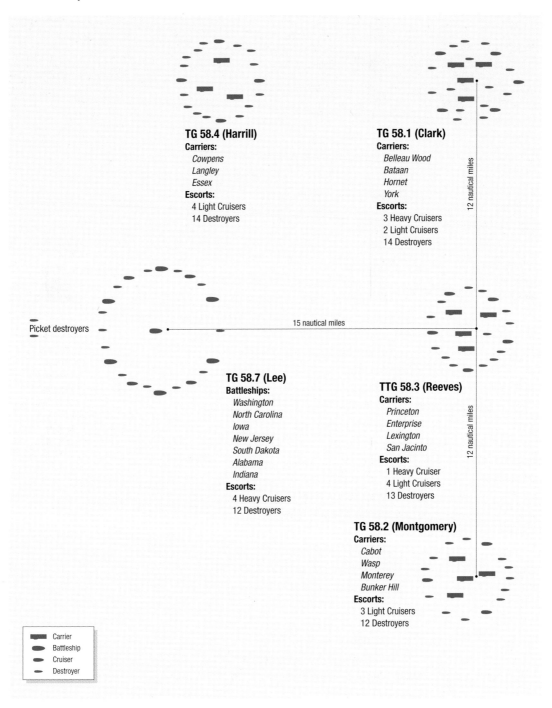

TG 58.4 (Harrill)
Carriers:
Cowpens
Langley
Essex
Escorts:
4 Light Cruisers
14 Destroyers

TG 58.1 (Clark)
Carriers:
Belleau Wood
Bataan
Hornet
York
Escorts:
3 Heavy Cruisers
2 Light Cruisers
14 Destroyers

12 nautical miles

Picket destroyers

15 nautical miles

TG 58.7 (Lee)
Battleships:
Washington
North Carolina
Iowa
New Jersey
South Dakota
Alabama
Indiana
Escorts:
4 Heavy Cruisers
12 Destroyers

TTG 58.3 (Reeves)
Carriers:
Princeton
Enterprise
Lexington
San Jacinto
Escorts:
1 Heavy Cruiser
4 Light Cruisers
13 Destroyers

12 nautical miles

TG 58.2 (Montgomery)
Carriers:
Cabot
Wasp
Monterey
Bunker Hill
Escorts:
3 Light Cruisers
12 Destroyers

Carrier
Battleship
Cruiser
Destroyer

The size of the forces involved were immense. The IJN mustered over 50 combatants, over 400 carrier aircraft on nine carriers, and some 300 land-based aircraft. But this was dwarfed by the USN's order of battle that included some 165 combatants, over 900 aircraft on 15 fleet and light carriers, and another 170 aircraft on seven escort carriers. As unbalanced as the forces were on paper, even more unbalanced was the level of training for the aircrew aboard the two carrier forces. Despite the fact that the IJN had been hoarding its carrier force for 20 months, it had been unable to make up previous losses and adequately train new carrier aircrews.

A Japanese bomber scores a near miss on *Bunker Hill* on June 19. The blast killed three and wounded 73, but damage to the ship was light. Despite several opportunities during the battle, the inexperienced Japanese aviators failed to score a single hit on a USN carrier. (Naval History and Heritage Command)

The Japanese plan to execute a series of long-range air strikes against the USN's fast carrier force appeared to go well. The USN commander, Admiral Spruance, decided to take a passive role to protect the landing force and let the Japanese launch the first attacks. After maneuvering to stay out of the range of USN carrier aircraft, the Japanese launched four major strikes on June 19. If this had been 1942, such an attack would have shattered any USN task force. But the nature of carrier warfare in the Pacific was very different in 1944.

To face the Japanese onslaught, the fast carriers mounted a strong CAP; just under 300 Hellcats reported engagements during the day. The well-directed CAP shredded the incoming Japanese waves. The first strike lost all but 17 of 69 aircraft and only succeeded in placing a single bomb on a battleship that caused little damage. The main Japanese attack of 128 aircraft was equally ineffective, and only 31 of the aircraft returned to their carriers. The third Japanese wave of 47 aircraft miscarried after it went after a false contact. The final wave of 82 aircraft also failed to hit anything. Most of its aircraft recovered on Guam, but never flew again. While the Japanese aerial debacle was in progress, USN submarines torpedoed and sank fleet carriers *Taiho* and *Shokaku*.

The following day Spruance went after the Japanese and was able to launch an afternoon strike of 216 aircraft. When the strike reached its target, light was fading so what resulted was a hurried series of attacks. Several ships were hit, but only carrier *Hiyo* was sunk by a torpedo. Two oilers were hit and later scuttled. With this parting shot, the Japanese escaped. The latest Japanese attempt to destroy the USN in a decisive battle turned out to be a decisive defeat. Of the 430 carrier aircraft available to the Japanese at the start of the battle, only 35 survived. This, and the loss of three more carriers, crippled the IJN's carrier force for the remainder of the war. USN losses were comparatively light – 130 aircraft and 76 aviators. No American ship was lost. Even though the battle was a resounding success, the victory seemed hollow to many American admirals since the bulk of the Japanese fleet had escaped.

VICTORY AT LEYTE GULF

As the Fast Carrier Task Force was making preparatory attacks against the Philippines in September 1944, Admiral Halsey noted that Japanese resistance was almost non-existent. He recommended to Nimitz that the planned invasion of Mindanao on October 25 be abandoned and the invasion of Leyte in the central Philippines planned for 15 November be moved up. The two-month advance in the schedule was quickly approved. On October 20, the Americans landed on Leyte. Covering the invasion was the Third Fleet with nine fleet carriers, eight light carriers, six battleships, four heavy and ten light cruisers, and 58 destroyers. The Seventh Fleet provided immediate protection to the landing with a force built around six old battleships and 18 escort carriers. The Third Fleet under Halsey reported to Nimitz and had the primary mission of engaging the IJN if it made an appearance. The Seventh Fleet was under MacArthur's command. This command structure was the cause of problems during the battle.

The IJN was determined to make an appearance, and in fact planned a supreme effort with all of its remaining strength. The essence of its plan was to draw Halsey's powerful force away from Leyte so a force of battleships and heavy cruisers could attack the invasion force inside Leyte Gulf. This plan was ill conceived for many reasons. Its primary fault was that the battleship force was scheduled to arrive in Leyte Gulf by October 25. By this time, the invasion force was ashore with 132,400 men and 200,000 tons of supplies. However, the myth persists that had the Japanese reached Leyte Gulf they could have turned the tide of the war by attacking the invasion fleet and the beachhead. In fact, the entire effort was without hope of success since all that was left in the gulf was empty transports and some resupply ships; the invasion force had long since unloaded and moved away.

The Battle of Leyte Gulf consisted of four major actions. In the first, the so-called IJN Center Force, with five battleships, ten heavy cruisers, and smaller escorts was subjected to intense air attack by the Third Fleet in the Sibuyan Sea on October 24. During the day, 259 aircraft attacked the Japanese force. Most of these sorties were directed at a single ship – the superbattleship *Musashi*. The 70,000-ton ship was eventually sunk after being battered by as many as 15 torpedoes and 16 bomb hits, but in so doing it absorbed so much punishment that the other ships in the Center Force (except for a heavy cruiser hit by a torpedo and forced to return to Singapore) were relatively undamaged. Halsey thought this beating rendered the Center Force ineffective, so headed to attack an IJN carrier force that had the primary mission of sacrificing itself to divert Halsey north.

Light carrier *Princeton* was the only fast carrier lost after the Battle of Santa Cruz in October 1942. It is shown here on fire after being bombed on the morning of October 24, 1944. Later in the day, the ship's torpedo magazine blew up and the ship was scuttled. (Naval History and Heritage Command)

Three major battles took place the following day. The first of these was fought during the early hours in the Surigao Strait when the IJN Southern Force, consisting of two old battleships, one heavy cruiser, and four destroyers, attempted to rush through the strait into Leyte Gulf. Facing them were six battleships (all but one veterans of Pearl Harbor), four heavy cruisers (one Australian), four light cruisers, and 28 destroyers. In the first phase of the battle, American destroyers delivered radar-directed torpedo attacks that sank battleship *Fuso* and three destroyers. In the gunnery phase, the surviving Japanese ships were detected on radar at 33,000 yards and engaged by the USN battleships at 22,800 yards. *West Virginia* hit battleship *Yamashiro* on its first salvo; deluged by hundreds of shells, *Yamashiro* finally sank after being hit by three torpedoes from USN destroyers. The Japanese heavy cruiser was hit by 10–20 shells and turned away. It was sunk later in the day by escort carrier aircraft. Only a single Japanese destroyer survived.

Hours later, the Center Force appeared off Samar Island headed south toward Leyte Gulf. At this point, the Center Force still numbered four battleships, six heavy cruisers, two light cruisers, and 11 destroyers. Just before 0700hrs, the Japanese encountered the Seventh Fleet's escort carrier force, which was broken down into three task groups. The nearest consisted of six escort carriers, escorted by three destroyers and four destroyer escorts. Facing what appeared to be overwhelming firepower, the USN force tried to escape at its top speed of 18 knots. The escort carriers came under a storm of fire; since it was at the rear of the formation, *Gambier Bay* took the brunt of Japanese attention. After taking as many as 26 hits, the ship slipped under the waves.

Common wisdom would have it that the slow and poorly armed escort carriers stood no chance against the Japanese and should have been annihilated in short order. Upon deeper examination, this belief is unfounded. The three escort carrier task groups embarked almost 500 aircraft. Total escort carrier sorties during the day against the Japanese force were 441– 209 fighters and 232 by Avengers (68 with torpedoes). This was more than the Fast Carrier Task Force mounted the day before that had sunk *Musashi*. The defense mounted by the escort carriers featured one of the most concerted USN air attacks on Japanese surface ships during the entire war. These attacks were not well coordinated and often failed to carry weapons suited for attacking ships but did keep the Japanese from overwhelming the slow escort carriers and accounted for three IJN heavy cruisers. The efforts of the escorts were also instrumental in saving the escort carriers from destruction. These cost the USN two destroyers and a destroyer escort. Just as the Japanese had closed to a position to seemingly complete the destruction of the American force, they broke off the action. It was an epic American victory, but one bought at a high price. Later the same day, the same group of escort carriers came under the first planned kamikaze attack of the war. Carrier *St. Lo* was hit by a skillful attack that caused it to roll over and sink within 30 minutes with the loss of 114 men. In the course of the surface battle and the kamikaze attack, the escort carrier task force lost 1,118 men.

The final battle was the most controversial. As Halsey was sending a series of strikes against the IJN carrier force consisting of four carriers, two battleships, three cruisers and eight destroyers, he got word of the plight of the escort carriers off Samar. By 1055hrs, he was forced to send the six fast battleships back to the south. They were too late by only a few hours to prevent the Center Force from escaping back through San Bernardino Strait. Over 500 sorties were devoted to hitting the Japanese carriers; *Zuikaku* was sunk, along with light carriers *Zuiho* and *Chitose*, and a destroyer. In the afternoon, an American cruiser-destroyer force finished off light carrier *Chiyoda* and another destroyer. The rest of the Japanese force fled, with another light cruiser being sunk by USN submarines.

Final Japanese losses were calamitous – four carriers, three battleships, six heavy cruisers, four light cruisers, and ten destroyers. The remaining ships did little during the war, most being restricted to port due to fuel shortages. It was the end of the IJN as an organized force.

FINAL CAMPAIGNS IN THE PACIFIC

From the first kamikaze attacks in October 1944 through July 1945, the USN was subjected to a suicide campaign of increasing ferocity. The final attacks in the Philippines were recorded on January 13, 1945 and were actually conducted by Imperial Japanese Army units. After a relative lull, kamikaze attacks picked up again when the Marines landed on Iwo Jima on February 19. Tethered to the beachhead, the invasion fleet was easy to find. On February 21, a single kamikaze hit escort carrier *Bismarck Sea* and sank the ship with 119 members of its crew.

The landing on Okinawa on April 1 brought the massed kamikaze attacks that the campaign was eventually known for. The first massed attack took place on April 6; it was followed by another nine, with the last taking place on June 21–22. Most of the suicide pilots selected the picket destroyers off the island for attack. The destroyers were susceptible to massed attacks and during 1945, 13 destroyers or destroyer-like ships were sunk. On May 11, the kamikazes scored one of their biggest successes of the war when two struck fleet carrier *Bunker Hill*. Huge fires were ignited on the flight and hangar decks. The crew saved the ship, but 346 were killed, 43 listed as missing, and 264 wounded.

Despite the carnage caused by some 3,000 kamikaze sorties, the USN was able to complete the occupation of the Philippines, maintain control of the waters around Okinawa, and then move to the waters off Japan to project power on a strategic level. But the cost was high. Of the 3,000 suicide missions, 367 hit or damaged a target. In total, 66 ships or craft (almost all American), were sunk or never repaired. Personnel casualties were extremely high with 6,190 killed and 8,760 wounded. After a spectacular debut during the Philippines campaign, the overall effectiveness of the kamikazes dropped during the Okinawa campaign. Success rates in the Philippines campaign were over 52 percent, but this fell to 16 percent in 1945. Despite being a prime target, kamikaze attacks were largely ineffective against fleet aircraft carriers. In 1944, fleet carriers were hit six times and none sunk. In 1945, ten were struck, and again none were sunk, but *Bunker Hill* came close. Two light carriers were hit during the war, and neither sank. Escort carriers were a different story. Sixteen were damaged and three sunk by kamikaze attack. As a military weapon, the kamikaze was not a success. It neither broke the morale of the sailors subjected to continual attacks nor succeeded in stopping the American advance.

THE USN'S WAR IN EUROPE

The Japanese attack on Pearl Harbor surprised not only the USN, but also the German Navy, which was in no position to attack shipping off the US East Coast when the war started. This situation was quickly rectified and on January 14, 1942 the first merchant ship was torpedoed by a U-boat east of Cape Cod. For the next six months, the German onslaught against the East Coast met a disorganized response from the unprepared USN. Merchant ships proceeded individually since the USN lacked the necessary escorts to organize convoys. When the USN finally reacted to the massacre, the Germans sent their U-boats into the Gulf of Mexico and the Caribbean to attacked undefended shipping there. From the opening of the attacks until mid-June, 127 ships were sunk, the vast majority American. In exchange, during the first six and a half months of the war, US forces accounted for only nine U-boats. The result was nothing less than a Second Pearl Harbor. The tardy institution of convoys in April decreased losses, first along the Atlantic, and later in the Gulf of Mexico. King's decision not to institute convoys at the onset of war was a disastrous mistake.

OPERATION *TORCH*

Unable to attack northern Europe directly in 1942, the Allies had to settle for an indirect strategy of invading French North Africa with the goal of clearing Axis forces from North Africa. The invasion, codenamed Operation *Torch*, was set for November 8 and divided into three parts. The Western Naval Task Force was a completely American operation to land an initial load of 35,000 US troops at three spots on Morocco. The Center Naval Task Force, targeted against Oran, and the Eastern Naval Task Force, targeted against Algiers, also included American troops but was escorted and covered by the RN.

The American part of Operation *Torch* was risky. The invasion force departed from Hampton Roads and had to transit across an entire ocean through waters invested with U-boats. The only air cover for the landings was provided by a single fleet carrier and four escort carriers. Waiting for the Americans was a large French force with heavy shore batteries, supported by air and naval forces. This was the largest USN operation of the war so far. Over 100 ships were involved including the five aircraft carriers, three battleships, three heavy and four light cruisers, 38 destroyers, four submarines, and 47 auxiliaries of various types, mostly transports.

The toughest battle was fought by the force assaulting nearest the major French base at Casablanca. The French Navy sortied with a light cruiser, seven destroyers, and eight submarines, supported by the 15in guns from the incomplete battleship *Jean Bart* and four shore batteries. After battleship *Massachusetts,* heavy cruisers *Wichita* and *Tuscaloosa*, and aircraft from carrier *Ranger* seemed to silence *Jean Bart* and the shore batteries, the landings proceeded. But the French weren't giving up. Seven destroyers sortied from Casablanca to attack the landing force, later joined by the light cruiser. Cruisers *Brooklyn* and *Augusta,* supported by eight destroyers, moved to protect the transports. The French fought bravely but took a serious beating. By the end of the day, four French destroyers had been sunk, and the light cruiser and two more destroyers heavily damaged. After resisting for three days, the French ceased hostilities.

THE CONVOY BATTLES OF 1943

The U-boat threat reached its peak in the first months of 1943. In May 1943, the Tenth Fleet was established to coordinate all USN antisubmarine warfare (ASW) activities. King designated himself as commander, but the

fleet was actually run by its chief of staff Rear Admiral Francis Low. This command shuffle coincided with a flood of new assets to fight the U-boats. By June, 42 destroyer escorts were in service; by the end of the year, 260 were operational. The first USN escort carrier committed to the defense of Atlantic convoys arrived just as the tide of the war against the U-boats was turning in the Allies' favor. The original intent was to use the escort carriers in the Central Atlantic. However, the first escort carrier, *Bogue*, was used in the North Atlantic in defense of convoys SC-123 and HX-235. *Bogue* recorded no U-boat kills in March or April, but in May its luck changed while in support of convoy ON-184. Beginning on May 21, aircraft from *Bogue* damaged three U-boats and sank another. In another deployment beginning on May 31, *Bogue* damaged two more German submarines and sank two. The reasons for these early successes were many. The newly established Tenth Fleet, exercising operational control of the escort carriers, made excellent use of Enigma intercepts that placed *Bogue* and its destroyer escorts where contact with U-boats was likely. At this point of the war, U-boats spent most of their time on the surface, so *Bogue's* air patrols came into regular contact with U-boats massing for attacks on convoys. The early success of *Bogue* demonstrated the effectiveness of the escort carriers combined with excellent tactical intelligence.

In June 1943, the Germans shifted the focus of U-boat operations to the Central Atlantic. This was right into the teeth of the USN's escort carrier operating area. *Core* and *Santee* were the first to benefit. In four days between July 13 and 16, the two carriers sank four U-boats. On July 30, *Santee* sank another southwest of the Azores. The escort carriers were increasingly freed from direct convoy protection and sent after known U-boat locations provided by Enigma intercepts. *Bogue* returned to action in July and accounted for two U-boats on July 23.

Card joined the fray in August and experienced immediate success. By the end of the month, it accounted for four U-boats sunk. Also active during the month was *Core* which sank two U-boats on August 24. During this period, the USN expanded the use of the Mark 24 mine, which was actually the world's first homing torpedo. Avengers flying from the escort carriers would force a U-boat to submerge with 500lb bombs and then drop a Mark 24 for the kill.

In September, U-boats returned to the North Atlantic in strength leaving the escort carriers in the Central Atlantic with few targets. In October, a spate of successes was recorded in the Central Atlantic. *Card* led the way with four confirmed U-boat kills. *Core* claimed another submarine on October 20 and *Block Island* made its first kill on October 28. For the last two months of 1943, *Card* and its escorts claimed another two submarines and *Bogue* another three with its escorts. The escort carriers, combined with Enigma-derived intelligence, had proven to be game-changers in the Battle for the Atlantic. In 1943, five escort carriers scored victories led by *Card*'s ten and *Bogue*'s eight.

THE BATTLE IS WON IN THE ATLANTIC

In 1944, more USN escort carriers entered the campaign. Accompanying the carriers were destroyer escorts that replaced the prewar flush-deck destroyers.

The first Casablanca-class escort carriers were *Mission Bay* and *Guadalcanal*. *Guadalcanal* scored quickly, sinking its first U-boat on January 16, 1944. On April 9 and 10, it sank another two enemy submarines. In June, it led its task group consisting of a destroyer and four destroyer escorts into the Central Atlantic where Enigma-derived information indicated *U-505* was operating. On June 4, one of its escorts detected the submarine on sonar and an ensuing series of attacks forced it to the surface. Boarding parties were sent over to capture the submarine and it was towed by *Guadalcanal* to Bermuda, arriving on June 19. This was the only German U-boat captured by the USN during the war.

In general, the Casablanca class was not able to handle sea conditions in the Atlantic as well as the Bogue class. Accordingly, most of the Casablanca-class ships were sent to the Pacific. *Tripoli*, *Solomons*, and *Wake Island* made brief combat appearances in the Atlantic, and only *Mission Bay* was active in combat operations through the end of the war. On June 15, aircraft from *Solomons* sank *U-860* for its only kill; *Wake Island*'s only kill came on July 2. *Mission Bay*'s task group accounted for another two submarines during the war, one on September 30 and the last on May 6, 1945.

The most active escort carrier of early 1944 was *Block Island*, which sank four U-boats in March. On May 6, *Block Island*'s task group encountered a U-boat that resulted in a close-range action with destroyer escort *Buckley* during which some of the U-boat's crew attempted to board the American ship. The submarine did not survive the action. *Block Island*'s brief but spectacular career came to an end on May 29 when *U-549* slammed three torpedoes into the carrier. The ship quickly sank, but only six men were lost. *U-549* was sunk the same day by the carrier's escorts. *Block Island* was the only USN escort carrier sunk in the Atlantic.

Bogue continued to enjoy success into 1944, sinking a U-boat in March and May, and an IJN submarine en route to Europe on June 24. Its last victory was recorded in August, making *Bogue* the top-scoring USN escort carrier of the Atlantic War. Other carriers scoring in 1944 included *Croatan* with four U-boats; *Card* sank one U-boat in July.

In 1945 U-boats were getting hard to find in the operating areas of USN escort carriers since most had been moved to areas closer to northern Europe. Those submarines still in the Atlantic increasingly used snorkels that reduced their time on the surface, making them harder to detect. In a last-ditch effort in 1945, six U-boats were deployed to attack targets off the US East Coast, giving the escort carriers a final chance to practice their ASW skills. Using Enigma-derived information, *Croatan* sank three submarines between April 15 and 21. *Core* scored its last kill on April 24.

The role of the escort carriers in the Atlantic campaign, while important, must be placed in perspective. Of the 785 U-boats sunk, only 177 were dispatched by USN forces. Of these, the escort carriers sank 53 and captured one. Escort carriers did not win the Battle of the Atlantic, but clearly they made an important contribution to winning the longest campaign of the war.

INVASIONS IN THE EUROPEAN THEATER

Once North Africa was cleared of Axis forces in May 1943, the logical next step was to invade Sicily. This was the biggest amphibious operation of the entire war if only initial assault forces are considered. Vice Admiral Kent Hewitt commanded the Western Naval Task Force consisting of some 580 ships. The invasion commenced on July 10. The following day, the American beach at Gela faced a German counterattack. For ten hours, light cruisers *Boise* and *Savannah*, supported by eight destroyers, rendered invaluable gunfire support that routed the German attack. After gaining a toehold, Allied forces cleared Sicily by August 17.

An invasion of the Italian mainland was next despite American objections to being sucked deeper into a Mediterranean war. The Bay of Salerno was selected as the landing site since it was the farthest point north still within Allied air range. The landings commenced on September 9 and met extremely heavy resistance from German troops. Resistance was so severe that the Army considered evacuating the troops already ashore. Led by cruisers *Philadelphia* and *Savannah* and four destroyers, naval gunfire support retrieved the situation. *Boise* joined the fight on September 14 replacing *Savannah*, which was struck by a German radio-controlled bomb. The weapon penetrated to the cruiser's lower shell handling room creating

Birmingham was one of five USN light cruisers assigned to support the July 1943 landings on Sicily. It is shown here firing on targets on July 10. Naval gunfire support was an essential component in overcoming contested landings. (Naval History and Heritage Command)

fires that almost sank the ship. Naval gunfire support was instrumental in the success of Salerno landings. The ships offshore delivered 11,000 tons of shells in support of the ground forces, a total not surpassed until Iwo Jima.

Stalemate in Italy resulted in an amphibious end-around at Anzio behind the German defenses. The landing was executed flawlessly on January 22, 1944. The Germans reacted quickly and turned the landing into a siege that was not broken until May 11. The USN gave support to the beachhead for the entire period, providing supplies, reinforcements, and gunfire support.

By June 1944, the Allies were ready to invade northern France. For this huge operation, the RN supplied the majority of gunfire support ships and the large majority of the hundreds of minesweeping units needed to clear the path to the invasion beaches. Most of the amphibious ships and craft used in the invasion were built in American yards. Leading up to the invasion, King was criticized for withholding what the RN considered to be adequate numbers of amphibious craft for the operation. Some American and British officers suspected that King was favoring the Pacific over the Normandy operation. There was also a competing requirement for the invasion of southern France, planned for the same time. In the end, the southern France operation was postponed to August and King found enough amphibious ships, primarily the ubiquitous tank landing ships, to satisfy demands.

The USN commanded the Western Naval Task Force, which was tasked to put troops ashore on Omaha and Utah beaches. A total of 931 ships and craft were required to deliver the troops assigned to the two beaches. Supporting USN warships included three battleships, three heavy cruisers, and 31 destroyers.

On June 6, the landings on Utah Beach went well, but on Omaha Beach it was a different story. At 0550hrs, *Arkansas* and *Texas* opened fire with their big guns. *Texas'* primary target was a heavily protected battery of six

155mm guns at Pointe du Hoc, 3 miles to the west of Omaha Beach. Housed in steel and concrete casemates in a position overlooking both Omaha and Utah Beaches, these guns posed the most dangerous threat to troops on the beaches and the transports offshore. For 34 minutes, *Texas* fired 255 14in shells at Pointe du Hoc until reports were received from its observation aircraft that the guns had been silenced. Actually the guns had been removed and taken a mile inland before the Allied assault. The craters from the 14in shells can still be seen there today. For much of the morning, the outcome of the landing on Omaha was uncertain. To relieve the pressure on the troops pinned down by German fire, seven destroyers closed to within 800 yards of the beach to deliver punishing fire. By late morning the troops on Omaha began to move inland.

The next task for *Arkansas* and *Texas* was supporting the ground assault on the fortified port of Cherbourg. On June 25 the two battleships, escorted by five destroyers, were tasked to neutralize a fortification located 6 miles east of Cherbourg known as Battery Hamburg. The battery was equipped with four 9.4in/40cal guns that were protected by steel shields and surrounded by reinforced concrete casemates. At 1208hrs while American troops assaulted Cherbourg from its landward side, *Arkansas* opened fire at 18,000 yards. It took the Germans 20 minutes to reply, and they quickly straddled *Texas*. *Texas* opened fire at 1239hrs. At 1316hrs, the Germans scored first. *Texas* was rocked when a shell bounced off the top of the armored conning tower and struck one of the navigation bridge's support columns. The resulting explosion sent shrapnel and rivets flying across the bridge, wounding almost everyone present. *Texas* got a measure of revenge when one of its salvoes placed a direct hit on one of Battery Hamburg's guns at 1335hrs. The inconclusive duel continued until 1501hrs when the battleships were ordered to retire to England. *Arkansas* had expended 58 12in shells and *Texas* had fired 206 14in shells.

Many of the ships that took part in the Normandy invasion moved into the Mediterranean to support the Allied invasion of southern France. The amphibious assault preceded much more smoothly than at Normandy. After providing pre-assault bombardments on August 15, *Arkansas*, *Texas*, and *Nevada*, along with heavy cruisers *Augusta*, *Quincy*, and *Tuscaloosa*, remained on station to offer fire support until the evening of August 17 when the beachheads were fully secured. Escort carriers *Tulagi* and *Kasaan Bay* conducted the USN's only escort carriers of the war in the Mediterranean in support of the invasion. By September 3, Marseilles and Toulon were opened to shipping and they played a critical role in supplying the advance into Germany.

CHAPTER 3
CARRIERS

PART 1: THE FLEET CARRIERS

In 1910, the USN established an early lead in naval aviation when it launched an aircraft off a wooden platform built on the cruiser *Birmingham*. The following year, the same aviator who had performed that feat landed an aircraft aboard armored cruiser *Pennsylvania* anchored in San Francisco Bay. However, the USN did not pursue this initial lead in carrier technology. Instead, seaplanes were preferred because of their economy and the fact that they did not impede the operations of the launching ship's guns. Experiments were begun with mounting catapults aboard large warships to support the use of seaplanes, but none were in service when World War I began. During the war, work on catapults continued. Successful catapult trials seemed to indicate that a major investment in aircraft carriers was unnecessary. The US entry into World War I in 1917 caught the USN without a single carrier or ship dedicated to operating aircraft. By the end of the war, the RN had clearly established a lead in naval aviation and the USN had yet to begin the construction of a single carrier. Fears of falling further behind the British and the realization that air supremacy was an essential part of modern naval operations compelled Congress to fund the conversion of a collier into an aircraft carrier in July 1919.

The initial role of USN carriers was to support the battle fleet. After World War I the battleship was still viewed as the arbiter of naval power and the carrier's role was to provide reconnaissance and spotting for the battle fleet while denying those advantages to the enemy. Use of aircraft to spot the fall of shot at long ranges exposed enemy ships to plunging fire against their weaker deck armor. Such an advantage was viewed as decisive by the battleship admirals. Carriers were also expected to protect the air space over their own fleet, thus denying the enemy the advantages of long-range spotting and

Santee photographed during Operation *Torch* in November 1942. On the left side of the flight deck are Douglas SBD-3 Dauntless scout-bombers with their non-folding wings which made them difficult to operate aboard escort carriers. To the right are Grumman F4F Wildcat fighters. (Naval History and Heritage Command)

scouting. Another important mission for carrier aircraft was antisubmarine patrol. Patrolling aircraft from carriers could keep enemy submarines submerged, and against a fast-moving force a submerged diesel-electric submarine with a top speed of less than 10 knots was effectively neutralized.

The USN gradually developed the carrier into an independent offensive platform. The first carrier aircraft were unable to carry torpedoes large enough to cripple or sink a capital ship. Of course, bombs could be carried, but these posed no real threat to ships maneuvering at speed to avoid attack. However, in the 1920s, the offensive capability of carrier aircraft was greatly increased by the development of dive-bombing, which for the first time

The USN's first three carriers in Bremerton, Washington about 1930. The immense size of the converted battlecruisers *Lexington* and *Saratoga* compared to the experimental *Langley* is striking. (Naval History and Heritage Command)

Early-war USN Carrier Air Groups

In the prewar period, and for almost two years into the war, the standard USN carrier air group had four squadrons. Spotting aircraft disappeared from the air group in the late 1920s, this mission being taken over by cruiser and battleship floatplanes. Evolving tactics and aircraft technology resulted in adjustments to the air group through the 1930s, but the basic structure was little changed going into World War II. By 1938, the standard prewar carrier air group had four squadrons of some 18 aircraft each, with another three in reserve. The fighter squadron was equipped with the Grumman F4F Wildcat. When the Douglas SBD Dauntless dive-bomber entered service, it was assigned to both the scouting and bombing squadrons. Dedicated scout squadrons were later disbanded and combined with the dive-bombing squadron. The fourth squadron was equipped with torpedo bombers that could also operate as level bombers.

At the start of the war, the standard torpedo bomber was the Douglas TBD Devastator that entered service in 1937.

Prewar carriers each had a permanently assigned air group. Each of the four squadrons was numbered after the hull number of the ship it was assigned to. For example, *Lexington*'s fighter squadron was designated VF-2, its dive-bomber squadron VB-2, its scout bomber squadron VS-2, and its torpedo squadron VT-2. After July 1938, air groups were known by the name of the ship. Thus, the squadrons listed above comprised the *Lexington* air group. By mid-1942, the entire air group was numbered to match its parent ship's hull number. With few exceptions, the permanence of the squadrons within an air group generally lasted through the Battle of Midway. After that, due to carrier losses or squadron exhaustion, carriers could have a mix of squadrons from two or three air groups.

allowed maneuvering ships to be struck with some degree of accuracy. Capital ships with heavy deck armor were still immune from attack, but carriers with their unarmored flight decks were now very vulnerable.

Reflecting the premise that carriers could not withstand significant damage, USN doctrine increasingly separated the carriers from the battle fleet in order that they escape early detection and destruction by the enemy. The primary task of the carrier was now to destroy opposing carriers, thus preventing their own destruction, and to set the stage for intensive attacks on the enemy battle fleet.

The requirement to generate maximum offensive power against enemy carriers drove USN carrier design. This meant provisions to launch a full deck of aircraft as quickly as possible. Open, unarmored hangars facilitated the quick launch of large numbers of aircraft. Doctrine called for most of the carrier's aircraft to be parked on the flight deck with the hangar deck used for aircraft maintenance and storage. This practice and the design of USN carriers meant that they operated larger air groups than their foreign contemporaries. The other factor driving USN carrier design was the tonnage restrictions of the 1922 Washington Naval Treaty. Up until the Essex class, the design of all USN carriers was impacted by this treaty.

The first American carrier was a conversion from a slow collier. Unable to procure funding from Congress for a modern carrier, the USN had to settle for a conversion in order that experimentation with aircraft from ships at sea could begin. When completed in March 1922, the ship was commissioned as *Langley* and given the designation CV 1 (the designation CV representing a fleet carrier and 1 being the first ship of this designation). It was never intended that *Langley* be anything more than a platform for experimentation. The conversion was very austere with a wooden flight deck built over a framework of beams and girders. The turbo-electric machinery of the collier was retained, but its top speed of only 14 knots meant that it was too slow to operate with any part of the fleet. The ship retained its six coal holds; one was used to store aviation gasoline, one contained the machinery for the aircraft elevator, and the other four provided aircraft storage. The aircraft were stored disassembled and were lifted out of the holds by means of a 3-ton gantry crane under the flight deck that moved over the four aircraft holds. There was no hangar deck. After removal from their hold, aircraft were assembled on the former collier upper deck. After assembly, the aircraft were moved to the flight deck by means of a single elevator. Despite its relatively small size, *Langley* usually embarked 30 aircraft, this being increased to as many as 42 on occasion.

When *Langley* entered service in 1924, the USN quickly gained an appreciation of the value of carrier aviation. *Langley* carried a large number

USN Antiaircraft Weapons

USN antiaircraft weapons were among the best used by any navy during the war. Since these were ubiquitous on all major USN ships, they will be covered here; heavier weapons unique to other types of ships will be covered in other chapters.

For long-range air defense, the mainstay weapon was the 5in/38cal dual-purpose gun. This weapon proved itself to be an excellent gun possessing good accuracy, a long barrel life, and, most importantly, a high rate of fire. It was the finest weapon of its type in service during the war and remained in service long after. In the middle of the war the effectiveness of the gun was further increased when the VT (variable timed) fuze, containing a tiny radio transmitter in the nose of the shell, entered service. The fuze sensed the reflected radiation off the target and detonated the shell within 30ft – a lethal range. When used with radar fire direction, it was a deadly combination. The Mark 37 director provided primary fire control for the 5in/38cal. This director was provided with Mark 4 radar to further increase its performance. The Mark 37 proved successful in handling all but the fastest targets. Later, the Mark 4 was replaced by the Mark 12 radar, which used the same antenna, but which offered a limited blind-fire capability. Introduced with the Mark 12 was the Mark 22 height-finder radar.

The next layer of air defense was provided by the 40mm Bofors gun. These were fitted in quadruple and twin mounts. Fire control for the 40mm Bofors was usually provided by the Mark 51 director. This was a simple and lightweight system and incorporated the Mark 14 gunsight. It proved effective out to about 3,000 yards. Beginning in late 1944, some Mark 51s were replaced by the similar Mark 57 with the Mark 29 radar. The Mark 57 provided a blind-fire capability. In 1945, the Mark 63 was introduced, which placed its associated radar directly on the 40mm mount. In some cases, both the Mark 51 and Mark 57 directors could be used to direct 5in guns, thus increasing the number of targets that could be engaged by the ship's 5in battery.

As dive-bombing came to be recognized as a threat, ships received short-range antiaircraft protection. This was originally provided by relatively large numbers of .50cal machine guns. These were the water-cooled version of the US Army's standard heavy machine gun placed on a naval mount. Fire control was accomplished by use of a ring sight and tracer rounds. Despite its high rate of fire of over 700 rounds per minute (rpm), the inherent inaccuracy of the weapon, combined with a small shell weight of under 2oz, made it ineffective. It remained in service, though, until replaced by the 20mm gun. Beginning in 1942, the Swiss-designed 20mm Oerlikon gun replaced the .50cal machine guns. Like the weapon it replaced, it was intended for last-ditch defense against aircraft and was fitted as a single mount. The 20mm gun was air-cooled. It required no external power source and was relatively lightweight, so it was introduced in large numbers and bolted anywhere with a free arc of fire. Later, a twin mount was introduced. The Mark 14 electric gunsight could be used as a director for the 20mm, which greatly increased its effectiveness.

Another early-war weapon was the 1.1in machine cannon. This weapon was four-barreled and water-cooled. Rate of fire was 140rpm firing a 1lb projectile. Fire control was accomplished locally or with the help of a director. In service, the weapon was heartily disliked by its crews as it was difficult to maintain and tended to jam in action. As production allowed, it was replaced by the quadruple 40mm mount.

Langley about 1932 with most of its air group on the flight deck. Though not operational as an aircraft carrier at the start of the war, *Langley* was instrumental in the development of USN ship-based aviation. (Naval History and Heritage Command)

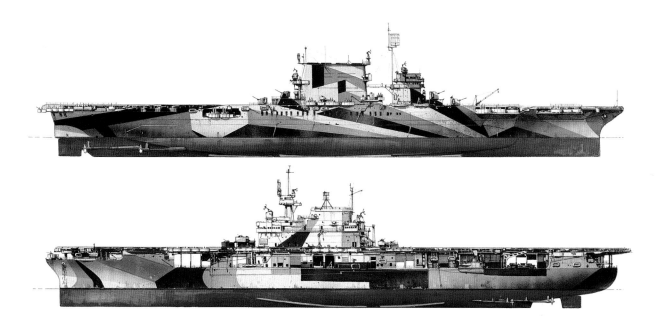

of aircraft for its size, a practice continued with every other prewar carrier. Exercises from *Langley* developed air combat and dive-bombing tactics. Employed during fleet exercises in the 1920s, *Langley*'s air group reinforced the importance of scouting and fleet air defense. It also demonstrated the offensive potential of carriers that could carry and launch large numbers of bombers. Despite its second-line status, *Langley* was retained as a carrier until 1936, probably because having been declared an experimental ship it did not count against the USN's carrier tonnage allocation under the Washington Naval Treaty.

In 1936, *Langley* was removed from service as an aircraft carrier. Between 1936 and 1937, the ship was converted to a seaplane tender, resulting in the removal of the forward 41 percent of the flight deck. Acting as an aircraft transport during the NEI campaign, *Langley* was bombed by IJN long-range medium bombers on February 27, 1942. After five direct bomb hits, the aged ship was scuttled by escorting destroyers.

Lexington Class

The question of whether the USN should build its first fleet carrier from the keel up or use a battlecruiser hull for conversion was solved by the Washington Naval Treaty, which forced the cancelation of all battlecruisers under construction or planned. Additionally, the treaty dictated that new carrier construction be limited to 23,000 tons, but an exemption was

THE TOP VIEW SHOWS *Saratoga* in its final wartime configuration. The differences from its mid-war appearance include an updated radar fit (with an SK in the pole mast aft of the island, an SM on the forward edge of the funnel, and an SC on the aft edge of the stack). The antiaircraft fit has been upgraded again and now includes an amazing 23 quadruple and two twin 40mm mounts. **THE BOTTOM VIEW IS OF** *Enterprise* in its 1944 configuration. *Enterprise* has the same radar fit as *Saratoga*. The ship retains its eight single 5in/38cal mounts and has received six quadruple 40mm mounts and several twin 40mm mounts. (Artwork by Tony Bryan, © Osprey Publishing)

granted for conversions up to 33,000 tons from existing capital ships. Even this was insufficient for battlecruiser *Lexington*'s conversion into a carrier. The conversion was only possible by a clause in the treaty that allowed the modernization of existing capital ships (and by extension carriers converted from capital ships) to protect them from air and torpedo attack with the addition of another 3,000 tons. Even at 36,000 tons, the conversion was still challenging.

THE TOP VIEW SHOWS *Saratoga* in its prewar configuration and colors. The battlecruiser hull is evident as is the enormous stack. Since it was nearly identical to *Lexington*, a large vertical stripe was painted on its stack to distinguish it. **THE BOTTOM VIEW SHOWS** *Saratoga* in its mid-war configuration. The 8in gun houses have been replaced by 5in/38cal dual gun mounts. The prewar 5in/25cal guns have also been replaced. Prewar machine guns have been replaced by a profusion of 20mm and 40mm guns. (Artwork by Tony Bryan, © Osprey Publishing)

Lexington Class Construction					
Ship	Built at	Laid down	Launched	Commissioned	Fate
Lexington (CV 2)	Bethlehem, Quincy (aka Fore River Ship and Engine Building, Quincy)	1/8/21	10/3/25	12/14/27	Sunk 5/8/42
Saratoga (CV 3)	New York Shipbuilding, Camden	9/25/20	4/7/25	11/16/27	Sunk 7/25/46 after atomic tests

When commissioned, these carriers became the largest carriers in service and would remain so until the completion of the IJN's *Shinano* in 1944. The hangar deck was entirely enclosed within the hull with the flight deck acting as the main load-bearing deck. This restricted the number of aircraft

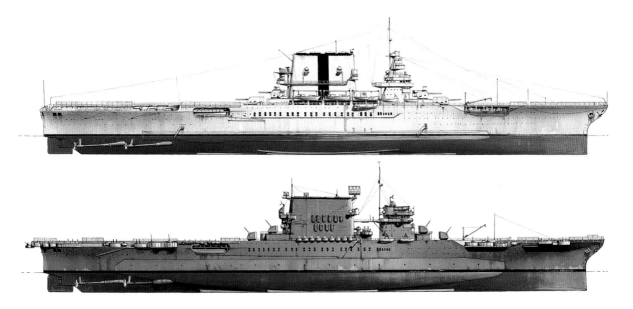

that could be carried and contrasted with later fleet carrier designs that featured open hangars and had the hangar deck as the main deck. Unusually for a USN carrier, the bow and stern of the ship were faired into the hull. The ships' most noticeable feature was the huge stack on the starboard side that was located aft and separate from the island. The turbo-electric machinery fitted was the most powerful in any USN ship and produced a top speed of 34 knots.

The aircraft hangar, huge for its day, was smaller than in subsequent carriers with only a fraction of *Lexington*'s displacement. As in subsequent fleet carriers, the 880ft-long flight deck was not armored but made of steel with a covering of wood planking. While providing minimal protection against bombs, this type of construction permitted the rapid repair of battle damage and a quick return to flight operations. Two large elevators were provided, and a single catapult was fitted on the flight deck. The original method of recovering aircraft was by a system of anchored longitudinal wires and weighted transverse wires. By 1931 this system was abandoned, and eight arresting wires were installed on the aft portion of the flight deck and provided with hydraulic controls to help stop landing aircraft. This became the norm for all later fleet carriers.

Armament and Service Modifications

As completed the Lexington class was armed to repel surface as well as air attack, the only USN fleet carriers so equipped. Eight 8in guns were fitted in four twin gun houses, two forward of the island and two aft of the stack. The 8in gun was chosen to allow the ships to deal with the fast "treaty" cruisers, which could also be equipped with guns up to 8in. In service, these guns were not effective since they could not fire across the flight deck without causing blast damage. For antiaircraft protection, 12 single 5in/25cal gun mounts were positioned in groups of three on sponsons on the corners of the flight deck.

This 1932 view of *Lexington* off Hawaii shows the ship's profile to full advantage. Note the huge stack, the separate small island, and the battlecruiser hull that enclosed the hangar deck. (Naval History and Heritage Command)

Saratoga photographed under way in September 1944 in its late-war configuration. The ship received a dramatically upgraded electronics and weapons suite from the start of the war as well as a camouflage scheme designed for its unique profile. (Naval History and Heritage Command)

Before the war both ships received little in the way of modernization since their prolonged absence from service could not be tolerated. *Lexington* was the more modern of the two sisters as it had its bow widened in 1936, expanding the size of the flight deck, and in 1940 a CXAM air search radar had been installed on the forward part of the stack. To counter the growing threat of dive-bombing, both ships received a large battery of .50cal machine guns. In 1940 1.1in quadruple machine cannons were installed. Five of these weapons were fitted, reducing the number of machine guns to 28. The outbreak of war saw the antiaircraft battery further reinforced. *Lexington* had its 8in guns removed in April 1942. When it was sunk the following month, it mounted a total of 12 quadruple 1.1in mounts, 32 20mm guns, and the 28 machine guns.

Early in the war *Saratoga* retained its 8in guns and had nine 1.1in mounts and 32 20mm guns; all its machine guns had been removed. In a yard period following damage from a submarine-launched torpedo in January 1942, it received most of the modifications planned prewar but never carried out. This included the provision of a large blister for torpedo defense. All the 8in guns were removed, and the antiaircraft battery was reinforced with 16 5in/38cal guns – eight in four turrets in place of the 8in gun houses and eight replacing the existing 12 5in/25cal guns. *Saratoga* also had its flight deck widened at the bow and lengthened aft. Other changes included the provision of a pair of Mark 37 directors (with Mark 4 radars) and four quadruple 40mm guns in place of the same number of 1.1in mounts (five 1.1in mounts remained), and the fitting of 30 20mm guns.

Saratoga's antiaircraft fit increased again following its August 1942 torpedoing. The last of the 1.1in mounts were replaced by 40mm quadruple mounts and an additional 22 20mm mounts were fitted. A refit from December 1943 to January 1944 brought a further increase in the ship's antiaircraft fit at the request of its commanding officer. Despite mounting top weight problems, another 14 40mm quadruple mounts were fitted. Two twin 40mm mounts were also fitted on the port side abeam the island. All but 16 of the 20mm guns were removed. By the end of the war, *Saratoga* had the standard carrier late-war radar suite of two air search and one fighter-director set.

The Lexingtons introduced the fleet carrier concept to the USN. In their day they were larger, faster, and carried more aircraft than any other carrier in the world. They were ideal platforms to test the theories of the Navy's aviation advocates during the prewar years and proved without doubt that large carriers were preferable to a number of smaller carriers, a notion that continues in the USN until this day. Despite not being based on any experience, their 1920s design was generally successful, and the ships were still capable of rendering excellent war service.

Lexington Class Specifications	
Displacement	Standard 36,000 tons; full 43,055 tons
Dimensions	Length 888ft; beam 105ft; draft 32ft
Propulsion	16 boilers and 4 turbo-electric transmission sets generating 180,000shp on 4 shafts; maximum speed 34kt
Range	10,000nm at 10kt
Crew	2,122 (prewar), 2,381 (*Saratoga*, 1944)

Ranger

Ranger was the first USN carrier designed and built as such from the keel up. Following the conversion of the two Lexingtons, 69,000 tons remained of the USN's allocated carrier tonnage under the Washington Naval Treaty. To use this remaining tonnage, many different designs were considered, but the final decision reflected the USN's desire to maintain numerical parity with the RN and the IJN. The eventual size selected (13,800 tons) was driven by a desire to produce five additional smaller carriers instead of a smaller number of larger carriers. This size was adequate for building a carrier that had sufficient aircraft capacity and handling facilities. When commissioned in 1934, *Ranger* introduced several features that would become common in future USN prewar carrier designs, including provision for an island, an open hangar, a gallery deck around the flight deck, and provision for cross deck catapults mounted on the hangar deck.

Ranger Construction					
Ship	Built at	Laid down	Launched	Commissioned	Fate
Ranger (CV 4)	Newport News Shipbuilding and Drydock, Virginia	9/26/31	2/25/33	6/4/34	Scrapped 1947

Many of *Ranger*'s features were compromised by the 13,800-ton design limit. The narrow hull had no underwater protection and only a single inch of steel was fitted on the hangar deck. The internal subdivision was inadequate, and the placement of the boiler and machinery rooms meant that a single hit could knock out the ship's entire propulsion system. Adequate space was not available to fit turbo-electric drive, so cruiser-type geared turbines were installed. Maximum speed was an inadequate 29.5 knots. Since the original design did not call for the provision of an island, the smoke from the six boilers was vented through six small stacks, three on each side of the aft hangar. During flight operations, the hinged stacks were rotated to a position parallel with the hangar deck.

Ranger pictured in October 1936. The lightness of its construction is evident. The small island is an afterthought as the original design called for a flush-deck ship. (Naval History and Heritage Command)

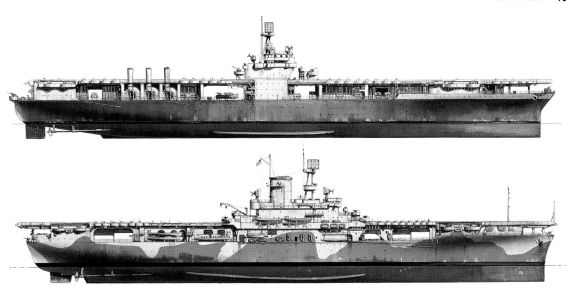

    Ranger's design was optimized to support the maximum number of aircraft. The hangar deck was larger than that of the Lexington class. Two elevators were fitted close together nearly amidships in an unusual arrangement driven by the desire to clear space for the hangar deck catapults (although they were never actually fitted). Originally it was planned to complete it with a flush deck to facilitate flight operations, but *Lexington* amply demonstrated the command and control advantages from even a small island, so a small starboard side island was added before completion. This placed *Ranger*'s final tonnage over the envisioned design limit and added to its top weight problems. Aircraft capacity was designed to be 76 including 36 fighters, 36 scout/dive-bombers, and four utility aircraft. At the time of its design, dive-bombing was the most potent antiship tactic, so no provision was made for torpedo storage and, until later in the war, no torpedo plane squadron was embarked. During the war, *Ranger* embarked as many as 72 aircraft; during the North African invasion, it embarked an air group of 54 Wildcats and 18 Dauntlesses.

Armament and Service Modifications

The 5in/25cal battery consisted of eight single mounts placed in four pairs on the corners of the flight deck. *Ranger* was among the first USN ships fitted with light automatic weapons to defend against dive bombing. Initially, 40 .50cal machine guns were fitted. Beginning in September 1941, *Ranger*'s antiaircraft protection was increased. Six 1.1in quadruple mounts were added at the expense of 16 of the original 40 .50cal machine guns. A refit following the ship's participation in the North African landings resulted in another augmentation of the ship's antiaircraft battery with six quadruple

THE TOP VIEW IS OF *Ranger* as it appeared during 1943 during its stint with the RN's Home Fleet. *Ranger* is armed with eight 5in guns, six 1.1in quadruple mounts, and 46 single 20mm guns. **THE BOTTOM VIEW IS OF** *Wasp* shown in its final configuration in September 1942 before its loss. *Wasp* mounts a mix of 5in, 1.1in, and 20mm guns. (Artwork by Tony Bryan, © Osprey Publishing)

40mm mounts replacing the 1.1in mounts and a total of 46 20mm guns being added. Additionally, *Ranger* retained its original battery of eight 5in/25cal guns.

By mid-war, the ship was heavily overweight and obsolescent. A comprehensive overhaul that would have provided some degree of underwater protection and the ability to operate modern aircraft was considered in late 1943 but was canceled when it was realized that the work would result in the delayed completion of two Essex-class carriers. A final refit in May–July 1944 confirmed that *Ranger* was no longer suitable for combat duties. It was equipped as a night training carrier: a new flight deck catapult was added, and its flight deck strengthened. Facilities to control night fighters were added, including a new SM height-finding radar. To compensate, all eight 5in guns were removed.

Of the seven prewar carriers, only *Ranger* saw no action in the Pacific. This alone speaks volumes on how it was viewed by the USN. Among the seven, it was the slowest and had the least adequate degree of protection and compartmentation. Its small size meant that it could not operate comfortably in common Pacific swells and was unable to operate aircraft in even moderate seas. *Ranger's* design was a false step. The experience gained in its construction at least meant that the same mistakes would not be made in the next class of carrier.

Ranger Specifications	
Displacement	Standard 14,500 tons; full 17,577 tons
Dimensions	Length 769ft; beam 80ft; draft 20ft
Propulsion	6 boilers and 2 geared turbines generating 53,500shp on 2 shafts; maximum speed 29.5kt
Range	9,960nm at 15kt
Crew	216 officers, 2,245 enlisted personnel

Yorktown Class

The Yorktown class was the first carrier class to be designed with the benefit of fleet experience. The basic design proved so successful that it was the basis for the even more successful Essex class. The genesis of the class came in the aftermath of what was generally viewed as the failed *Ranger* design. With the remaining Washington Naval Treaty carrier tonnage, it was decided to build two larger ships of some 20,000 tons rather than another *Ranger*-sized design. This would permit the correction of *Ranger's* most glaring weakness

– lack of protection. A carrier of some 20,000 tons had sufficient size to allow a real degree of protection against torpedo attack, a primary design feature in the Yorktown class. A 4in side armor belt was fitted over the machinery spaces, magazines, and gasoline storage tanks. The bottom 4ft of the belt below the waterline was tapered to 2.5in. Vertical protection was limited to 1.5in of armor over the machinery spaces. The ends of the machinery spaces were protected by a 4in armor bulkhead. Underwater protection was further enhanced by a side protective system that extended the same length as the side armor. This system consisted of three tanks intended to absorb the shock of any torpedo; the inner tank was a void and the outer two were filled with liquids. The entire length of the ship was double-bottomed.

Yorktown Class Construction					
Ship	Built at	Laid down	Launched	Commissioned	Fate
Yorktown (CV 5)	Newport News, Virginia	5/21/34	4/4/36	9/30/37	Sunk 6/7/42
Enterprise (CV 6)	Newport News Virginia	7/16/34	10/3/36	5/12/38	Scrapped 1958
Hornet (CV 8)	Newport News Virginia	9/25/39	12/14/40	10/20/41	Sunk 10/27/42

Yorktown photographed in October 1937 just after its commissioning. Note the large island and the forward starboard sponson with two 5in/38cal guns. (Naval History and Heritage Command)

TOP *Enterprise* was the USN's most famous carrier of the war. This is the ship maneuvering at high speed during the Battle of Midway at which its aircraft sank three IJN fleet carriers. (Naval History and Heritage Command)

ABOVE This is *Hornet* in October 1941. The ship was a virtual repeat of the prior two ships in the class except for some minor bridge modifications. (Naval History and Heritage Command)

Many other design features were carried over from *Ranger*. The main deck was the hangar deck with the unarmored flight deck being built of light steel. Much of the hangar deck could be opened using large roller curtains. This allowed aircraft to warm up prior to launch. The curtains could be closed to accommodate weather conditions or tactical requirements. The largest island yet fitted on a USN carrier was included, providing room for conning and navigation, aircraft control, and fire control. A large stack was designed into the island, making this the first USN carrier with a combined island/stack. All the boilers were located forward of the two engine rooms. The close location of the two engine rooms proved a major design fault.

The first two ships of the class, *Yorktown* and *Enterprise*, were commissioned in 1937 and 1938 respectively. The third ship of the class, *Hornet*, did not enter service until 1941. When the Washington Naval Treaty expired, and additional carrier construction was authorized, the best design available was the Yorktown class. Instead of being delayed waiting for a new design, *Hornet* was built to a slightly modified Yorktown-class design. As such, it was the last USN carrier affected by treaty limitations.

The Yorktown class was designed to operate 90 aircraft, including 84 combat aircraft and six utility aircraft. To support the large air group, all three ships were fitted with three elevators and two deck catapults. Another catapult was fitted flush to the hangar deck immediately aft of the forward elevator. The hangar deck catapult was intended to permit launching of scout aircraft even when the flight deck was occupied by preparations for a full-deck strike.

Armament and Service Modifications

The Yorktown class carriers were some of the first USN ships equipped with the new 5in/38cal dual-purpose guns. For intermediate and close-in protection, four 1.1in quadruple mounts were placed fore and aft of the island, and a total of 24 .50cal machine guns were fitted on the gallery deck.

Most modifications concerned the antiaircraft battery. Even before the war, the USN planned to substitute twin 40mm mounts for the 1.1in

mounts and 20mm for the .50cal machine guns. However, shortages precluded this from taking place until after the war had begun. By June 1942, all three ships had received 20mm guns – 24 in *Hornet* and *Yorktown*, and 32 in *Enterprise*. *Yorktown* and *Hornet* were lost before their 1.1in mounts could be removed. In August 1942, more 20mm guns were added: 38 in *Enterprise* and 32 in *Hornet*. *Hornet* was lost before any further modifications were made. During repairs to *Enterprise* in November 1942, four quadruple 40mm mounts replaced the 1.1in mounts located around the island and the number of 20mm guns was increased to 46. *Enterprise's* first major refit and modernization took place beginning in July 1943. It emerged with a greatly modified antiaircraft battery of six quadruple 40mm mounts, eight twin 40mm mounts and 48 20mm guns. Two Mark 37 directors replaced the old Mark 33s and the radar suite was modernized. The first facilities to handle night fighters were fitted and a new Combat Information Center was built in the island. With the addition of new blisters for increased stability and enhanced underwater protection, *Enterprise's* fully loaded condition increased to 32,060 tons.

THE TOP VIEW SHOWS *Yorktown* in its prewar colors and configuration. Note the large combined island/stack with a large foremast. **IN THE BOTTOM VIEW,** *Yorktown* is seen in its June 1942 appearance at the time of its loss. The CXAM radar added to its foremast is evident. Less obvious are the many 20mm guns and .50cal machine guns that now line its gallery deck. (Artwork by Tony Bryan, © Osprey Publishing)

LEFT *Enterprise* pictured at Noumea in November 1942 after the defeat of the final Japanese attempt to re-take Guadalcanal. For this crucial period, *Enterprise* was the USN's sole operational carrier in the Pacific. (Naval History and Heritage Command)

Enterprise's last refit and modernization occurred in 1945 following its last wartime damage. The advent of the kamikaze had demonstrated the uselessness of the light 20mm guns and it was considered necessary to mount as many 40mm guns as possible. *Enterprise* emerged with a battery of 54 40mm guns (11 quadruple and five twin). To compensate, the twin 40mm on the bow was removed and the number of 20mm mounts reduced to 16 twins.

The Yorktown class was undoubtedly one of the most successful and influential carrier designs by any navy. The class showed an amazing ability to sustain damage, far beyond its design expectations. It also proved remarkably adaptive, taking continually larger aircraft as the war progressed while remaining capable of operating a large air group. Until the introduction of the Essex class, it provided the bulk of the USN's carrier air power.

Yorktown Class Specifications	
Displacement	Standard 19,576 tons; full 25,500 tons
Dimensions	Length 810ft (*Hornet* 825ft); beam 110ft (*Hornet* 114ft); draft 25ft
Propulsion	9 boilers and 4 sets of geared turbines generating 120,000shp on 4 shafts; maximum speed 32.5kt
Range	11,200nm at 15kt
Crew	227 officers, 1,990 enlisted personnel

Wasp

Wasp's unique design was driven solely by the desire to use the remaining 14,700 tons of the USN's treaty carrier allocation. With less than 15,000 tons, it was impossible to build a repeat of the Yorktown class, but designers tried to fit many features of the larger ship into *Wasp*. However, what resulted was a slightly improved version of *Ranger* with all the major shortcomings of the earlier design. Several unique design features were used on *Wasp* to reduce its weight, such as an asymmetrical hull to compensate for the weight of the starboard side island without the use of ballast, and the fitting of the first deck-edge elevator, but the ship came in over its design displacement at 15,400 tons. This resulted in stability problems in service.

Wasp Construction					
Ship	Built at	Laid down	Launched	Commissioned	Fate
Wasp (CV 7)	Bethlehem, Quincy	4/1/36	4/4/39	4/25/40	Sunk 9/15/42

Wasp in 1940 during sea trials prior to its commissioning. After brief service in the Mediterranean, it was sunk soon after arriving in the Pacific. (Naval History and Heritage Command)

Wasp's hull was shorter than *Ranger*'s by some 40ft and possessed a slightly greater beam; consequently, an additional 21,000 shaft horsepower (shp) was provided, but the top speed of 29.5 knots was not entirely satisfactory. An unusual machinery arrangement was used with the forward and aft engine rooms separated by two sets of three-abreast boiler rooms. As on *Yorktown*, the boiler uptakes were vented out of a stack that was part of the starboard side island. The ship's key weakness was its light protection. Even though better torpedo compartmentation was provided compared to *Ranger*, no side belt was fitted, although provision was made to fit one in the event of war. The hangar deck was armored up to 1.25in, and 3.5in bulkheads protected the after magazine and steering compartment.

Wasp was also unique in that it had catapults installed in both ends of its hangar deck, not just forward as in *Yorktown*. Two flight deck catapults were also installed. In addition to the two deck elevators, a deck-edge elevator was fitted on the port side of the forward hangar bay. This T-shaped platform could be folded up for storage. Its success made it a standard design feature in subsequent fleet carriers. As designed, an air group of 72 aircraft was envisioned. Initially, as with *Ranger*, no provision was made for embarking torpedo aircraft. However, in 1942, just before its loss, a small torpedo squadron was embarked. When sunk, *Wasp* embarked an air group of 32 fighters, 28 dive-bombers, and ten torpedo planes.

Armament and Service Modifications

Wasp was armed much like the preceding Yorktown class. Eight 5in/38cal guns were arranged in pairs on the port and starboard bow and quarter. Four 1.1in quadruple mounts were fitted forward and aft of the island. Close-in air defense was provided by water-cooled .50cal machine guns arranged on the gallery deck around the flight deck. During its short service life, little was done to *Wasp* other than to enhance its antiaircraft protection. By January 1942, this had been increased by 34 20mm guns with all but six of the machine guns having been removed. The 5in battery and the 1.1in mounts were retained and their splinter protection improved. Though it was intended to replace the 1.1in mounts, only a single quadruple 40mm mount was fitted before its loss.

Wasp Specifications	
Displacement	Standard 14,700 tons; full 19,116 tons
Dimensions	Length 749ft; beam 81ft; draft 20ft
Propulsion	6 boilers and 2 steam turbines generating 70,000shp on 2 shafts; maximum speed 29.5kt
Range	12,000nm at 15kt
Crew	201 officers, 2,046 enlisted personnel (Sep 42)

The Transformation of the USN's Carrier Force

By the middle of 1942, the USN's prewar carriers had halted the Japanese advance. Losses had been heavy – only *Saratoga* and *Enterprise* remained in the Pacific. However, in 1943, the bounty of US industrial production arrived and changed the nature of the war in the Pacific. Accompanying the

Essex during the Okinawa campaign in May 1945 with its late-war air group. By this point in the war, over 70 percent of the air group consisted of fighters like the F6F Hellcats and F4U Corsairs in this view. (Naval History and Heritage Command)

USN Mid- and Late-war Carrier Air Groups and Aircraft

Essex-class carriers, as commissioned, had an air group with a large fighter squadron of 36 fighters, plus 18-aircraft scout, dive-bomber, and torpedo squadrons. One additional dive-bomber for liaison duties was included for a total air group of 91 aircraft. There were also nine reserve aircraft. By 1944, the need for a dedicated scout bomber squadron was gone, so the two squadrons equipped with dive-bombers were combined into a single 24-aircraft squadron. The fighter squadron grew and included special radar-equipped night fighter and photo-reconnaissance fighter variants. As the kamikaze threat became paramount, the number of fighter aircraft was again increased in December 1944. Now a single 73-aircraft fighter squadron was embarked, and the number of strike aircraft reduced to 30, organized into two 15-aircraft dive-bomber and torpedo squadrons. With 73 aircraft and 110 pilots, the fighter squadron had become too unwieldy. In January 1945 it was split into two squadrons, one with 36 fighters, the other with 36 fighter-bombers. In practice, the two squadrons were interchangeable. In 1945, two air groups discarded their dive-bomber squadron and operated 93 fighters and 15 torpedo aircraft.

Most Essex-class carriers took different air groups into action. With a large pool of aviators available, the USN could rotate tired air groups. In addition to casualties, the air groups had to contend with fatigue brought on by incessant combat. In January 1944, it was decided that air groups would be rotated after six to nine months of combat. This was later shortened in April to six months as the pace of the war intensified. It became necessary to rotate some air groups after only four months. This contributed to the requirement to bring Marine Corps fighter squadrons aboard the fleet carriers in late 1944. Eventually, two air groups were planned for each carrier.

The arrival of the new carriers coincided with the arrival of new aircraft. Most prominent among these was the Grumman F6F Hellcat. The first mass-produced variant, the F6F-3, entered service in 1943 and was faster and better protected and had more firepower than its Japanese counterparts. The Hellcat was the USN's mainstay fighter with over 12,000 built. The improved F6F-5 began to enter service in April 1944. Late in the war, some air groups received the Vought F4U Corsair. Introduced in 1943, the Corsair remained land-based until late 1944 when the kamikaze crisis and a fighter shortage brought it aboard fleet carriers on a permanent basis. With its speed and ruggedness, it proved to be the best carrier fighter of the war.

Into the mid-war period, the dive-bomber role continued to be filled by the Douglas SBD Dauntless. The upgraded Dauntless SBD-5 was not finally replaced until July 1944. Its replacement was the Curtiss SB2C Helldiver. This aircraft experienced a long gestation period before being wholly accepted for fleet use. Difficult to handle, it possessed no greater range than the Dauntless, carried a similar bomb load, and proved more difficult to maintain. It was, however, faster and more rugged. The torpedo bomber mission was handled by the Grumman TBF Avenger from mid-1942 to the end of the war. This aircraft also performed in a level bomber role. Some 7,500 were built under the TBF and the General Motors TBM designation.

This photograph of *Essex* during its workups in May 1943 shows the offensive potential of these ships. In this view, SBD Dauntless dive-bombers are visible aft, as well as TBF Avengers and F6F Hellcats with their wings folded. (Naval History and Heritage Command)

USN Radar

A critical development during the prewar years with a great impact on USN capabilities and operations was the introduction of radar. During the war, the USN deployed improved radars that widened the radar gap compared to the Axis navies. Radar allowed the USN to compensate for the superior night-fighting capabilities of the IJN, and eventually to eclipse them. Air search radars were central to the USN's air defense doctrine and greatly improved the survivability of USN ships to air attack. Radar was eventually deployed to almost every ship in the combat zone and aboard land and carrier-based aircraft. In the Atlantic, radar was a key weapon in the fight against the U-boats.

Primary USN World War II Radars			
Radar Type	**Primary Purpose**	**Maximum Range**	**Fitted On**
CXAM	Air search	70nm	6 ships in 1940
CXAM-1	Air search	70nm	14 ships in 1941
SC/SC-1	Air search	30nm	Carriers through destroyers
SC-2	Air search	80nm	Carriers through destroyers
SK/SK-2	Air search	100nm	Battleships, carriers, cruisers beginning in Jan 1943
SM	Height finding	50nm	Mostly carriers beginning in late 1943
SP	Height finding	70nm	Battleships and cruisers beginning in 1945
SR	Air search	110nm	Carriers through destroyers
SG	Surface search	22nm	All major ships beginning in Apr 1942

arrival of the Essex-class fleet and Independence-class light carriers was a number of doctrinal changes that turned the newly created Fast Carrier Task Force into a war-winning weapon. The early-war practice of operating only one or two carriers in a task group was abandoned. Now the arrival of new ships permitted up to four separate carrier task groups to be formed under the Commander, Fast Carrier Force Pacific. Each would operate up to five carriers (usually four) in a mix of fleet and light carriers. These would typically be escorted by a division of battleships, four cruisers, and a dozen or so destroyers. To provide the best protection against air attack, the carriers were placed in the middle of a circle of escorts. Task groups usually steamed in formation with 12nm between their centers, leaving 8nm from screen to screen. This cruising disposition was based on the effective range of the formation's heavy antiaircraft guns. In addition to presenting any attacker with a continuous wall of antiaircraft fire, it provided enough room for maneuver. It also provided overlapping radar coverage.

By 1943, the USN had transformed naval warfare in the Pacific. Not only did the numbers of carriers in service dramatically increase, but so did the effectiveness of each ship and its air group. A new generation of aircraft manned by well-trained pilots, improvements in air search and fire-control radars, the effectiveness of the Combat Information Center concept that fuzed information on a real-time basis, and the growing number and effectiveness of shipboard antiaircraft guns combined to make USN fast carrier task groups largely immune to conventional air attack. This defensive capability forced the Japanese to rely on night attacks and eventually on kamikaze aircraft. Together with these technological advances, there was a corresponding operational leap. A sophisticated mobile logistics capability was developed which allowed the USN to forward deploy to fleet anchorages and operate the Fast Carrier Task Force at sea for months at a time using underway replenishment. This maintained a high operational tempo, keeping the Japanese off-balance, and provided the capability not just to raid, as the IJN's carrier task force had done early in the war, but to project power on a sustained basis. It was a war-winning formula.

Essex Class

The Essex class had its roots in the prewar Yorktown class. Design work for what was to become the Essex class began in June 1939. The most important design feature of the new class was the requirement to operate a larger air group. It was recognized that the latest aircraft were larger and heavier,

Essex was launched on July 31, 1942, many months ahead of schedule. The Essex class was the largest class of fleet carriers ever built and constituted an unmatched display of industrial might and efficiency. (Naval History and Heritage Command)

requiring more deck space to handle the large air group. This could not be achieved on a Yorktown-size hull. It was also desired that the new class possess increased protection. Moreover, endurance was an important factor, since the ships were designed for a war in the Pacific. Eventually, what emerged was a design of some 27,000 tons with an air group of 90 aircraft, a range of 15,000nm at 15 knots, and a top design speed of 33 knots.

Essex Class Construction					
Ship	Built at	Laid down	Launched	Commissioned	Fate
Essex (CV 9)	Newport News, Virginia	4/28/41	7/31/42	12/31/42	Scrapped 1975
Yorktown (CV 10)	Newport News, Virginia	12/1/41	1/21/43	4/14/43	Preserved as a museum ship in Charleston, SC
Intrepid (CV 11)	Newport News, Virginia	12/1/41	4/26/43	8/16/43	Preserved as a museum ship in New York City
Hornet (CV 12)	Newport News, Virginia	8/3/42	8/30/43	11/29/43	Preserved as a museum ship in Alameda, CA
Franklin (CV 13)	Newport News, Virginia	12/7/42	10/14/43	1/31/44	Scrapped 1966
Ticonderoga (CV 14)	Newport News, Virginia	2/1/43	2/7/44	5/8/44	Scrapped 1974
Randolph (CV 15)	Newport News, Virginia	5/10/43	6/28/44	10/9/44	Scrapped 1975
Lexington (CV 16)	Bethlehem, Quincy	7/15/41	12/23/42	2/17/43	Preserved as a museum ship in Corpus Christi, TX
Bunker Hill (CV 17)	Bethlehem, Quincy	9/15/41	12/7/42	5/25/43	Scrapped 1973
Wasp (CV 18)	Bethlehem, Quincy	3/18/42	8/17/43	11/24/43	Scrapped 1973
Hancock (CV 19)	Bethlehem, Quincy	1/28/43	1/24/44	4/15/44	Scrapped 1976
Bennington (CV 20)	Brooklyn Navy Yard (New York Navy Yard)	12/15/42	2/28/44	8/6/44	Scrapped 1994
Bon Homme Richard (CV 31)	Brooklyn Navy Yard	2/1/43	4/29/44	11/26/44	Scrapped 1992
Shangri-La (CV 38)	Norfolk Navy Yard	1/15/43	2/24/44	9/15/44	Scrapped 1988

In addition to the 14 ships that saw wartime service, another three were commissioned in 1945 but did not arrive in time to see active service. These were all long-hull ships and included *Boxer* (CV 21), *Antietam* (CV 36), and *Lake Champlain* (CV 39). *Antietam* was present at the Japanese surrender in September 1945. Ships completed after the war included *Leyte* (CV 32), *Kearsarge* (CV 33), *Princeton* (CV 37), *Tarawa* (CV 40), *Valley Force* (CV 45), and *Philippine Sea* (CV 47). The final ship to enter service was *Oriskany* (CV 34), which was completed in 1950 to a modified design.

The first ship in the class, CV 9, later *Essex*, was ordered as part of the Naval Expansion Act of 1938. However, as events in Europe unfolded, it was obvious that the USN would require dramatic expansion. The Two-Ocean Navy Act of June 1940 allocated funds for three more carriers. Following the fall of France, another seven carriers were funded in August 1940. After the attack on Pearl Harbor, another two were funded. A second wave of an additional ten ships was ordered in August 1942 and three more were ordered in June 1943. Of the 26 ships ordered, all but two were completed. Of the 17 completed before war's end, 14 would arrive in the Pacific in time to see action.

Five shipyards were involved in the Essex class building program. The Newport News shipyard in Virginia and

This fine view shows *Franklin* upon its commissioning in February 1944. The ship's heavy defensive armament and large island are clearly visible. The ships were able to handle extensive additions of electronics and antiaircraft weapons as the war progressed. (Naval History and Heritage Command)

the Bethlehem Quincy shipyard in Massachusetts delivered most of the early ships. Other facilities to complete Essex carriers were the Navy Yards at Norfolk, Philadelphia, and New York. Construction on the class went smoothly, aided by the high priority accorded to carrier production. The lead ship was completed in only 17 months – some 15 months early. Construction and design emphasized economical use of materials, both to reduce use of steel and therefore weight, and to keep construction as easy as possible, thus speeding completion. Where possible, all steel parts were kept straight and flat. The high priority of carriers and the efficiency of American yards meant that an Essex-class ship could be completed in as little as 14 months, and no more than 22.5 months, with the average being 18.5 months.

There were two Essex-class sub-types. Most ships were built to the "short-hull" design with an overall length of 872ft. Of the 14 ships to see combat service in the Pacific, four ships were completed to a "long-hull" design with an overall length of 888ft. The difference was the clipper bow fitted to the long-hull units; both sub-types had the same waterline length. The clipper bow improved sea keeping and allowed for the provision of two bow-mounted 40mm quadruple mounts.

For the first time on a USN carrier, underwater protection was provided by a system with two outboard voids filled with liquids and two inboard voids. In theory, the liquid layers would absorb the shock of a torpedo explosion and the voids would contain any fragments and leakage. This system extended about the same length as the armored belt and protected the ship's vitals. Protection was designed to be adequate against 500lb of TNT. The triple bottom system consisted of two layers on the bottom of the hull. The inner bottom ran the whole length of the ship, but the third bottom only covered the vitals.

Hancock was the first long-hull Essex-class ship to be commissioned and the ninth overall. The clipper bow of the long-hull version and the two 40mm quadruple mounts on the bow are clearly visible. (Naval History and Heritage Command)

The flight deck was not armored, as the weight penalties for this would have been prohibitive. The main deck (the hangar deck) armor of 2.5in was designed to be sufficient to stop penetration by a 1,000lb bomb dropped from 10,000ft. Another 1.5in of armor was fitted on the fourth deck. Side armor was sufficient to defeat 6in shells, which designers believed would be sufficient against cruiser attack. The belt armor had a maximum depth of 4in tapering to 2.5in. The area protected totaled 508ft including the ship's machinery, magazines, and aviation gas storage. Steering gear was protected by 4.5in of side armor, with an aft bulkhead of 4in, and was covered by 2.5in and closed on the bottom with .75in of armor. There was also a .63in armored platform over the forward and aft magazines.

Propulsive machinery was fitted into six compartments below the fourth deck, with each separated by a watertight bulkhead. The positioning of the engine and boiler rooms was alternated so that a single hit could not destroy all propulsive power. The Essex class was the first US carrier to use the concept of two independent groups of machinery. This was an important design upgrade from the previous Yorktown class. The ship's four propellers were driven by four sets of Westinghouse steam turbines driven by steam from eight Babcock and Wilcox oil-fired boilers. This machinery produced 150,000shp. With oil bunkerage of between 6,161 and 6,331 tons, the ships possessed enormous range – up to 17,250nm for the long-hull ships. The propulsive system proved very efficient in service, providing excellent range and no major maintenance difficulties. This was a result of the USN's development of high-power, lightweight machinery that provided weight savings and advantages in fuel consumption.

Aircraft-handling Facilities

The central design feature of the Essex class was the ability to handle a large air group. Because the air group was so large, it could not be accommodated in the hangar deck and the practice of using a continuous deck park was adopted. The flight deck was 108ft wide and 862ft long. After favorable reports were gained on the performance of the deck edge elevator on *Wasp*, this was approved for the Essex class. Thus, three large elevators were installed, one centerline forward, one offset to starboard near the island, and the deck edge elevator located on the port side amidships. Elevator cycle time was 45 seconds, including time to load the aircraft on and off the elevator.

To speed aircraft launch times, one flush deck catapult was mounted forward. This was the 18,000lb capacity H (hydraulic) Mark 4B. Use of the catapult was not common in the early stages of the war. If aircraft were not too heavy to make a rolling take-off, this was the easier and preferred method. However, as aircraft became heavier, use of catapults increased. By war's end, some carriers were making 40 percent of launches by catapult. Doing so also increased flight deck flexibility as it permitted a launch to be made in any wind condition and allowed for a launch of a larger deck load.

An open hangar deck was retained – this allowed aircraft to be warmed up on the hangar deck and then moved to the flight deck, greatly speeding launch times. A series of large roller curtains were used to close the hangar to accommodate tactical requirements or weather conditions. The hangar itself was 654ft by 70ft with 18ft clearance. Six ships received a double-action type catapult mounted athwartships in the forward hangar bay. This attempt to improve tactical flexibility proved impracticable and all were eventually removed. Another impracticable feature was the inclusion of a full set of arresting gear forward. This would allow the ship to retain its aviation capabilities if bomb damage destroyed the recovery facilities in the rear of the ship. Despite its lack of feasibility, the forward arresting gear was not removed from the ships until 1944.

The amount of aviation gasoline was increased from 178,000 gallons in the Yorktown class to between 225,000 and 232,000 gallons for short-hulled ships and between 209,000 and 242,000 gallons for long-hulled ships. The amounts varied as different modifications were incorporated for protection of the gasoline storage system. Later ships had the aviation tanks moved aft to better-protected locations and the tanks were modified to insert seawater into the area of consumed gasoline. The total aviation ordnance that could be stored in two primary magazines was 625.5 tons.

Armament and Service Modifications

The protective antiaircraft armament of the Essex class was much increased over the Yorktown class. For long-range antiaircraft protection, a total of 12 5in/38cal guns were fitted. Four twin mounts were fitted on the starboard side, two forward and two aft of the island. These were on the flight deck, so presented a slight impediment to flight operations. On the port side, four additional guns were fitted in single mounts. These were placed in pairs on sponsons just below the flight deck to minimize the impact on the size of the flight deck.

The Essex class was originally designed to carry eight 40mm quadruple mounts. These were situated one on the bow, one at the stern (offset to port), two on the port side adjacent to the pairs of single 5in guns fore and aft, and four on the island (two forward and two aft). Throughout the war, the number of these weapons was increased. Additions included two mounts on the hangar deck level port side in place of the hangar deck catapult, and an additional mount on the stern. In mid-1943, further additions were approved, including two mounts on sponsons on the hangar deck level on the starboard quarter. These were originally fitted in recessed mountings so as not to interfere with a Panama Canal passage, but later they were placed in sponsons to provide a better arc of fire. Three additional mounts were added below the island on detachable sponsons. Finally, two mounts were added on platforms just below the flight deck on the port side. The only decrease in the 40mm fit was the removal of one of the quadruple mounts on the forward part of the island to allow the flag bridge to be expanded. When ships were under refit, some or all these modifications were added. Short-hull ships could receive all but a second 40mm mount on the bow,

THESE VIEWS SHOW *Yorktown* in the configuration typical among early Essex-class ships. The starboard side view shows the early radar fit consisting of an SK antenna on the forward part of the radar platform and an SC-2 antenna mounted on a platform on the starboard side of the stack. An SG radar is mounted on the topmast and there is a small radar platform for a second SG on the aft part of the stack. *Yorktown* carried 12 5in/38cal guns, ten 40mm quadruple mounts and 23 20mm single mounts during this period. (Artwork by Tony Bryan, © Osprey Publishing)

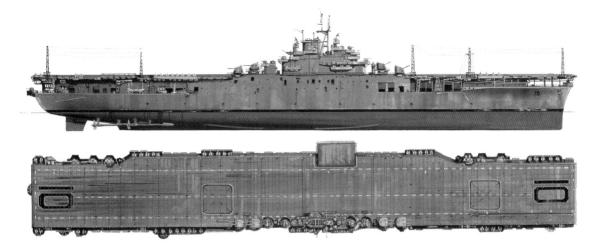

LEFT *Shangri-La* was another long-hull Essex-class carrier and the next to last to see combat service during the war. The ship carries a late-war electronic suite, but some modifications have not been incorporated, shown by the lack of starboard-side sponsons for 40mm quadruple mounts. (Naval History and Heritage Command)

BELOW *Bon Homme Richard*, the last Essex-class carrier completed in time to see wartime service, shows all late-war modifications to this class. These include five starboard-side sponsons for 40mm quadruple mounts, a modified bridge, and the placement of the SK-2 radar on a platform on the starboard side of the stack. (Naval History and Heritage Command)

making for a possible total of 17 quadruple mounts. With a second quadruple mount on the bow, long-hull ships embarked as many as 18 quadruple mounts. The addition of these extra quadruple mounts posed a great increase in top weight but was considered essential to enhance the ship's antiaircraft protection.

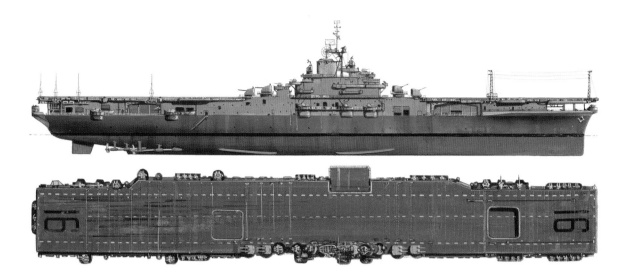

THESE VIEWS SHOW *Lexington* in May 1945 after a refit that reflected all the late-war weapons and electronics modifications made to Essex-class ships. The starboard side view shows the late-war radar fit, consisting of an SM antenna on the forward part of the radar platform and the new SR antenna mounted on the aft portion of the radar platform in place of an SC-2. The SK-2 is mounted on a platform on the starboard side of the stack. By this period *Lexington* carried 17 40mm quadruple mounts and dual 20mm mounts. *Lexington* was one of two ships to receive Army quadruple .50cal machine-gun mounts. (Artwork by Tony Bryan, © Osprey Publishing)

As designed, the Essex class mounted 46 20mm guns on platforms just below the flight deck level. This number rose to as many as 58 on some ships by the summer of 1943. By 1945, in response to the kamikaze threat, the twin 20mm mount was introduced, taking the place of some of the single mounts. Also, in response to the kamikaze threat, in 1945 *Wasp* and *Lexington* received Army quadruple .50cal machine-gun mounts on a trial basis.

The Essex class proved able to accommodate many wartime modifications. The total of these changes made the ships seriously top heavy and therefore less stable. It was estimated that, with the reduction of stability, three or four torpedo hits would have resulted in a high probability of loss. It was fortunate that none of the ships suffered war damage that threatened their stability. *Franklin* suffered extensive topside damage but developed stability problems due to the use of massive amounts of fire-fighting water. The only ships that took torpedo hits, *Lexington* and *Intrepid*, took only a single hit astern and were not threatened with sinking. Wartime modifications also made for severe overcrowding conditions. On trials, *Essex* had a crew of 226 officers and 2,880 enlisted men, several hundred more than its original design. In 1945, *Intrepid* had a crew of 382 officers and 3,003 enlisted men. This made berthing and messing difficult and living conditions in tropical areas were particularly uncomfortable.

It is hard to overstate the importance of the Essex class to the USN's Pacific campaign. The class was the most numerous of any USN fleet carrier (in fact, of any fleet carrier in history), a fact that pays testimony to the utility of the basic design and to the productiveness of American shipyards. While the design was far from perfect, and numerous wartime additions

made the ships dangerously top heavy, this potential weakness was never tested. By 1945, the carriers were very overcrowded. Nevertheless, with their large air group, high speed, and great endurance, these were the ships that broke the back of the IJN and carried the war to the Japanese homeland itself.

THESE VIEWS SHOW *Ticonderoga*. The only difference between this carrier and its short-hull sisters is the clipper bow that provided better sea-keeping qualities and allowed the fitting of a second 40mm quadruple mount on the bow with a better field of fire. *Ticonderoga* was commissioned with 11 40mm quadruple mounts as seen here. (Artwork by Tony Bryan, © Osprey Publishing)

Essex Class Specifications	
Displacement	Standard 27,500 tons; full 33,000 tons
Dimensions	Length 872ft (888ft for long hull); beam 93ft; draft 27ft, 6in (full load)
Propulsion	8 boilers and 4 geared turbines generating 150,000shp on 4 shafts; maximum speed 33kt
Range	15,440nm at 15kt
Crew	3,448

PART 2: THE LIGHT CARRIERS

The USN operated only one class of light carriers during the war. The Independence class was a crash conversion program brought about by wartime expediency. In 1941, it appeared that the lead ship of the Essex class would not be delivered until early 1944. The idea behind the Independence class was a program to bridge that gap. The person pushing the concept was none other than President Roosevelt, who proposed using some of the Cleveland-class light cruisers for conversion into light carriers. The Navy had already considered several schemes for carrier conversions,

Princeton was launched on October 18, 1942 at Camden, New Jersey. Though forced on the USN by President Roosevelt, the Independence-class carriers proved an important part of the Fast Carrier Task Force. (Naval History and Heritage Command)

but rejected Roosevelt's proposals on the grounds that the ships could not be completed before the expected arrival of the Essex-class units, and, when completed on a light cruiser hull, would be inferior units. The conversions that the USN had in mind were much more complex than anything that Roosevelt envisioned, so the early rejection of his proposals is not surprising. Roosevelt insisted that the Navy consider a more austere conversion, and

CONFIDENTIAL
U. S. S. PRINCETON CVL 23

in October 1941 it agreed that a light carrier conversion could be completed more quickly if design limitations were accepted. On this basis, and in accordance with Roosevelt's wishes, the first conversion was ordered in January 1942 using one hull, and by June 1942 the conversion program had grown to nine of the 36 planned Cleveland-class light cruisers.

Independence Class Construction					
Ship	Built at	Laid down	Launched	Commissioned	Fate
Independence (CVL 22)	New York Shipbuilding, Camden	5/1/41	8/22/42	1/14/43	Scuttled 1951
Princeton (CVL 23)	New York Shipbuilding, Camden	6/2/41	10/18/42	2/25/43	Sunk 10/24/44
Belleau Wood (CVL 24)	New York Shipbuilding, Camden	8/11/41	12/6/42	3/31/43	To France 1953 as Bois Belleau; scrapped 1960
Cowpens (CVL 25)	New York Shipbuilding, Camden	11/17/41	1/17/43	5/28/43	Scrapped 1960
Monterey (CVL 26)	New York Shipbuilding, Camden	12/29/41	2/28/43	6/17/43	Scrapped 1971
Langley (CVL 27)	New York Shipbuilding, Camden	4/11/42	5/22/43	8/31/43	To France 1951 as La Fayette; scrapped 1963
Cabot (CVL 28)	New York Shipbuilding, Camden	3/16/42	4/4/43	7/24/43	To Spain 1967 as Dedalo; scrapped 2001
Bataan (CVL 29)	New York Shipbuilding, Camden	8/31/42	8/1/43	11/17/43	Scrapped 1961
San Jacinto (CVL 30)	New York Shipbuilding, Camden	10/26/42	9/26/43	11/14/43	Scrapped 1971

With a displacement of 10,000 tons and a waterline length of 600ft, the Cleveland-class cruisers were the smallest hulls that the USN considered suitable for conversion into a carrier with a useful air group and the speed to operate with the fleet. However, use of a light cruiser hull resulted in

This view of *Langley* clearly shows the hull lines of the Cleveland-class light cruiser upon which the conversion of Independence-class light carriers was based. The placement of the small island and the four small stacks outside the hull lines is also evident. (Naval History and Heritage Command)

many problems. The narrow hull constrained the size of the hangar and flight deck and the latter would be further restricted by an island. Additionally, the sheer of the cruiser hull posed problems for the placement of aircraft elevators and the construction of the hangar deck, which obviously required a level deck. To overcome these problems, it was decided that a flight deck short of the bow was acceptable. An island was included in the final design, but it was small and was built outside the line of the flight deck. The sheer of the cruiser hull meant that in order to maintain the structural strength of the main deck the new hangar deck was built 4ft above the main deck, and that elevators were placed farther aft, though this was not optimum for flight deck operations. All nine ships were built at New York Shipbuilding in Camden, New Jersey. Five ships were laid down as Cleveland-class cruisers and the last four as carriers. All were commissioned in 1943, with the building time reduced to a mere 13.5 months for the last ship of the class.

The cruiser hull was completed up to the main deck. With displacement increasing to 11,000 tons and much of the weight located high up on the ship, the hulls were blistered to increase stability. The blisters were also used to increase fuel stowage. Originally the ships were designed without an island. However, fleet experience demonstrated the advantages of even a small island, so one was added, and a radar mast incorporated. The small escort carrier-sized island was built entirely outside the line of the flight deck and hull to ease aircraft-handling problems. Only a pilot house and a chart house were contained in the island. The Combat Information Center and the radar control rooms were on the gallery deck. Just forward of the island was an aircraft crane to lift aircraft from the pier to the flight deck. This flight deck level crane was required as it was impossible to lift planes to the enclosed hangar deck. Disposal of exhaust gases was conducted by venting each of the four boilers through a separate small stack arranged on the starboard side aft of the small island. To counterbalance the small island, the crane, the four small funnels, and 82 tons of concrete ballast were added to the port side tanks.

Armor was minimal, and there was no flight deck protection. The main armored deck was only 2in thick, while the main belt was a maximum of 5in, tapering to 3.25in (the first two ships in the class had no belt protection because of a shortage of armor). Bulkheads over magazines and steering gear were as much as 5in deep. The torpedo storage area was given additional splinter protection and bomb elevators and ammunition hoists also received additional protection.

Aircraft-handling Facilities

The flight deck was 552ft long and 73ft wide. Originally, a single flush deck catapult was fitted. There were two centerline elevators. Extra space was provided on the flight deck by the forward elevator so that aircraft could bypass the elevator. Eight arresting gear wires were fitted aft; these were the same type found on the Essex class. The hangar was limited in size and width, being only 285ft long and 55ft wide. Aviation ordnance storage was not generous. A total of 331 tons of aviation ordnance could be carried, with the original cruiser magazines converted to store bombs. Seventy-two each 1,000lb and 500lb bombs were carried. A space aft of the hangar was converted to store 24 torpedoes. Aviation gas capacity was 122,000 gallons.

The light carrier's air group was originally a smaller version of a fleet carrier air group. This mixed group was to include 24 F4F Wildcat fighters, 12 Dauntless dive-bombers, and nine Avengers. When the larger F6F Hellcat replaced the Wildcat, fewer fighters could be carried, so in October 1943 the light carrier air group was reduced to 12 fighters, nine dive-bombers, and nine torpedo planes. Dauntlesses with their non-folding wings were soon discarded, and by November 1943 the air group was set at 25 Hellcats and nine Avengers. Frequently during the war, the light carrier

air groups were tasked to provide CAP over the task group, freeing the larger fleet carrier air groups to focus on strike missions. In accordance with this doctrine, proposals were made throughout the war to make the Independence class into all-fighter carriers. Just before the end of the war this was approved, and the air group was set at 36 Hellcat or Corsair fighters. However, only a single carrier, *Cabot*, saw action with an all-fighter air group. In 1944, *Independence* was assigned duties as a night carrier with an air group of 19 F6F-5N Hellcat fighters and eight TBM-1D Avenger bombers. Night carrier duties were later assumed by the larger fleet carriers that could more safely conduct night flight operations.

Armament and Service Modifications

The lead ship of the class was originally fitted with a 5in/38cal single mount on the bow and the stern to counter surface attack. At the request of *Independence*'s commanding officer, these were replaced by 40mm quadruple mounts after only six weeks. In addition to the two quadruple 40mm mounts, standard weapons fit for the Independence class was eight twin 40mm and 14 20mm guns. In February 1943, a ninth twin 40mm mount was added on the forward port side of the flight deck. Only *Independence* was completed with just eight 40mm mounts; the other eight ships received all nine twin mounts before completion. Seven Mark 51 directors were fitted to provide fire control for the 20mm and 40mm batteries. Standard radar fit for the light carriers included an SK air search radar between the

OPPOSITE *Princeton* during its shakedown cruise in May 1943. Visible aft are nine SBD Dauntless dive-bombers; because of their non-folding wings that made them difficult to operate on small flight decks, they were later removed from light carrier air groups. *Princeton* was the only Independence-class carrier lost during the war. (Naval History and Heritage Command)

THESE VIEWS SHOW *Independence* in its late-war configuration. The small size of the island is evident. The primary modification following commissioning was the removal of the 5in mounts in favor of two quadruple 40mm mounts. In addition, the ship now fits nine dual 40mm mounts. The SK radar remains between the four small stacks, but the SC-2 has been replaced by an SM antenna on the radar platform. On the topmast is an SG radar. (Artwork by Tony Bryan, © Osprey Publishing)

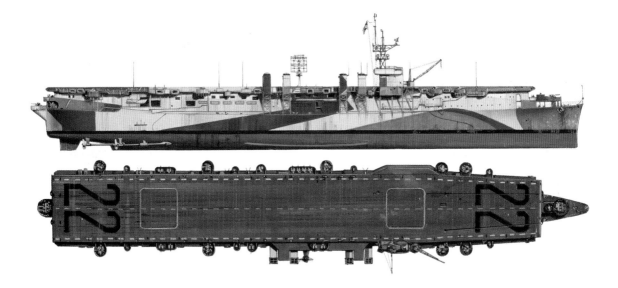

San Jacinto under way in January 1944. Despite the problems with flight and hangar deck flexibility, increased vulnerability to damage, and uncomfortable living conditions, the Independence-class ships were still successful conversions. (Naval History and Heritage Command)

two groups of small stacks on the starboard side, with an SC-2 radar in the radar mast. The wide separation of these two radars made for a better radar performance than that of the Essex class, where the closely grouped radars suffered from mutual interference.

Modifications were largely restricted to upgrading the antiaircraft armament. As completed, *Independence* had 14 20mm guns. The number of 20mm mounts was increased to 22 on some ships by adding new platforms along the flight deck. Later, the single mounts were replaced with five twin mounts (six in *Monterey*). Increasing top-weight problems required the deletion of some of the 20mm mounts, including the mounts on the bow and stern. It proved impossible to fit more 40mm guns in place of the ineffective 20mm mounts owing to weight problems. In 1944 the radar fit was modified when the back-up SC-2 air search radar on the front part of the radar mast was deleted in favor of a height-finder radar. *Independence* received the SM radar and other units (except *Princeton*) the lighter SP set.

The quick conversion of the nine Independence-class ships was a significant achievement. Even with their small air groups, the nine ships represented the equivalent aircraft capacity of approximately four fleet carriers. Keeping in mind that they entered service before the expected 1944 arrival of the Essex-class ships, the Independence class provided needed insurance. This proved especially important given the heavy attrition of the prewar carriers during 1942. On the minus side, the operation of these smaller deck carriers resulted in a much higher accident rate. Their austere design offered speed of completion but also presented the problems associated with a small air group, lack of flight deck and hangar deck flexibility, increased vulnerability to damage, and uncomfortable living conditions. On balance, the class proved a success and certainly compared favorably to the largely ineffective conversions that constituted the IJN's light carriers.

Independence Class Specifications	
Displacement	Standard 11,000 tons; full 15,100 tons
Dimensions	Length 622ft 6in; beam 71ft 6in; draft 26ft
Propulsion	4 boilers and 4 geared turbines generating 100,000shp on 4 shafts; maximum speed 31kt
Range	8,325nm at 15kt
Crew	140 officers and 1,321 men, increased to 1,569 in service

PART 3: THE ESCORT CARRIERS

The USN explored the concept of small aircraft carriers immediately following the Washington Naval Treaty in 1922. Serious consideration was given to building a hybrid cruiser-carrier known as a "flying deck cruiser." This concept never came to fruition since traditional carriers and cruisers were judged to be more valuable. However, another concept proved to be more prescient. This called for the conversion of ten passenger ships into carriers in wartime. Passenger liners were suited for this conversion since they usually possessed high speeds and were larger than regular merchant ships. For reasons explained later, when conflict came the USN did not use passenger liners as the basis for complex carrier conversions but did use regular merchant hulls to build quickly and cheaply what came to be known as escort carriers.

The impetus to convert merchant ships into small carriers was the war in Europe. The German U-boat threat to trans-Atlantic convoys was apparent, and a small carrier dedicated to convoy escort seemed a worthy investment. However, the USN was resistant to the entire notion of building and employing conversions of patently inferior small carriers with a limited

When first commissioned, *Long Island* had a short 362ft flight deck as is evident in this July 8, 1941 view. *Long Island* was active in the South Pacific in 1942 where it transferred the first Marine aircraft to Guadalcanal before spending the remainder of the war on training duties. (Naval History and Heritage Command)

Escort Carrier Air Groups

Because of their small size, escort carriers carried a limited number of aircraft. The standard escort carrier fighter was the Grumman F4F Wildcat. The later FM-2 version was designed for escort carrier operations since it was lighter, mounted a more powerful engine, and had a taller vertical stabilizer to counteract the torque from the bigger engine. The larger, more powerful Grumman F6F Hellcat was also embarked on escort carriers, but almost always the larger Sangamon-class ships. The primary strike aircraft aboard escort carriers was the reliable and sturdy TBF/TBM Avenger which could carry a large payload of torpedoes, bombs, or depth charges. The USN treated the Sangamon class as mini-fleet carriers, as shown by the fact that they carried Douglas SBD Dauntless dive-bombers until mid-1944. This aircraft did not have folding wings, which made it difficult to fit aboard escort carriers.

The Sangamon-class ships were considered large enough to carry air groups, each consisting of two squadrons. One squadron was equipped with 12–14 fighters and the other with a mix of nine Avengers and nine Dauntlesses. The Hellcat replaced the Wildcat on most of these ships, and by mid-June 1944 the dive-bombers were removed. In October 1944, these ships embarked an air group of up to 24 fighters and nine Avengers. During the Okinawa campaign, they carried 18 Hellcats and 12 Avengers.

Bogue and Casablanca-class ships carried a similar number of aircraft, but these were organized into composite squadrons. For ASW operations in the Atlantic, Bogue-class ships initially embarked a fighter-heavy mix of 12 Wildcats and nine Avengers. In May 1943, this was reversed to 12 Avengers and nine Wildcats that made for crowded conditions. Later in 1943, this was changed to 12 Avengers and only six fighters.

The Casablanca-class ships also embarked a composite squadron of Avengers and Wildcats. The standard organization called for 16 FM-2 Wildcats and 12 TBM Avengers. This number could fluctuate depending on operational and combat losses and the availability of replacement aircraft.

Air groups and composite squadrons were rotated regularly on escort carriers since the high tempo of operations caused combat fatigue necessitating regular turnover. As many as 22 escort carrier air groups and 84 composite squadrons were formed during the war. Many of the USN's escort carriers were never deployed on combat duties, so many never embarked an operational air capability.

Card under way in the Atlantic on June 15, 1943. On its flight deck are six F4F Wildcat fighters and seven TBF/TBM Avenger torpedo bombers – over half of its total complement. The carrier has been upgraded with an SK air-search radar on its mast. (Naval History and Heritage Command)

Suwannee at anchor in Kwajalein Harbor, Marshall Islands on February 7, 1944. The aircraft of CVEG-60 include SBD dive-bombers, F6F fighters and TBF torpedo planes. The ship's antiaircraft fit has been greatly augmented as is evident by the 20mm guns fitted on the bow and the two twin 40mm mounts on the port bow. (Naval History and Heritage Command)

aircraft capacity and little or no protection. The driving force behind what would become escort carriers was again none other than President Roosevelt. In late October 1940, he directed the Navy to acquire a merchant ship for conversion into an aircraft carrier. Roosevelt had an austere conversion in mind which was in direct contradiction to what the USN wanted. The ship to be converted had to be between 6,000 and 8,000 tons and have a top speed of not less than 15 knots. The ship had to be able to carry 8–12 helicopters or aircraft. The carrier-to-be was viewed as an asset for convoy escort. Pushed into action, the USN decided to obtain two C-3 type merchant ships for conversion. It was still obvious that the Navy did not fully understand Roosevelt's concept when it stated it needed 18 months to convert the ships into carriers. Roosevelt gave them three months. A proposal on January 17, 1941 was accepted by Roosevelt and the first ship slated for conversion, *Mormacmail,* was scheduled to be available on March 1. A second ship, *Mormacland*, was also set for conversion and subsequently assigned to the RN.

Long Island and *Charger*

The first escort carrier conversion was completed on June 2, 1941, just within Roosevelt's directed three-month period. The ship was commissioned as *Long Island*. To meet the deadline, the conversion was austere. A 362ft flight deck was placed over a small hangar. The ship had no island, only a single elevator aft, and a catapult forward. Its diesel engines generated a top speed of just under 17 knots. Trials indicated that the short flight deck was inadequate, and the ship returned to the yards for the addition of another

Long Island photographed in November 1941 following the extension of its flight deck. The open forward section of its hangar deck is evident. Its merchant ship origin is obvious. (Naval History and Heritage Command)

77ft. *Long Island*'s sister ship was completed as HMS *Archer* and handed over to the RN. The only difference was that it received a small island on the starboard side.

Not surprisingly, *Long Island* was found to be operationally limited. The main requirements for the next class of escort carriers were a longer flight deck, a second elevator, and additional antiaircraft armament. The next escort carrier design, still based on the C-3 merchant ships, addressed many of these shortcomings.

Long Island and Charger Construction					
Ship	Built at	Laid down	Launched	Commissioned	Fate
Long Island (CVE 1)	Federal Shipbuilding, Kearny	3/13/39	11/4/39	8/25/42	Converted to merchant use and scrapped 1977
Charger (CVE 30)	Federal, Kearny	6/3/38	3/4/39	9/24/42	Scrapped 1962

Charger was a sister ship of *Long Island* converted from a C-3 type cargo ship with diesel propulsion. It was part of a class of four ships built for the RN. On October 4, 1941, it was returned to USN service and recommissioned in March 1942, keeping its British name. The carrier spent its career on the East Coast as a training ship for British aviators. In almost every respect, *Charger* was identical to *Long Island*, the major difference being that as with all RN escort carriers, it was fitted with a small island.

Armament

Long Island was fitted with a 5in/51cal single mount on the stern for defense against surface attacks. Antiaircraft protection was provided by two 3in/50cal single mounts on the bow and four .50cal machine guns fitted along both sides of the flight deck. The machine guns were replaced with single 20mm guns, and in 1942, before it went to the South Pacific, a total of 20 20mm guns were fitted. *Charger* had an identical armament.

Long Island Specifications (Charger similar)	
Displacement	Standard 8,390 tons; full 13,890 tons
Dimensions	Length 492ft; beam 69ft 6in; draft 25ft 9in
Propulsion	2 boilers and geared turbines generating 7,965shp on 1 shaft; maximum speed 16.5kt
Range	Not available
Crew	970

Bogue Class

There were 45 ships of this class built, and of these 34 served in the RN. Of the first 21 built in 1942, the USN received 10 and the RN 11. The 1943 build program totaled 24 ships, and all but one went to the British. The USN retained only *Prince William* which spent the war as a training carrier. The only difference between *Prince William* and the British ships was the arrangement of the 40mm gun battery. All the USN ships were built in Tacoma, Washington.

Bogue Class Construction (USN ships only)					
Ship	Built at	Date Purchased by USN	Launched	Commissioned	Fate
Bogue (CVE 9)	Todd Dry Dock and Construction, Tacoma	5/1/42	1/15/42	9/26/42	Scrapped 1960
Card (CVE 11)	Todd, Tacoma	5/1/42	4/21/42	11/8/42	Scrapped 1971
Copahee (CVE 12)	Todd, Tacoma	2/1/42	10/21/41	6/15/42	Scrapped 1961
Core (CVE 13)	Todd, Tacoma	5/1/42	5/15/42	12/10/42	Scrapped 1971
Nassau (CVE 16)	Todd, Tacoma	5/1/42	4/4/42	8/20/42	Scrapped 1961
Altamaha (CVE 18)	Todd, Tacoma	5/1/42	5/25/42	9/15/42	Scrapped 1961
Barnes (CVE 20)	Todd, Tacoma	5/1/42	5/22/42	2/20/43	Scrapped 1959
Block Island (CVE 21)	Todd, Tacoma	5/1/42	6/6/42	3/8/43	Sunk 29 May 1944
Breton (CVE 23)	Todd, Tacoma	5/1/42	6/27/42	4/12/43	Scrapped 1972
Croatan (CVE 25)	Todd, Tacoma	5/1/42	8/3/42	4/28/43	Scrapped 1971
Prince William (CVE 31)	Todd, Tacoma	5/18/42	8/23/42	4/9/43	Scrapped 1961

The Bogue class was a direct attempt to address the design problems identified with *Long Island*. The C3-S-A1 merchant hull was the basis for the design. The diesel engines on *Long Island* proved troublesome, so for increased reliability and speed, the Bogue class shifted to steam turbines. The new top speed was 18 knots which represented a marginal increase.

The length of the flight deck was expanded to 442ft 3in and the width to 111ft 6in. The single port side catapult forward was retained. To increase the speed and safety of handling aircraft on such a small deck, two elevators, nine arresting wires, and three crash barriers were provided. Stability was improved by lowering the flight deck by 4ft. The size of the hangar deck was also expanded to about 240ft in length between the elevators. Aircraft handling on the hangar deck was a real challenge since the original sheer and camber of the merchant hull was retained. This meant that aircraft handling required pulleys that made moving aircraft difficult at best and often impossible in rough seas.

The primary visual difference on the new class was the addition of a small island on the starboard side. The island was a mere 6ft across but included a pilot house, a chart room, and cabins for the captain and navigator. Atop the island was the mast for radar and other equipment.

A major deficiency of all escort carriers was that they were essentially unprotected. The only exception was some splinter protection around the island, some gun positions, and other key areas including the torpedo stowage area in the hangar. There was no underwater protection which made them

OPPOSITE *Bogue* under way in Puget Sound, Washington on November 3, 1942, shortly after its commissioning in September. The carrier was completed with an SC radar and a light antiaircraft suite, both of which are evident in this view. The obvious difference of the Bogue class compared to *Charger* was the fully enclosed hangar deck. (Naval History and Heritage Command)

THESE VIEWS SHOW *Bogue*, the lead unit in a class of 11 escort carriers built for the USN. This conversion was based on the same merchant hull as *Long Island* but featured a small island and a fully enclosed hangar. (Artwork by Paul Wright, © Osprey Publishing)

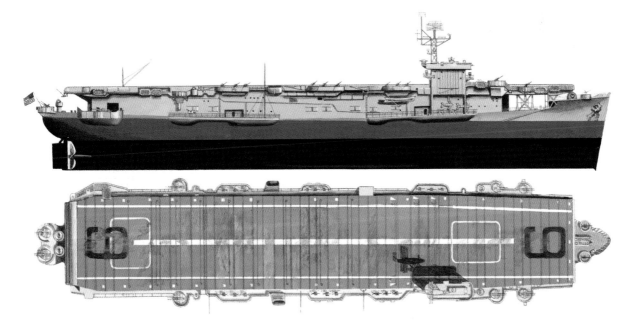

vulnerable to torpedoes. From 1943, escort carriers were provided with some additional magazine protection by adding a 1in thick longitudinal bulkhead outboard of the magazine with water ballast between the bulkhead and the outer hull in an attempt to provide some protection against torpedoes.

The Bogue-class conversion was a success. The ship proved able to handle an air component of some 20 aircraft, including the large Avenger torpedo bombers, and these could be launched in rough sea conditions. The ships proved easy to handle and maneuverable, even on their one screw. Living conditions aboard were also judged to be above average.

Armament

The weak defensive armament on *Long Island* was identified as a deficiency, so it was increased on the Bogue-class ships. Two 5in/51cal guns were originally fitted for protection from surface attack, but this was changed to the 5in/38cal which was capable of engaging surface and air targets. As completed, antiaircraft armament consisted of eight twin 40mm mounts and 20 single 20mm mounts. Some ships received additional 20mm single mounts on the sponsons along the hangar deck.

Bogue-Class Specifications	
Displacement	Standard 8,390 tons; full 13,890 tons
Dimensions	Length 495ft 8in; beam 69ft 6in; draft 23ft 3in
Propulsion	2 boilers and geared turbines generating 8,500shp on 1 shaft; maximum speed 18kt
Range	26,000nm at 15kt
Crew	890

Sangamon Class

The Sangamon-class escort carriers were an anomaly in early-war escort carrier design. This class of only four ships was based on a tanker hull, which since it was much larger than a C3 merchant hull provided the basis for a balanced design. These ships possessed greater endurance, were more stable, and could carry more aircraft than earlier designs. Had more tanker hulls been available, this is the class the USN would have preferred to build in mass numbers.

The 1942 escort carrier conversion program was set for 24 ships, but only 20 C3 hulls were available. The difference was made up by four Cimarron-class fleet oilers. These valuable ships were originally built in 1939 as mercantile tankers and taken over by the USN in 1940 for

conversion into fleet oilers. In 1942, the four ships were selected for conversion to escort carriers and sent to three different yards. Their size and speed made them the basis for the best early-war escort carrier conversion. The four ships were hurried to completion so they could participate in the planned invasion of French North Africa. Two were commissioned in August and the other two in September 1942.

Santee photographed mid-October 1942 shortly before it participated in the invasion of North Africa. The openings low on its hull betray its origin as an oiler and provide a good recognition feature. Aircraft on its flight deck include (from aft) Dauntless dive-bombers, Wildcat fighters, and Avenger torpedo planes. (Naval History and Heritage Command)

Sangamon Class Construction					
Ship	Built at	Laid down	Launched	Commissioned	Fate
Sangamon (CVE 26)	Federal (Kearny)	3/13/39	11/4/39	8/25/42	Scrapped 1948
Suwannee (CVE 27)	Federal (Kearny)	6/3/38	3/4/39	9/24/42	Scrapped 1962
Chenango (CVE 28)	Sun Shipbuilding	7/10/38	1/4/39	9/19/42	Scrapped 1962
Santee (CVE 29)	Sun Shipbuilding	5/31/39	3/4/39	8/24/42	Scrapped 1960

These were large ships with a full load displacement of 23,875 tons and an overall length of 553ft. The flight deck measured 503ft by 105ft and the hangar deck of 220ft in length had no sheer, which made aircraft handling much easier. One catapult was originally fitted, with a second one added in 1944. The flight deck was much lower to the water (42ft versus 54ft on the Bogue class), so the ship was more stable and able to operate aircraft in more challenging sea conditions.

Speed was increased by use of two turbines driving twin screws. However, both turbines were in a single engine room which made the ship's propulsive power vulnerable to a single torpedo hit. Endurance was also increased. In addition to the fuel carried in the bunkers, these ships retained extra fuel capacity and the equipment to service other ships.

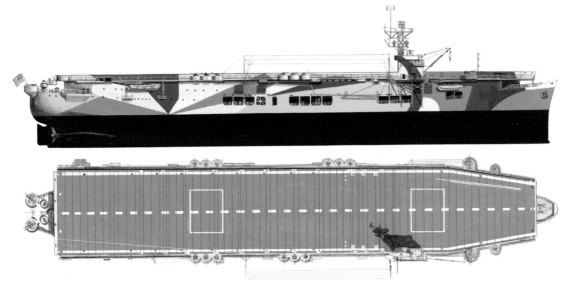

Armament

Two single 5in/38cal guns were fitted aft. The original 40mm fit was four twin mounts, but from 1943 this was modified to two quadruple and ten twin mounts. Each ship also carried 12 single 20mm mounts when commissioned; this was later increased to 19.

Sangamon Class Specifications	
Displacement	Standard 10,500 tons; full 23,875 tons
Dimensions	Length 553ft 6in; beam 75ft; draft 30ft 7in
Propulsion	4 boilers and geared turbines generating 13,500shp on 2 shafts; maximum speed 18kt
Range	23,900nm at 15kt
Crew	1,080

Casablanca Class

The next class returned to a smaller conversion mounted on a merchant hull. President Roosevelt was again involved in the design process. Henry J. Kaiser, a well-known shipbuilding magnate, proposed an escort carrier design to Roosevelt capable of 20 knots that could be built quickly and cheaply. Roosevelt was quick to agree and in June 1942 called members of the USN's Bureau of Ships and the Maritime Commission (responsible for merchant construction) to the White House to tell them of his desire to build Kaiser's carriers. These ships were also known as the Kaiser class and were the first escort carriers built as such from the keel up. The design of the ship was not actually the work of Kaiser, but of the naval architect firm of Gibbs and Cox.

The design was not as capable as the Navy would have liked, but since Roosevelt's desires were clear, planning continued. A S4-S2-BB3 merchant hull was selected as the basis for the new design. The hulls were built to merchant specifications and modified as necessary to naval standards. The plan was to build all 50 ships at Kaiser's Vancouver, Washington yard using all-welded and extensive modular construction. Fitting out took place at the naval base in Astoria, Oregon. The lead ship of the class, *Casablanca*, was scheduled for delivery in February 1943 but various problems delayed its commissioning until July 8. Once Kaiser's yard hit its stride, it completed the entire program by July 8, 1944, an awesome achievement by any measure. Some of the later ships were completed and commissioned in under four months. The ships were viewed by the USN with initial suspicion but turned out to be timely additions to the fleet.

Casablanca, on the right, about to be launched at Henry J. Kaiser's shipyard in Vancouver, Washington, on April 5, 1943. Two of its 49 sister ships are under construction at left. *Casablanca*'s commissioning was delayed to July, but by July of the following year all 50 Casablanca-class escort carriers were in service. (Naval History and Heritage Command)

Casablanca Class Construction					
Ship	Built at	Laid down	Launched	Commissioned	Fate
Casablanca (CVE 55)	Kaiser, Vancouver	11/3/42	4/5/43	7/8/43	Scrapped 1947
Liscome Bay (CVE 56)	Kaiser, Vancouver	12/9/42	4/19/43	8/7/43	Sunk 11/24/43
Anzio (CVE 57)	Kaiser, Vancouver	12/12/42	5/1/43	8/27/43	Scrapped 1960
Corregidor (CVE 58)	Kaiser, Vancouver	12/17/42	5/12/43	8/31/43	Scrapped 1960
Mission Bay (CVE 59)	Kaiser, Vancouver	12/28/42	5/26/43	9/13/43	Scrapped 1960
Guadalcanal (CVE 60)	Kaiser, Vancouver	1/5/43	6/5/43	9/25/43	Scrapped 1960
Manila Bay (CVE 61)	Kaiser, Vancouver	1/15/43	7/10/43	10/5/43	Scrapped 1960
Natoma Bay (CVE 62)	Kaiser, Vancouver	1/17/43	7/20/43	10/14/43	Scrapped 1960
St. Lo (CVE 63)	Kaiser, Vancouver	1/23/43	8/17/43	10/23/43	Sunk 10/25/44
Tripoli (CVE 64)	Kaiser, Vancouver	2/1/43	9/2/43	10/31/43	Scrapped 1960
Wake Island (CVE 65)	Kaiser, Vancouver	2/6/43	9/15/43	11/7/43	Scrapped 1947
White Plains (CVE 66)	Kaiser, Vancouver	2/11/43	9/27/43	11/15/43	Scrapped 1959
Solomons (CVE 67)	Kaiser, Vancouver	3/19/43	10/6/43	11/21/43	Scrapped 1947
Kalinin Bay (CVE 68)	Kaiser, Vancouver	4/26/43	10/15/43	11/27/43	Scrapped 1947
Kasaan Bay (CVE 69)	Kaiser, Vancouver	5/11/43	10/24/43	12/4/43	Scrapped 1960
Fanshaw Bay (CVE 70)	Kaiser, Vancouver	5/18/43	11/1/43	12/9/43	Scrapped 1959
Kitkun Bay (CVE 71)	Kaiser, Vancouver	5/31/43	11/8/43	12/15/43	Scrapped 1947
Tulagi (CVE 72)	Kaiser, Vancouver	6/7/43	11/15/43	12/21/43	Scrapped 1947
Gambier Bay (CVE 73)	Kaiser, Vancouver	7/10/43	11/22/43	12/28/43	Sunk 10/25/44
Nehenta Bay (CVE 74)	Kaiser, Vancouver	7/20/43	11/28/43	1/3/44	Scrapped 1960
Hoggatt Bay (CVE 75)	Kaiser, Vancouver	8/17/43	12/4/43	1/11/44	Scrapped 1960
Kadashan Bay (CVE 76)	Kaiser, Vancouver	9/2/43	12/11/43	1/18/44	Scrapped 1960
Marcus Island (CVE 77)	Kaiser, Vancouver	9/15/43	12/16/43	1/26/44	Scrapped 1960
Savo Island (CVE 78)	Kaiser, Vancouver	9/27/43	12/22/43	2/3/44	Scrapped 1960
Ommaney Bay (CVE 79)	Kaiser, Vancouver	10/6/43	12/29/43	2/11/44	Sunk 1/4/45
Petrof Bay (CVE 80)	Kaiser, Vancouver	10/15/43	1/5/44	2/18/44	Scrapped 1959
Rudyerd Bay (CVE 81)	Kaiser, Vancouver	10/24/43	1/12/44	2/25/44	Scrapped 1960
Saginaw Bay (CVE 82)	Kaiser, Vancouver	11/1/43	1/19/44	3/2/44	Scrapped 1960
Sargent Bay (CVE 83)	Kaiser, Vancouver	11/8/43	1/31/44	3/9/44	Scrapped 1959
Shamrock Bay (CVE 84)	Kaiser, Vancouver	11/15/43	2/4/44	3/15/44	Scrapped 1959
Shipley Bay (CVE 85)	Kaiser, Vancouver	11/22/43	2/12/44	3/21/44	Scrapped 1961
Sitkoh Bay (CVE 86)	Kaiser, Vancouver	11/23/43	2/19/44	3/28/44	Scrapped 1961
Steamer Bay (CVE 87)	Kaiser, Vancouver	12/4/43	2/26/44	4/4/44	Scrapped 1959
Cape Esperance (CVE 88)	Kaiser, Vancouver	12/11/43	3/3/44	4/9/44	Scrapped 1961
Takanis Bay (CVE 89)	Kaiser, Vancouver	12/16/43	3/10/44	4/15/44	Scrapped 1960
Thetis Bay (CVE 90)	Kaiser, Vancouver	12/22/43	3/16/44	4/21/44	Scrapped 1966
Makassar Strait (CVE 91)	Kaiser, Vancouver	12/29/43	3/22/44	4/27/44	Wrecked 1961

Windham Bay (CVE 92)	Kaiser, Vancouver	1/5/44	3/29/44	5/3/44	Scrapped 1961
Makin Island (CVE 93)	Kaiser, Vancouver	1/12/44	4/5/44	5/9/44	Scrapped 1947
Lunga Point (CVE 94)	Kaiser, Vancouver	1/19/44	4/11/44	5/14/44	Scrapped 1966
Bismarck Sea (CVE 95)	Kaiser, Vancouver	1/31/44	4/17/44	5/20/44	Sunk 2/21/45
Salamaua (CVE 96)	Kaiser, Vancouver	2/4/44	4/22/44	5/26/44	Scrapped 1947
Hollandia (CVE 97)	Kaiser, Vancouver	2/12/44	4/28/44	6/1/44	Scrapped 1960
Kwajalein (CVE 98)	Kaiser, Vancouver	2/19/44	5/4/44	6/7/44	Scrapped 1961
Admiralty Islands (CVE 99)	Kaiser, Vancouver	2/26/44	5/10/44	6/13/44	Scrapped 1947
Bougainville (CVE 100)	Kaiser, Vancouver	3/3/44	5/16/44	6/18/44	Scrapped 1960
Mantanikau (CVE 101)	Kaiser, Vancouver	3/10/44	5/22/44	6/24/44	Scrapped 1960
Attu (CVE 102)	Kaiser, Vancouver	3/16/44	5/27/44	6/30/44	Scrapped 1949
Roi (CVE 103)	Kaiser, Vancouver	3/22/44	6/2/44	7/6/44	Scrapped 1947
Munda (CVE 104)	Kaiser, Vancouver	3/29/44	6/8/44	7/8/44	Scrapped 1960

The Kaiser-built ships shared similar dimensions to the Bogue class, but featured improved streamlining, a square stern, and two boiler uptakes on each side of the flight deck. The aircraft-handling facilities on the new ships virtually mirrored those on the Bogue class. The flight deck was 477ft long and 108ft wide. These ships were fitted with two elevators, nine arresting wires, three crash barriers, and a single catapult. The size of the hangar deck was enlarged to 257ft between the elevators and its utility enhanced by not incorporating the ships' sheer.

The crush of wartime production meant that no turbines or diesels were available to power these ships. Instead, old-fashioned reciprocating engines were used. Each generated 9,000 indicated horsepower (ihp) and

This overhead view of *Wake Island* on November 9, 1944 in Hampton Roads shows very clearly the location of the ship's elevators and armament. Note the 5in/38cal gun on the stern, the two twin 40mm mounts on each quarter and the single 20mm mounts along the flight deck. *Wake Island* was one of the few escort carriers to see action in both theaters during the war. (Naval History and Heritage Command)

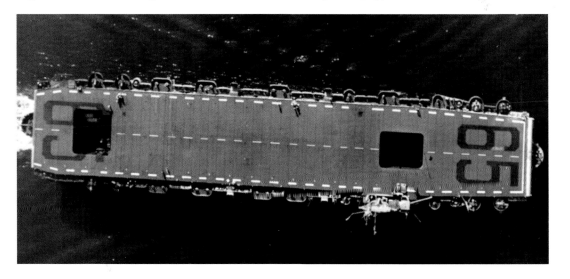

drove one of the two shafts. Design speed was 19 knots, but *Casablanca* made almost 21 knots on trials. The engine rooms were not located together which offered increased protection from a single torpedo hit. The ship was very maneuverable with a tactical diameter of only 540 yards. These ships were the fastest and most maneuverable USN escort carriers. The extra speed of even a few knots was important to sustain flight operation in low-wind conditions.

Armament

These carriers were inadequately armed with only one 5in/38cal gun on the stern, 16 40mm guns on eight mounts and 20 20mm guns in single mounts. When the kamikaze threat emerged in October 1944, this shortcoming became a real issue.

Casablanca Class Specifications	
Displacement	Standard 8,200 tons; full 10,900 tons
Dimensions	Length 512ft 3in; beam 65ft 2in; draft 20ft 9in
Propulsion	4 boilers and reciprocating engines generating 9,000ihp on 2 shafts; maximum speed 19kt
Range	10,200nm at 15kt
Crew	860

Commencement Bay Class

The final class of escort carriers represented a return to the larger and more capable Sangamon design. These ships incorporated lessons learned in wartime escort carrier operations. Improvements included better aircraft-handling facilities, a larger island, and an improved armament suite. The design was based

Puget Sound photographed at anchor in Tokyo Bay, Japan, in October 1945. This view shows the characteristics of a Commencement Bay escort carrier with its large tanker-like hull, enlarged island and heavy antiaircraft armament. (Naval History and Heritage Command)

on an oiler hull and approved on December 1, 1942. Twenty-three ships were approved, and all were assigned to the Todd-Pacific Yard in Tacoma, Washington. The lead ship, *Commencement Bay*, was not commissioned until November 27, 1944; only three of the 19 ships completed saw combat before the end of the war. Altogether, 27 ships of this class were ordered from Todd and eight from Kaiser. Of the 19 ships completed, two were never commissioned. Work on another four was suspended in August 1945 and the ships broken up. Twelve more were canceled at the same time without work ever having begun.

Commencement Bay Class Construction					
Ship	Built at	Laid down	Launched	Commissioned	Fate
Commencement Bay (CVE 105)	Todd, Tacoma	9/23/43	5/4/44	11/27/44	Scrapped 1972
Block Island (CVE 106)	Todd, Tacoma	10/25/43	6/10/44	12/30/44	Scrapped 1960
Gilbert Islands (CVE 107)	Todd, Tacoma	11/29/43	7/20/45	2/5/45	Converted to communications ship and re-named *Annapolis*, scrapped 1979
Kula Gulf (CVE 108)	Todd, Tacoma	12/16/43	8/15/44	5/12/45	Scrapped 1971
Cape Gloucester (CVE 109)	Todd, Tacoma	1/10/44	9/12/44	3/5/45	Scrapped 1971
Salerno Bay (CVE 110)	Todd, Tacoma	2/7/44	9/29/44	5/19/45	Scrapped 1962
Vella Gulf (CVE 111)	Todd, Tacoma	3/7/44	10/19/44	8/9/45	Scrapped 1971
Siboney (CVE 112)	Todd, Tacoma	4/1/44	12/9/44	5/14/45	Scrapped 1971
Puget Sound (CVE 113)	Todd, Tacoma	5/12/44	11/30/44	6/18/45	Scrapped 1962
Rendova (CVE 114)	Todd, Tacoma	6/15/44	12/28/44	10/22/45	Scrapped 1971
Bairoko (CVE 115)	Todd, Tacoma	7/25/44	1/25/45	7/16/45	Scrapped 1961
Badoeng Strait (CVE 116)	Todd, Tacoma	8/18/44	2/15/45	11/14/45	Scrapped 1972
Saidor (CVE 117)	Todd, Tacoma	7/30/44	3/17/45	9/4/45	Scrapped 1971
Sicily (CVE 118)	Todd, Tacoma	10/23/44	5/14/45	2/27/46	Scrapped 1961
Point Cruz (CVE 119)	Todd, Tacoma	12/4/44	5/18/45	10/16/45	Scrapped 1971
Mindoro (CVE 120)	Todd, Tacoma	1/2/45	6/27/45	12/4/45	Scrapped 1960
Rabaul (CVE 121)	Todd, Tacoma	1/2/45	7/14/45	Never	Completed and not commissioned; scrapped 1972
Palau (CVE 122)	Todd, Tacoma	2/19/45	8/6/45	1/15/46	Scrapped 1960
Tinian (CVE 123)	Todd, Tacoma	3/20/45	7/5/45	Never	Completed and not commissioned; scrapped 1971

The class appeared externally like the Sangamon-class ships and shared similar dimensions. There were some important differences, like a flight deck and elevators able to handle up to a 17,000lb aircraft instead of the previous 14,000lb. The elevators operated more quickly, and two catapults were fitted. The width of the island was increased.

The design speed of 19 knots was achieved by steam turbines able to generate 16,000shp. Many ships exceeded the design speed on trials. The engine rooms were separated to increase survivability. Two more transverse bulkheads were fitted for extra strength and better subdivision was incorporated.

Armament

The armament on these ships was greatly expanded, addressing a shortcoming of every previous escort carrier class. Two 5in/38cal single guns were fitted on the stern. The antiaircraft suite was much improved. Since the 40mm gun was better at handling kamikaze attacks, and the quadruple 40mm mount was favored in particular, three quadruple mounts were fitted (one on the bow and two on the fantail), and another 12 40mm twin mounts were fitted in gun tubs mostly below the flight deck level. Twenty single 20mm guns were fitted along the flight deck in groups of five.

Commencement Bay Class Specifications	
Displacement	Standard 11,373 tons; full 24,275 tons
Dimensions	Length 557ft 1in; beam 75ft; draft 32ft 2in
Propulsion	4 boilers and geared turbines generating 16,000shp on 2 shafts; maximum speed 19kt
Range	8,320nm at 15kt
Crew	1,066

The contribution of the USN's escort carriers during World War II was significant but has also been largely forgotten. Most escort carriers served in the Pacific. They proved supremely versatile, performing in their originally envisioned roles of convoy escort, and providing ground support during amphibious invasions. They also served in other roles which were not envisioned, like providing air defense for amphibious invasions and even as the centerpiece of a fleet engagement during the Battle of Leyte Gulf in October 1944. Not surprisingly, since they were not designed for air defense or fleet actions, they were not entirely successful in those roles. Nevertheless, their presence at all major amphibious operations after November 1943 provided adequate air defense against low-level Japanese attacks which allowed the Fast Carrier Task Force to be directed at targets to degrade Japanese air power at an operational level. In the Atlantic, USN escort carriers proved successful in the overall context of Allied ASW efforts against the German U-boat threat.

Another attribute was the basic cheapness of the escort carrier concept that allowed these ships to be produced in large numbers. Operating together, escort carriers provided significant numbers of aircraft for a variety of missions. A total of 77 escort carriers were commissioned into USN service during the war. In addition, American shipyards built 38 escort carriers for the RN. In comparison, the IJN built only five escort carriers, and these were mostly used for aircraft transport duties.

The evolution of USN escort carrier design eventually produced a ship which was virtually as capable as a light flight carrier, but with a reduced speed. The initial escort carrier, *Long Island*, possessed limited capabilities, but proved the viability of the entire escort carrier concept and its utility in the basic aircraft transport role. The Bogue class proved adequate in its intended role as an ASW hunter-killer carrier. The similar Casablanca class faced a higher threat environment in the Pacific. While the mass production of this class allowed the USN to include large task groups of escort carriers in major amphibious operations, this front-line duty revealed the deficiencies of the Casablanca class and of escort carriers in general. The lack of protection was glaringly obvious when *Liscome Bay* was torpedoed and sunk with massive personnel casualties off the Gilbert Islands in November 1943. Fortunately for the USN, that was the only occasion when a CVE was exposed to torpedo damage in the Pacific War. The real danger to escort carriers operating in the Pacific was from air attack. Operating in groups, escort carriers could cope with the limited threat from conventional Japanese air attack, but against kamikaze attack the vulnerabilities of the escort carriers were fully revealed. Even in groups, escort carriers could not generate adequate air cover, and singly a CVE did not possess adequate antiaircraft capabilities to defend against a suicide attacker. Worst of all, when struck, a CVE often did not have the damage control capabilities to cope with a hit in a vulnerable area. As a result, three CVEs were lost to kamikazes and 16 damaged.

Instead of an escort carrier with limited capabilities, the USN really wanted an escort carrier with capabilities approaching that of a real carrier. The Sangamon class came close to this aspiration and was used as de facto fleet carriers early in the war. The Sangamons proved to be superior escort carriers with their expanded air groups and a greater ability to survive damage. The Commencement Bay class was the ultimate USN escort carrier which was virtually a light carrier in terms of combat capability.

Because of their small aircraft complements, escort carriers had to operate in groups to be effective. In this view, a group of CVEs practice formation and maneuver exercises in Hawaiian waters on January 13, 1944. The photograph was taken from *Manila Bay* and the ships astern are *Anzio*, *Corregidor*, *Natoma Bay*, and *Nassau*; all but the last are Casablanca-class ships. The first three saw action in the invasion of the Marshalls shortly thereafter. (Naval History and Heritage Command)

CHAPTER 4
BATTLESHIPS

The USN went to war in December 1941 with 17 battleships in commission, which gave it the largest battle fleet in the world. The two North Carolina-class battleships commissioned in 1941 were the USN's first new battleships since 1923. These were the first of ten modern battleships that recorded productive and high-profile wartime careers. However, of the 17 battleships in service in late 1941, 15 were older units, with the earliest dating back to 1912. These were still seen as the heart of the fleet and critical to the Navy's war plans.

PART 1: THE PREWAR BATTLESHIPS
The Impact of Naval Treaties on USN Battleship Development

After World War I, the battleship was still considered the arbiter of naval power. In the aftermath of the war, Great Britain, Japan, and the United States all had plans for major battleship building sprees. The ambitious USN plan would have moved it ahead of the RN and greatly surpassed Japan's battle fleet. None of the three naval powers were in a position to fully execute their incredibly expensive building programs, so when the Americans proposed a naval disarmament conference to be convened in Washington, DC at the end of 1921, all major naval powers accepted the offer. The resulting Washington Naval Treaty of February 8, 1922 contained a limit to overall battleship tonnage for each power (for the USN it was 525,000 tons, which gave it parity with the RN (not achieved until 1931), and also set limits for the ships themselves. Each ship could not displace more than 35,000 tons and could not carry a main gun larger than 16in. The treaty was

An aerial starboard bow view of *West Virginia* on June 1, 1944 shows the result of its modernization. An entire new superstructure is evident with a Mark 34 director equipped with the Mark 8 radar on top. The large radar above the superstructure is the SK and an SG radar is fitted on top of both pole masts. The extensive antiaircraft battery of quadruple 40mm and single 20mm mounts is evident, as is the new secondary battery of twin 5in/38cal mounts. (Naval History and Heritage Command)

American Battleship Main Battery Weapons

All but one World War II USN battleship carried a main battery of 14in or 16in guns. The real difference between the 14in and the 16in guns was in their penetrative power. The heavier shell of the larger 16in gun gave it considerably more hitting power. The 14in had the ability to penetrate 13.6in of armor at 12,000 yards; in comparison, the 16in could penetrate 18.9in at 12,000 yards.

USN Battleship Main Guns				
Gun	Muzzle Velocity (ft/sec)	Maximum Range (yd)	Rate of Fire (rpm)	Fitted on
12in/50	2,900	23,900	2–3	Arkansas
14in/45	2,600	23,000	1–2	New York, Nevada, and Pennsylvania classes
14in/45 (post modernization)	2,600	34,300	1–2	New York, Nevada, and Pennsylvania classes
14in/50	2,700	36,300	1–2	Tennessee class
16in/45	2,520	35,000	1–2	Colorado class
16in/45	2,300	36,900	2	North Carolina and South Dakota classes
16in/50	2,500	42,345	2	Iowa class

binding for 15 years. Because the USN was already over its allowable limit, it had to scrap older dreadnoughts and scrap or cancel new ships already begun or projected. With new battleship construction forbidden, the USN was forced to concentrate on modernizing existing units during the interwar period. The London Naval Treaty of 1930 kept the building limits in place until the system of naval arms control collapsed at the end of 1936. The high costs of building dreadnoughts and the displacement restrictions of the naval treaties meant that each USN battleship design had to carefully weigh the requirements for firepower, speed, and protection and find an appropriate balance among the three. Generally, American designers emphasized firepower and then protection, with speed coming in a distinct third.

Wyoming Class

The two ships of the Wyoming class were among the USN's first-generation dreadnoughts. Each first-generation class made incremental improvement from the previous one. The Wyoming class featured firepower and protection improvements from the preceding Florida class.

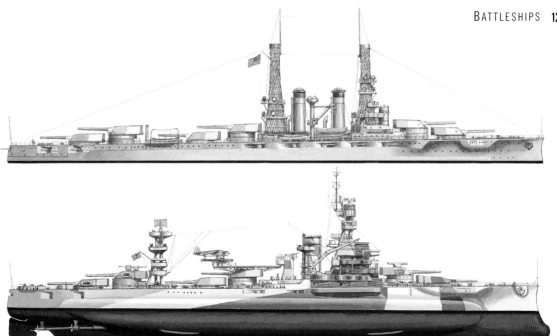

The design was also driven by the RN's new class of "superdreadnought" that possessed a significantly greater displacement over previous designs and new 13.5in main battery guns. The USN wanted ships with similar capabilities. This proved difficult since the USN's new 14in/45cal gun was still in the design stage. The primary issue for the Wyoming class' design was whether to design a ship around a new gun that had yet to be tested and whether it would be worth the considerable delay for these guns to be constructed and tested. Two new designs were prepared that used the 14in/45cal gun (one mounting eight, the other ten), but ultimately an alternative design was selected that mounted twelve 12in/50cal guns in six twin turrets. The 12in/50cal gun, which had a higher muzzle velocity over its 12in/45cal predecessor, was also a new design but one that could be completed and tested much sooner than the 14in/45cal gun. This was a conservative decision at the time, but ballistics experts calculated that a broadside of twelve 12in/50cal guns carried almost the same weight as ten 14in/45cal guns.

THE TOP VIEW IS OF *Arkansas* in 1917 in its original configuration. It was the only USN 12in armed battleship to survive until World War II. Note the main battery arranged in six twin-gun turrets. **THE BOTTOM VIEW IS OF** *Arkansas* in its final configuration in 1945. While the main battery remains as built, almost every other part of the ship was rebuilt. Note the profusion of radars and the light antiaircraft battery of ten 3in guns, nine quadruple 40mm mounts, and 28 single 20mm guns. (Artwork by Paul Wright, © Osprey Publishing)

Wyoming Class Construction					
Ship	Built at	Laid down	Launched	Commissioned	Fate
Wyoming (BB 32)	William Cramp and Sons, Philadelphia	2/9/10	5/25/11	9/25/12	Scrapped 1947
Arkansas (BB 33)	New York Shipbuilding, Camden	1/25/10	1/14/11	9/17/12	Sunk 7/5/46 as atomic target

Arkansas photographed in January 1945. The ship did not receive a large-scale modernization during the war, but did have its antiaircraft and radar fits improved as can be seen in this view. Note the arrangement of the 12in main battery. (Naval History and Heritage Command)

Principal aspects of the class' protection scheme included a main belt 11in thick at the top, tapering to 9in on the bottom, and stretching from the forward to the aft 12in turret barbettes. The barbettes were provided with armor 11in thick; the turrets had 12in of frontal armor. Horizontal armor was limited to a maximum of 2.5in.

Armament and Service Modifications

The main battery of twelve 12in/50cal guns was mounted in six twin turrets. One pair of superimposed turrets was placed forward, and two pairs of superimposed turrets were placed aft of the superstructure. The secondary battery of 21 5in/51cal guns were fitted in 17 casemates below the main deck and four guns in open positions in the superstructure. Two submerged 21in torpedo tubes were also fitted.

The Wyoming class survived the Washington Naval Treaty and was given top priority for modernization in the mid-1920s. This extensive modernization included conversion to fuel oil. Additional protection was provided in the form of torpedo bulges, and horizontal protection was increased to a maximum of 3.5in of armor. Most of the casemated secondary batteries located below the main deck were relocated to open-top sponsons built on the sides of the main deck, and the ships now carried eight 3in antiaircraft guns. The torpedo tubes were removed.

Wyoming was converted to a training ship under the terms of the 1930 London Naval Treaty. *Arkansas* remained in service, but it was considered a second-class unit. Accordingly, it was not extensively modified during the war. By the end of the war, it had been upgraded with radar and its antiaircraft suite consisted of ten 3in guns, nine 40mm quadruple mounts, and 28 20mm Oerlikons in single mounts.

Wyoming Class Specifications (as built)	
Displacement	Standard 26,417 tons; full 27,680 tons
Dimensions	Length: 562ft; beam 93ft 2in; draft 28ft 7in
Propulsion	12 boilers and 4 direct-drive turbines generating 28,000ihp on 4 shafts; maximum speed 20.5kt
Range	8,000nm at 10kt
Crew	1,063

New York Class

The two New York-class ships were authorized on June 24, 1910. With the successful testing of the 14in/45cal gun earlier in the year, the new class would be the first USN dreadnought fitted with a 14in gun. The design was the ten 14in/45cal-gun ship drawn up earlier for the Wyoming class. The new class was similar in layout and appearance to the Wyoming class but had five twin turrets instead of six. Consideration was given to using triple-gun turrets to eliminate the amidships turret, but time was of the essence since the USN was falling behind Germany in dreadnought construction.

New York Class Construction					
Ship	Built at	Laid down	Launched	Commissioned	Fate
New York (BB 34)	Brooklyn Navy Yard	9/11/11	10/30/12	5/15/14	Sunk as target 7/8/48
Texas (BB 35)	Newport News, Virginia	4/17/11	5/18/12	3/12/14	Preserved as museum near Houston, TX

Another major difference between the New York and Wyoming classes was the installation of vertical triple-expansion engines in the New York class. This decision was the result of disappointing performance of the turbines in the recently commissioned *North Dakota*. The USN felt compelled to revert to vertical triple-expansion machinery if the desired range was to be achieved.

ABOVE *Texas* is the oldest surviving dreadnought battleship remaining in the world. This is a recent photograph in its berth near Houston, Texas. (Cristian Sorto, CC BY-SA 4.0)

ABOVE RIGHT A German 240mm shell from Battery Hamburg lands astern of *Texas* during the naval bombardment of Cherbourg on June 25, 1944. *Texas* fired 206 14in shells during the action and was credited with one 240mm gun destroyed. It suffered minor damage from one hit. (NARA)

The protection scheme of the new class incorporated slight improvements. The main armored belt was 12in thick at the top, tapering to 10in at the bottom. The conning tower and the barbettes both featured armor up to 12in thick, and the turret face armor was increased to 14in. Horizontal protection remained limited to a maximum of 2in.

Armament and Service Modifications

In addition to the main battery described above, the New York class was fitted with a secondary battery of 21 5in/51cal single guns in the same general arrangement as the Wyoming class. Four submerged 21in torpedo tubes were also fitted.

Between 1925 and 1927, both ships received an extensive and lengthy modernization. This was like that given to the Wyoming class and included new masting and superstructure, the provision of new oil-fired boilers, and a protection upgrade with an additional 3,000 tons of armor and torpedo bulges. Wartime modifications focused on the upgrade of the ships' radar and antiaircraft suites. By the time *Texas* went to the Pacific in December 1944, its full load displacement had risen to 34,000 tons and its crew to 1,723. At this point its secondary battery had been reduced to six 5in/51cal guns, but its antiaircraft fit totaled ten 3in/50cal guns, ten quadruple 40mm, and 44 single 20mm mounts. *New York* displayed similar wartime modifications.

New York Class Specifications (as built)	
Displacement	Standard 27,433 tons; full 28,822 tons
Dimensions	Length 573ft; beam 95ft 3in; draft 29ft 7in
Propulsion	Two vertical triple-expansion engines, coal-fired by 14 boilers producing up to 28,100ihp on 2 shafts; maximum speed 21kt
Range	7,060nm at 10kt
Crew	1,042

Nevada Class

These ships represented the second generation of American dreadnought design. They featured a 14in gun main battery and introduced the design innovation of the "all or nothing" protection scheme.

Nevada Class Construction					
Ship	Built at	Laid down	Launched	Commissioned	Fate
Nevada (BB 36)	Bethlehem, Quincy	11/4/12	7/11/14	3/11/16	Sunk as target 7/31/48
Oklahoma (BB 37)	New York Shipbuilding, Camden	10/26/12	3/23/14	5/2/16	Sunk under tow 5/17/47

THE TOP PROFILE DEPICTS *Oklahoma* as it appeared in December 1941 when it was sunk at Pearl Harbor. **THE LOWER PROFILE SHOWS** *Nevada* as it appeared in 1945 after it returned to the Pacific. The ship is bristling with antiaircraft guns, including the four 5in/38cal mounts visible, and a robust electronics suite. The bridge structure has been modified and the unique stack configuration is apparent. (Artwork by Paul Wright, © Osprey Publishing)

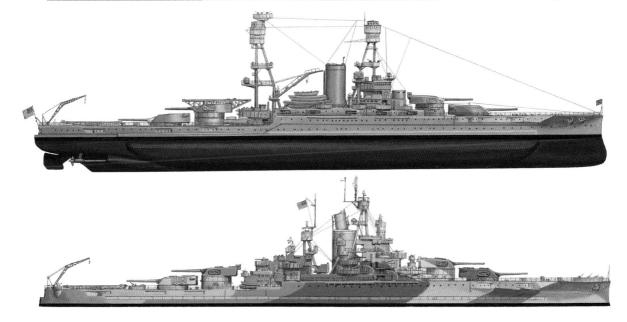

Protection

The "all or nothing" concept meant that only vital areas were protected by armor with other areas being unprotected. This provided the vital areas with greater protection. The Nevada class compared favorably to its European and Japanese counterparts of 1916, particularly in horizontal protection. Of the ship's waterline length of 575ft, only 400ft was protected. This allowed a greater emphasis on horizontal protection. Total weight of armor was 11,162 tons of which only 3,788 was allocated to the main belt. The armored deck and the splinter deck had a combined 3,291 tons. Overall, armor was 40 percent of the design displacement.

The main armor belt was a maximum of 13.5in thick. Almost half of the main belt was below the waterline, which tapered to 8in at its lowest point. The armored citadel was completed forward and aft by armored bulkheads with a maximum armor thickness of 13in. The turret barbettes received 13in of armor, the coming tower 16in, and the turret faces 18in. Horizontal protection totaled 3in of armor in three different layers that extended over the same length as the main belt.

Propulsion

Prior USN battleships relied on coal with a supplement of oil. The advantages of going to an all-oil arrangement were considerable since oil took less space, had a greater thermal content, made replenishment at sea possible, and dispensed with the issue of dealing with coal dust on sensitive equipment. Oil-fired ships required smaller boiler rooms that reduced the area requiring protection. *Nevada* was the first USN battleship to go all-oil.

Oklahoma in September 1930 after the completion of its modernization. The prominent piece of equipment on top of the bridge is the primary rangefinder for the main battery. A back-up rangefinder can be seen on top of Turret 2. (Naval History and Heritage Command)

Armament and Service Modifications

To mount the ten 14in guns, it was decided to use triple gun turrets for the first time. *Nevada* used two of these, one fore and aft, combined with a twin turret fitted in a superfiring position. The secondary battery of 21 5in/51cal guns was mounted in hull casemates, but to improve their usefulness in moderate or heavy seas, 14 of them were mounted one deck higher than on preceding battleships. Two submerged 21in torpedo tubes were also fitted. These proved totally useless in practice and all USN battleships had their submerged torpedo tubes removed during their major reconstruction.

As already mentioned, USN battleships underwent extensive modernization during the interwar period. For the Nevada class this took place from 1927 to 1929. Both ships lost their cagemasts in favor of heavy tripod masts and the bridge structure was substantially enlarged. Two catapults were added, one on the aft twin 14in turret and the other on the quarterdeck aft. Antitorpedo bulges were added which increased the depth of torpedo protection to 22ft. In addition, the boiler rooms were provided with torpedo bulkheads and a triple bottom also incorporated. The upper armored deck was increased to 5in and parts of the lower armored deck increased to as much as 3in. All told, an extra 1,906 tons of armor was added.

Both ships also had six new boilers installed and *Nevada* had its reciprocating engines replaced by new geared turbines from the canceled battleship *North Dakota*. This kept its speed at 20.5 knots, but the addition of the bulges in *Oklahoma* with no new machinery reduced its speed to 19.7 knots.

In addition to providing the main guns with increased elevation (greatly increasing range), all casemate 5in guns were moved one deck up. The 3in guns were replaced by 5in/25cal high-angle guns. A light antiaircraft capability was added in the form of eight .50cal machine guns. When completed, the ships displaced 30,500 tons. Additional efforts were made to

Nevada pictured on July 1, 1943 off San Francisco shortly after the completion of its modernization. This work was not as extensive as on those battleships more heavily damaged at Pearl Harbor, but it has still transformed the ship's appearance. The aft tower mast has been removed, but the forward one remains. The most obvious new weaponry is the four twin 5in/38cal mounts on each side. The single stack has been lengthened giving it a unique recognition feature. (Naval History and Heritage Command)

increase the ships' antiaircraft protection before the war. In its February 1941 refit, *Oklahoma* was earmarked to receive four 1.1in quadruple machine cannons, but since these were not available, four 3in/50cal guns were fitted instead. The four 36in searchlights were moved from the stack to the mainmast to get them higher up.

Nevada was the first of the battleships that were severely damaged at Pearl Harbor to be refitted. The ship was refloated on February 12, 1942, departed for Puget Sound Naval Shipyard on April 22, and underwent modernization that took until December. A new superstructure was fitted, and a raked extension of the stack added to keep smoke clear of the bridge. The secondary and antiaircraft batteries were removed and replaced with a dual-purpose battery of 16 5in/38cal guns in eight twin mounts. Ten 40mm quadruple mounts and 38 single 20mm mounts were also added. To compensate for all this new top weight, the mainmast, the armored conning tower, the catapult on the aft turret, 300 tons of fuel oil, 200 tons of reserve feed water, and a number of main battery rounds were all removed. Efforts to improve the ship's antiaircraft fit continued during the war. *Nevada*'s final fit in August 1945 was 16 5in/38cal guns, ten 40mm quadruple mounts, 20 twin and five single 20mm mounts.

Nevada Class Specifications (as built)	
Displacement	Standard 27,500 tons; full 28,400 tons
Dimensions	Length: 583ft; beam 95ft; draft 28ft 6in
Propulsion	12 boilers and 4 direct-drive turbines (reciprocating engines on *Oklahoma*) generating 25,500shp (24,800ihp on *Oklahoma*) on 4 shafts; maximum speed 20kt
Range	8,000nm at 10kt
Crew	864

Pennsylvania Class

The Navy requested four ships for the next battleship class, but this ran into Congressional opposition. A compromise resulted in a single ship being authorized in August 1912. This became *Pennsylvania*. The second ship of the class, *Arizona*, was not authorized until March 1913 to an almost identical design. Consideration was given to making these two ships a repeat of the Nevada class, but it was decided to implement incremental improvements. The primary difference was a requirement to fit 12 14in guns. This and some improvements in protection required a slightly longer hull. *Pennsylvania* was fitted as the fleet flagship and could be distinguished from its sister ship by its higher conning tower.

Pennsylvania Class Construction					
Ship	Built at	Laid down	Launched	Commissioned	Fate
Pennsylvania (BB 38)	Newport News, Virginia	10/27/13	3/16/15	6/12/16	Scuttled 2/10/48 after atomic tests
Arizona (BB 39)	Brooklyn Navy Yard	3/16/14	6/19/15	10/17/16	Sunk 12/7/41

Protection

The Pennsylvania class enjoyed the same level of main belt protection as the preceding Nevada class, but the new class did introduce changes in underwater protection. The main armor belt was 444ft long and 17.5ft wide. Maximum thickness was 13.5in, tapering to 8in on the lower edge. Half of the main belt was below the waterline. The armored bulkheads had a maximum thickness of 13in. The turret barbettes received 13in of armor, the coming tower 18in, and the turret faces 18in. Horizontal protection was increased with the provision of a lower armored deck. The uppermost armored deck remained at 3in arranged in three layers, but the lower armored deck added another 1.5–2in arranged in two layers. Protection over the steering machinery was increased to 6.25in on the upper deck. The vulnerable boiler room uptakes were provided with 15in of armor protection. Since underwater protection was already seen as a potentially critical weakness on the Nevada class, this was addressed in the new class. A 3in torpedo bulkhead 9.5ft inboard from the outer hull was fitted with a width of almost 12ft. It was calculated that it could withstand an explosion of 300 pound of TNT. Overall, protection was superior to RN dreadnoughts of the day and was equivalent to German designs.

Pennsylvania pictured before the beginning of its modernization period in June 1929. Note the cagemasts and the large ship's boats amidships. (Naval History and Heritage Command)

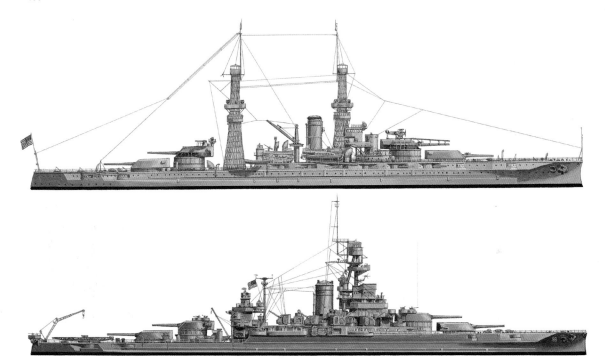

Armament and Service Modifications

The success of the triple 14in turret allowed an increase to 12 14in guns
fitted into four triple turrets. The secondary battery totaled 22 5in/51cal
single guns, almost all in casemates. For the first time, antiaircraft protection
was included in the design in the form of four 3in guns. The two 21in
submerged torpedo tubes were also fitted when the ship was completed.

The class' major modernization began in 1929. Both ships received new
boilers and turbines, but speed was not increased since the modernization
added some 3,100 tons of weight. Protection was enhanced with another
layer placed on the upper armored deck bringing its thickness to 4.75in.
This, and other small additions, added over 1,000 tons of additional armor.
A new 4.67ft deep antitorpedo blister was added and an extra torpedo
bulkhead added in the area of the boiler rooms. The overall depth of torpedo
protection was now 19ft.

Firepower augmentations included increasing the elevation of the 14in
turrets to 30 degrees. Antiaircraft protection was greatly increased with
eight 5in/25cal dual-purpose guns and eight .5cal machine guns. The
torpedo tubes were removed, and two new catapults fitted.

As war loomed, more efforts were made to increase antiaircraft protection.
During *Arizona*'s June 1941 refit, eight .50cal machines were added.
Positions for the 1.1in quadruple guns were provided, but none were fitted
because of shortages. *Pennsylvania* received similar modifications before the

war. After the Pearl Harbor raid, *Pennsylvania* was fitted with four 1.1in quadruple mounts and 16 20mm single guns in early 1942.

From October 1942 to February 1943, *Pennsylvania* underwent refit and major modification. The armored conning tower was removed to save top weight; similarly, the mainmast was removed and replaced by a small superstructure upon which the after main battery director rested. A new deckhouse was built to take a dual-purpose battery of eight twin 5in/38cal mounts. One catapult was removed, as were all the 5in/51cal guns. The new antiaircraft suite included ten 40mm quadruple and 51 20mm single mounts, and even the eight prewar machine guns were retained.

A March–July 1945 refit added the Mark 34 main battery director on the aft superstructure that was equipped with the modern Mark 8 fire-control radar. The antiaircraft suite was further augmented in the face of the kamikaze threat. In August 1945, the antiaircraft battery consisted of 42 40mm and 71 20mm guns.

This fine port beam view shows *Arizona* in August 1935. The casemates on the main deck for the 5in/51cal secondary battery are visible, as is the single 5in/51cal mount and the four port side 5in/25cal antiaircraft guns on the deckhouse. This is the configuration that the ship was in on December 7, 1941, when it was destroyed at Pearl Harbor. (Naval History and Heritage Command)

Pennsylvania Class Specifications (as built)	
Displacement	Standard 31,400 tons; full 32,567 tons
Dimensions	Length 608ft; beam 97ft; draft 28ft 10in
Propulsion	12 boilers and 4 geared turbines generating 31,500shp (34,000shp *Arizona*) on 4 shafts; maximum speed 21kt
Range	8,000nm at 10kt
Crew	915 (this increased to 1,574 during World War II)

New Mexico Class

Following the completion of design work on the Pennsylvania class, the USN saw a need for an entirely new battleship design to keep pace with European and Japanese ships. This new design was to be over 35,000 tons, possess better protection, and be fitted with the more powerful 16in gun. This was an expensive proposition, and the Secretary of the Navy did not approve it, so the 1914 battleship building program was essentially a repeat of the Pennsylvania class with minor improvements. Two ships were proposed, *New Mexico* and *Mississippi*, but the sale of pre-dreadnoughts *Idaho* and *Mississippi* to Greece in 1914 brought enough funds for a third ship that became *Idaho*.

The three ships of the New Mexico class shown together proceeding in column in January 1938. *Idaho* leads *Mississippi* and *New Mexico*. These were considered by the USN as their most powerful battleships before the war. When the Atlantic Fleet had to be reinforced in mid-1941, the New Mexico class was selected and when King pressured Nimitz to commit the older battleships to combat in the South Pacific, these ships came the closest to seeing action. (Naval History and Heritage Command)

New Mexico Class Construction					
Ship	Built at	Laid down	Launched	Commissioned	Fate
New Mexico (BB 40)	Brooklyn Navy Yard	10/14/15	4/13/17	5/20/18	Scrapped 1947
Mississippi (BB 41)	Newport News, Virginia	4/5/15	1/25/17	12/18/17	Scrapped 1956
Idaho (BB 42)	New York Shipbuilding, Camden	1/20/15	6/30/17	3/24/19	Scrapped 1947

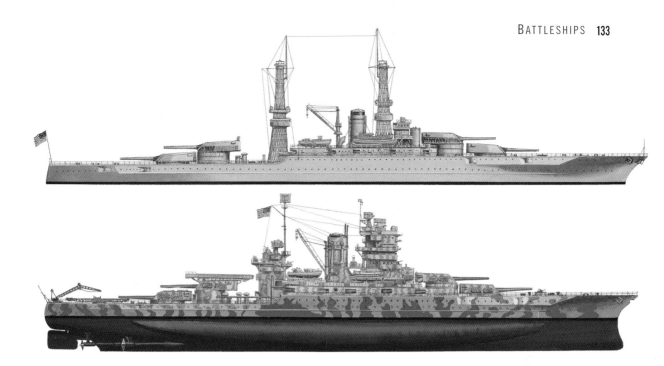

There were important visual differences to the new design. This was primarily due to the clipper bow to address the wetness problem in place of the ram bow on previous USN dreadnoughts. Displacement was marginally larger, and the hull was some 16ft longer. The only difference between the protection scheme of the New Mexico class and the preceding Pennsylvania class was the upper armored deck which was thickened to 3.5in.

The machinery was like that on the Pennsylvania class with nine boilers driving four direct-drive turbine shafts. *New Mexico* was fitted with a turbo-electric power plant to test the suitability of the system on battleships. The promise of turbo-electric drive was greater efficiency which translated into greater range and the ability to provide much greater internal sub-division in the machinery spaces. The system proved successful and was adopted for use on subsequent battleship classes.

Armament and Service Modifications

The main battery was comprised of 12 of the new 14in/50cal guns placed in redesigned turrets that allowed each gun to elevate independently. The guns could be elevated to 30 degrees resulting in a big improvement in range. The secondary battery was reduced to 14 5in/51cal guns, but these were placed in the deckhouse which permitted them to be worked in all types of seas. Four 3in guns were provided for antiaircraft protection and the two useless submerged 21in torpedo tubes were retained.

Between 1931 and 1934, these ships received the most extensive modernization of any USN dreadnought. This meant that at the start of the

THE TOP PROFILE IS *Mississippi* in 1917 in its original appearance. The ship looks much like the two preceding classes of superdreadnoughts with the most notable exception of the clipper bow. THE BOTTOM PROFILE IS *New Mexico* as it appeared in January 1942 before being deployed to the Pacific. The appearance of the *New Mexico* class during this period was marked by its large bridge structure and lack of large control tops or tripod masts. (Artwork by Paul Wright, © Osprey Publishing)

ABOVE This aerial view of *Idaho's* starboard bow was taken in January 1938 and shows the post-modernization configuration of the New Mexico ships. The ship presents a powerful and graceful appearance with its clipper bow, large bridge structure and four triple 14in turrets. (Naval History and Heritage Command)

Pacific War, the New Mexico class was the most modern in the fleet, aside from the newly completed North Carolina class. Horizontal protection was increased from 3.5in to 5.5in on the upper armored deck. The splinter deck over the machinery spaces was increased to 2.75in. To increase torpedo protection, a blister was fitted, and an additional bulkhead fitted outside the existing one; this increased the beam by 9ft. Propulsion was also upgraded with the original nine large-tube boilers being replaced. All three ships were fitted with turbo-electric drive, and even *New Mexico* which already had electric drive had it replaced to standardize with the rest of the class. Speed remained just over 21 knots, but the increased power (40,000shp) made up for the blisters and the increased displacement.

RIGHT An aerial port quarter view of *Mississippi* under way in July 1945. The ship is bristling with a heavy antiaircraft battery including 16 5in/25cal single guns and 12 40mm quadruple mounts – the most of any ship in its class. A single catapult remains on the quarterdeck, and an SK radar is on the mainmast. (Naval History and Heritage Command)

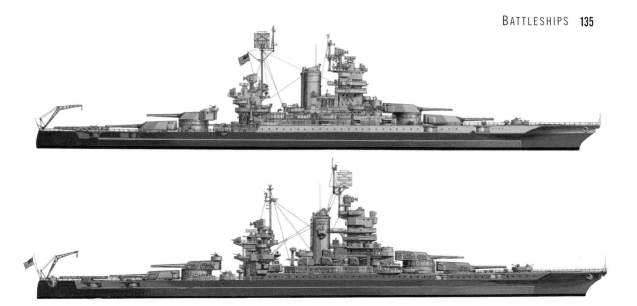

The alteration to the armament was not as dramatic. The 3in guns were replaced by 5in/25cals, and eight .50cal machine guns were added. The submerged torpedo tubes were removed. In 1941, the entire class was scheduled to receive 1.1in quadruple mounts, but these were unavailable, so four 3in guns were added. The two 5in/51cal guns in open mounts on the forward deck house were removed. Before dispatch into the Pacific after Pearl Harbor, the ships were given radar, 1.1in quadruple mounts, and 14 20mm single guns.

The ships were needed in service, so there was little chance for major reconstruction during the war. The desired antiaircraft fit in November 1942 called for the removal of the 5in/51cal guns, the retention of the eight existing 5in/25cal mounts and the addition of ten 40mm quadruple mounts and 40–45 20mm single mounts. Eventually all three ships received at least this level of antiaircraft protection. *Idaho* had an extensive late-war refit which the other ships did not. Between October 1944 and January 1945, ten single 5in/38cal in enclosed mounts replaced the open 5in/25cal mounts.

THE TOP PROFILE IS *Mississippi* in 1943 as its appearance begins to change with new antiaircraft guns and radar. The electronics upgrade is evident with the SK air search on the mainmast and the SG surface search radar on the foremast. All the fire-control directors for the main and secondary batteries are radar-equipped. All but six of the 5in/51cal guns have been removed, and ten 40mm quadruple mounts are visible along with many single 20mm mounts.

THE BOTTOM PROFILE DEPICTS *Idaho*, the most heavily modified New Mexico-class ship. All 5in/51cal casemate guns and the 5in/25cal guns have been deleted and replaced by ten single 5in/38cal mounts. The number of 40mm quadruple mounts has now reached 12. (Artwork by Paul Wright, © Osprey Publishing)

New Mexico Class Specifications (as built)	
Displacement	Standard 32,000 tons; full 33,000 tons
Dimensions	Length 624ft; beam 97ft 6in; draft 30ft
Propulsion	9 boilers driving 4 direct-drive turbines generating 32,000shp on 4 shafts, maximum speed 21kt (*New Mexico* 2 electric generators and 4 electric motors generating 27,000shp on 4 shafts; maximum speed 21kt)
Range	8,000nm at 10kt
Crew	1,084

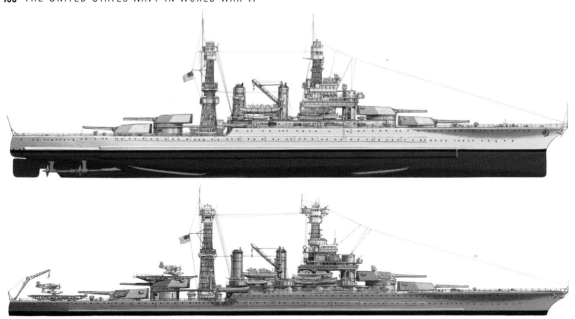

Tennessee Class

THE TOP PROFILE DEPICTS
Tennessee as it appeared in 1922 shortly after being completed. The ship gives a clean and balanced appearance overall with its symmetrical main battery layout, two prominent cage masts, and clipper bow.
THE LOWER PROFILE DEPICTS
California in its early-war configuration at Pearl Harbor in December 1941. No major modifications were made after its commissioning, but the two catapults are evident. (Artwork by Paul Wright, © Osprey Publishing)

For the 1915 battleship building program, Congress approved the normal two ships. The final design was not completed until March 1916 due to modifications on a new underwater protection scheme and a decision to adopt turbo-electric propulsion.

Tennessee Class Construction					
Ship	Built at	Laid down	Launched	Commissioned	Fate
Tennessee (BB 43)	Brooklyn Navy Yard	5/15/17	4/30/19	6/3/20	Scrapped 1959
California (BB 44)	Mare Island Navy Yard	10/25/16	11/20/19	8/10/21	Scrapped 1959

Protection

The main armor belt displayed a maximum thickness of 13.5in that tapered to 8in on its lower edge. Half of the main belt was below the waterline and it was backed by concrete, not wood. The armored bulkheads at both ends of the belt had a maximum thickness of 13.5in. The turret barbettes received between 14in and 16in of armor, the conning tower 16in and the turret faces 18in. Horizontal protection consisted of a main armored deck with 3.5in arranged in two layers, and the lower armored deck of another 2in over the machinery spaces and 1.5in elsewhere. The main armored deck was

designed to explode armor-piercing shells, while the lower armored deck, also called the splinter deck, was designed to prevent shell fragments from entering the ship's vitals.

Underwater protection was greatly enhanced. A series of longitudinal splinter bulkheads covered the area between the double bottom to the lower armored (splinter) deck. The spaces between these bulkheads were designed to absorb the force of a blast against the side of the ship by either being void or filled with liquid. Eventually, it was decided that the most effective arrangement was to have the outer compartment left as a void, the next three filled with a liquid (either fuel oil or water), and the innermost compartment left void to take the compression of the expanding liquid. The maximum depth of this system was 17ft 3in from the outer hull. The system was designed to withstand the blast of 400lb of TNT. This concept was well in advance of its time and gave the USN the best underwater protection of any dreadnought designed before World War II. The system was so successful that all future USN battleships used it as the basis for their underwater protection systems.

California ended up on the bottom of Pearl Harbor following progressive flooding from two torpedo hits. The ship was raised in March 1942 and later sent to Bremerton for reconstruction. (Naval History and Heritage Command)

Propulsion

New Mexico had been fitted with a turbo-electric power plant to test its suitability for use on battleships. Trials were successful, and they were designed into the Tennessee class. The new ships had eight boilers powering

two electric generators which produced power for four electric motors. The steam turbines were coupled directly to alternators. The current produced was fed to motors which were coupled to the propellers. This provided 26,800shp on four shafts which was adequate for the design speed of 21 knots. The boilers were placed in individual compartments inboard of the antitorpedo system forming another protective layer. The two turbo-generators were on the centerline and were not located near one another.

Armament and Service Modifications

The Tennessee class retained the proven 14in/50cal gun fitted in four triple turrets making them the last USN battleships to use 14in guns. The secondary battery consisted of 14 5in/51cal single guns, almost all in casemates. Antiaircraft protection was provided by four 3in guns. Two 21in submerged torpedo tubes were also fitted. Before the war, the antiaircraft suite had been upgraded to eight 5in/25cal guns, four 3in/50cal guns, and eight .50cal machine guns. The submerged torpedo tubes were removed.

Both ships were damaged at Pearl Harbor and eventually both were rebuilt from the main deck up. *California* was the first to begin reconstruction, which started in June 1942. The work was so extensive that it did not re-enter service until January 1944. The entire superstructure was replaced with one based on the South Dakota class. The armament was almost entirely renewed. The main battery remained but was provided with two Mark 34 directors placed on two new towers. The old secondary and long-range antiaircraft batteries were removed. In their place, a battery of 16 dual-purpose 5in/38cal guns was fitted.

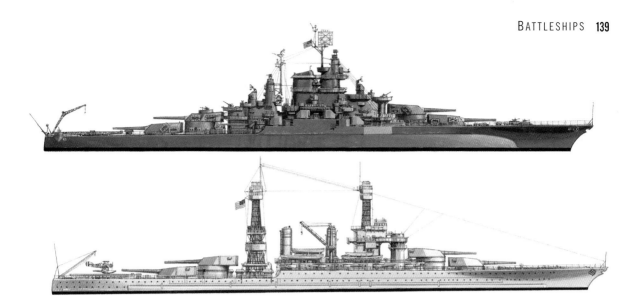

Another dramatic improvement was the ships' light antiaircraft battery – 14 40mm quadruple mounts and 52 single 20mm guns were added.

Protection was also enhanced. The most important addition was a torpedo blister that increased overall beam to 114ft making the ship too wide to use the Panama Canal. In addition to the blister, more internal longitudinal bulkheads were added to increase underwater subdivision. Horizontal protection was increased by 2in of armor (3in over the magazines) for a total of 7in (8in over the magazines). The roofs of the turrets also received additional armor, bringing them up to 7in.

After this transformation, full load displacement increased to almost 41,000 tons. New boilers increased power to 32,500shp, but this was negated by the increased displacement. Post-modernization speed was a maximum of 20.5 knots. The ship's crew grew to 2,375 men, more than double the original crew when the ship was launched.

Tennessee ended up in the same basic configuration as *California* after the ship was taken out of service in September 1942 for modernization. The light antiaircraft battery was different with ten quadruple 40mm mounts along with 43 single 20mm guns. The ship's complement grew to 2,240 men.

THE TOP PROFILE DEPICTS *Tennessee* in 1945 after being rebuilt. Only its original main battery remains unaltered. The secondary battery and original antiaircraft batteries have been replaced with dual-purpose 5in/38cal mounts and a host of 40mm quadruple and 20mm single mounts. The prominent cage masts are gone and have been replaced with compact fire-control towers. **THE BOTTOM PROFILE FEATURES** *West Virginia* in 1924 shortly after entering service. The ship looks like the Tennessee class except for the main battery which consists of four twin 16in gun turrets. (Artwork by Paul Wright, © Osprey Publishing)

OPPOSITE The aerial bow view of *Tennessee* in December 1943 shows the battleship after reconstruction. The new superstructure is evident, as are the eight twin 5in/38cal twin mounts. Three of the Mark 37 directors for the 5in/38cals are visible forward and on both sides of the superstructure. The Mark 34 director with the Mark 8 radar for the main battery is visible on top of the superstructure. (Naval History and Heritage Command)

Tennessee Class Specifications (as built)	
Displacement	Standard 32,300 tons; full 33,190 tons
Dimensions	Length 624ft; beam 97ft 5in; draft 30ft 2in
Propulsion	8 boilers powering 2 electric generators and 4 electric motors generating 28,600shp on 4 shafts; maximum speed 21kt
Range	8,000m at 10kt
Crew	1,083

Colorado Class

The new class took the same dimensions, propulsion systems, and protection scheme as on *Tennessee* and *California* and substituted the new 16in/45cal gun for the standard 14in/50cal. The move to the 16in gun had been contemplated for some time and work was already advanced on the USN's first gun of this caliber. Intelligence that the Japanese were planning to equip the Nagato class forced the decision to move to the 16in gun on the Colorado class.

Colorado Class Construction					
Ship	Built at	Laid down	Launched	Commissioned	Fate
Colorado (BB 45)	New York Shipbuilding, Camden	5/29/19	3/22/21	8/30/23	Scrapped 1959
Maryland (BB 46)	Newport News, Virginia	4/24/17	3/20/20	7/21/21	Scrapped 1959
Washington (BB 47)	New York Shipbuilding, Camden	6/30/19	9/1/21	Never	Sunk as target 1924
West Virginia (BB 48)	Newport News, Virginia	4/12/20	11/17/21	12/1/23	Scrapped 1959

A classic aerial oblique view of *Colorado* in 1934. The crew are manning the rails in their Winter Blue uniforms. The ship gives a clean and balanced appearance with its symmetrical main battery and two prominent cage masts. (Naval History and Heritage Command)

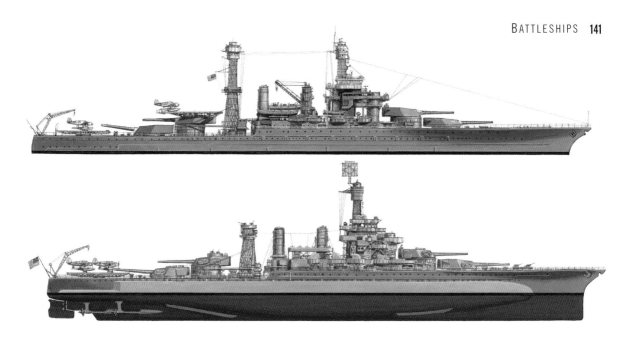

As the class was being completed, the Washington Naval Treaty, signed in February 1922, came into effect. Only *Maryland* was already in service, and it appeared that the other ships would never be completed. The Japanese fought hard to keep the new 16in battleship *Mutsu*, and in compensation the USN was allowed to complete *Colorado* and *West Virginia*. The last ship of the class, *Washington*, was never finished.

As mentioned, the protection of the USN's first 16in battleship was identical to that of the preceding Tennessee class. By USN standards, the ship was under-armored since the thickness of the main belt did not equal the caliber of the main battery guns. The total weight of armor in the class was 12,353 tons which equated to 35.8 percent of the ship's normal displacement.

Armament and Service Modifications

The eight 16in gun main battery used a four-turret layout. Even with the number of main battery guns reduced from 12 to eight, the broadside of the Colorado class was virtually identical to that of the preceding Tennessee class. Eight 16in guns delivered a broadside of 17,920lb compared to the 18,000lb broadside of a ship equipped with 12 14in guns. More importantly the heavier 16in shell possessed greater penetrative powers against armored targets.

The secondary battery consisted of 12 5in/51cal single guns; none of these was mounted on the hull, which gave the ships a cleaner appearance. Antiaircraft protection was provided by eight 3in guns. Two 21in submerged torpedo tubes were also fitted amidships when the ship was completed, but these were removed early in the ships' careers. In 1928–29, the eight 3in guns were replaced with the 5in/25cal gun.

THE TOP PROFILE DEPICTS *Colorado* as it appeared in 1941 before going into refit and limited modernization before the opening of war. The ship retains its two prominent cage masts and two catapults. The secondary battery of six 5in/51cal guns is evident with five of the guns in casemates. The sixth gun is located on the second level abaft Turret 2. The starboard side antiaircraft guns include four 5in/25cal mounts without shields on the second level and two single 3in guns. **THE SECOND PROFILE IS OF** *Maryland* in early 1943 as it appeared in mid-war after minor modifications. The ship retains ten 5in/51cal guns in casemates and eight 5in/25cal mounts with shields. The aft cage mast has been cut down and three 20mm single guns placed on top. Other 20mm guns are evident on two galleries built abeam the forward stack and near Turrets 2 and 3. The turret-mounted catapult has been removed. (Artwork by Paul Wright, © Osprey Publishing)

Maryland shown in 1944 after the aft cage mast had been removed and replaced with a small superstructure. The electronics fit can be seen with SK radar on the forward cage mast and SG radars atop both pole masts. The Mark 3 fire control is evident on top of the directors atop the remaining cage mast and the aft superstructure. (Naval History and Heritage Command)

The wartime modernization of the three Colorado-class ships took different paths. The most drastic modernization belonged to *West Virginia*, which was sunk at Pearl Harbor. From the summer of 1942 until June 1944, *West Virginia* was rebuilt. The work was very similar to that done on *Tennessee* and *California* with the same superstructure and massive torpedo bulges. The main battery remained, but all the old 5in guns were replaced by eight twin 5in/38cal mounts. Ten 40mm quadruple mounts and 40 20mm single guns were added. Fire control was drastically improved with Mark 34 directors with Mark 8 radars for the main battery and Mark 37 directors with Mark 4 radars for the secondary battery. This was equivalent to the fire-control suite given to the fast battleships. By 1945 the 20mm suite was modified to 58 single, one twin, and one quadruple mount; displacement had risen to 40,396 tons full load.

Maryland and *Colorado* were never given extensive modernizations. *Colorado* did not receive a prolonged refit until November 1943. By 1944, the light antiaircraft battery had been raised to ten 40mm quadruple mounts and 40 20mm single mounts, but the ship retained its 5in/25cal single mounts. *Maryland*'s first large modernization occurred in early 1944; after another refit later in 1944, the ship carried ten 40mm quadruple mounts and 48 20mm guns. In the ship's final refit in May 1945, all 5in/51cal casemate guns were removed along with the 5in/25cal battery and were replaced with eight twin 5in/38cal mounts. The 20mm battery was reduced to 18 twin mounts.

Colorado Class Specifications (as built)	
Displacement	Standard 31,800; full 33,590 tons
Dimensions	Length 624ft; beam 97ft 5in; draft 30ft 2in
Propulsion	8 boilers powering 2 electric generators and 4 electric motors generating 28,900shp on 4 shafts; maximum speed 21kt
Range	8,000m at 10kt
Crew	1,083

USN Prewar Battleships – an Analysis

As designed and modernized, USN prewar battleships were superior to their British and Japanese contemporaries in overall protection, particularly horizontal protection. Like almost all battleships of the day, the Achilles heel of USN prewar battleships was inadequate underwater protection. In the area of speed, older USN battleships were inferior to British and Japanese ships, and this could have been an important tactical consideration had the decisive battle fleet engagement envisioned by both the USN and IJN ever occurred. Overall though, the USN's emphasis of superior sustainability in the form of greater protection was probably a better choice than higher speed that the IJN seemed to have an enduring fascination for. In terms of hitting power, the standard USN prewar battleship with its 10–12 14in guns possessed a slight potential advantage over its Japanese counterparts. Both navies fielded battleships carrying eight 16in guns, but superior USN fire control was a critical advantage. During the interwar period, USN fire control was on parity with RN and IJN battleships since all were using the same basic technology. However, with the advent of radar, the USN applied it more quickly and effectively.

The fully modernized *Tennessee*, *California*, and *West Virginia* were near equivalents to the USN's new battleships in combat capabilities. Their fire-control systems were equivalent to the newer ships, as were their antiaircraft capabilities. Protection was also essentially equivalent in terms of horizontal protection and antitorpedo defenses, and these ships carried thicker main belts. However, the lack of speed of all the USN's prewar battleships was so low as to take them out of any fleet role and relegate them to supporting amphibious invasions.

There is an extremely limited basis on which to directly compare USN prewar battleships with their Japanese peers. The only occasion when any of these ships took part in a surface engagement against Japanese battleships was in October 1944 at the Battle of Surigao Strait. This was not a true test, however, since it featured an overwhelming USN force of six battleships and eight cruisers against a Japanese force which had been whittled down to a single battleship already damaged by USN destroyer torpedoes and an accompanying heavy cruiser by the time the gunnery phase of the engagement took place. The outcome in this case was not in doubt, but it is still noteworthy that no major USN ship was even damaged in the engagement and the Japanese battleship was sunk.

The outcome at Surigao Strait was no surprise since USN battleships were better protected than their IJN dreadnought contemporaries and possessed superior fire-control systems for their main batteries. The only wild card in

USN Prewar Battleship Operations

Principal USN Prewar Battleship Operations		
Operation	Time Period	Ships Participating
Pearl Harbor	December 1941	*Nevada, Oklahoma, Pennsylvania, Arizona, Tennessee, California, Maryland, West Virginia*
Task Force 1 (eastern Pacific defense)	January–October 1942	*Pennsylvania, Tennessee, Maryland, Colorado, New Mexico, Mississippi, Idaho*
Aleutians campaign	May–August 1943	*Nevada, Pennsylvania, Mississippi, Idaho, Tennessee*
Gilberts invasion	November 1943	*Pennsylvania*
Marshalls invasion	January–February	Same as for Gilberts
Bombardment of Kavieng	March 20, 1944	*New Mexico, Mississippi, Idaho, Tennessee*
Invasion of northern France	June 1944	*Nevada, Arkansas, Texas*
Marianas invasion	June 1944	*Pennsylvania, New Mexico, Idaho, California, Tennessee, Colorado, Maryland*
Invasion of southern France	August 1944	Same as for northern France
Palaus invasion	September 1944	*Pennsylvania, Mississippi, Tennessee, Maryland, West Virginia*
Leyte invasion	October–November 1944	*Pennsylvania, Mississippi, Tennessee, California, Maryland, West Virginia, New Mexico* (November), *Colorado* (November)
Luzon invasion	January–February	*Pennsylvania, New Mexico, Mississippi, California, West Virginia, Colorado*
Iwo Jima invasion	February 1945	*Nevada, Idaho, Tennessee, Texas, New York, Arkansas*
Okinawa invasion	April–June 1945	*Nevada, New Mexico, Mississippi, Idaho, Tennessee, Colorado, Maryland, West Virginia, Texas, New York*
East China Sea sweep	July 1945	*Nevada, Pennsylvania, Tennessee, California, Arkansas, Texas*

As clearly shown in the accompanying table, the older battleships were busy from May 1943 until the end of the war. They were part of almost every major USN operation. The largest amphibious operation of the war, the invasion of Okinawa in April–June 1945, included ten older battleships. Beginning in May 1943, when the USN invaded Attu Island in the Aleutians, the older battleships found a role supporting amphibious invasions. They proved well suited for this role. Their main battery was extremely powerful in a shore bombardment role and the ships formed a covering force able to take on any likely IJN attempt to intervene with the invasion force. While the IJN's older battleships sat in home waters with no role except to wait for the increasingly unlikely major fleet surface engagement, the older USN battleships were constantly busy providing antiair and surface screening to amphibious forces. Their most useful contribution was providing gunfire support to American ground troops as they attempted to expel well dug-in Japanese defenders from a seemingly endless succession of Pacific islands. In this capacity, they excelled by all accounts. The old battleships were ideally suited for this role since they possessed a combination of endurance on station, great range and accuracy of fire, and immense destructive power. Though they never were the centerpiece of a decisive naval engagement against the IJN, they did make real contributions to the USN's victorious Pacific campaign.

such an engagement was whether the USN battleships would be exposed to an intense IJN torpedo threat. Even after their prewar modernization, the record of older USN battleships against Japanese torpedoes was not good. The case of *Oklahoma* was exceptional since any battleship of its era would have been overwhelmed by five torpedo hits, but the fact that *Nevada* and *Pennsylvania* were severely damaged by a single torpedo at different points in the war demonstrated that underwater protection was still a weakness. *West Virginia* was overwhelmed by seven torpedo hits at Pearl Harbor, and *California* was caught in an unprepared condition and settled on the harbor's floor after only two torpedo hits. This was against the IJN's Type 91 air-launched torpedo with a 529lb warhead, and the Type 93 torpedo carried by IJN cruisers and destroyers had a much larger 1,080lb warhead. Two of these were sufficient to sink a USN prewar heavy cruiser, and a similar number would have likely crippled any USN prewar battleship.

It is generally thought that the older USN battleships played little part in the war. This was probably for two reasons. These ships lacked the speed to escort the fast carriers, leaving this duty to the North Carolina, South Dakota and Iowa classes. Perhaps, more importantly, the attack on Pearl Harbor gave the mistaken impression that the Pacific Fleet's battle line had been wiped out, a perception reinforced by the fact that the older battleships were not employed in the forward areas through 1942. The lightly damaged survivors of Pearl Harbor, *Pennsylvania*, *Tennessee*, and *Maryland*, were joined by the undamaged *Colorado* and the three ships of the New Mexico class to form a powerful battle line in early 1942. This force, known as Task Force 1, was not employed in the forward areas despite the constant prodding by Admiral King to Admiral Nimitz to find active employment for them. Nimitz declined to use the ships primarily for logistical concerns, but the real reason was probably more to do with his assessment of the ability of the ships to withstand the Japanese torpedo threat. This speaks volumes of how the older battleships were viewed by the USN. Not fast enough to escort carriers, and not capable enough to operate as front-line units in the face of a major IJN threat, they were judged to be suitable only for support to amphibious forces and for dealing with the odd Japanese unit which might penetrate to the invasion area.

PART 2: THE FAST BATTLESHIPS

The USN placed ten "fast" battleships in commission from 1941 to 1944. These possessed the requisite speed to operate with the new battle fleet – the carrier task forces. The six ships of the North Carolina and South Dakota classes were directly affected by the Washington Naval Treaty, having been designed to adhere to the treaty's 35,000-ton limit for battleships. The Iowa class was the USN's last battleship class but was still impacted by treaty restrictions.

North Carolina Class

The North Carolina class battleships were the first USN battleships to be built since *West Virginia* was commissioned on December 1, 1923. The design process for the North Carolina class was prolonged and was greatly restricted by the 35,000-ton treaty limit and the requirement to keep the beam under the limit of the Panama Canal. The General Board, responsible for approving design specifications, wanted a battleship capable of 30 knots with a main battery of nine 14in guns. Such a ship could act as part of the "fast wing" of the battle fleet to catch the IJN's Kongo-class fast battleships and be fast enough to hunt down and destroy Axis commerce raiders. The design that was finally approved constituted a shift in USN battleship design priorities. The approved version provided for a ship capable of only 27 knots, but with maximum firepower of 12 14in guns in quadruple turrets. The ship was to be protected against 14in shellfire. The design was changed after construction began because of concerns that Japan would not commit to the restrictions of the Second London Naval Treaty of 1936. The treaty included escalator clauses for main battery guns for the signatory nations to counter developments by non-signatory powers. When Japan refused to commit to the Second London Naval Treaty's 14in limit for battleship guns, the Secretary of the Navy approved changing the main armament for the North Carolina-class battleships from 12 14in to nine 16in/45cal guns in July 1937. This change was possible because the turret size for quadruple 14in guns was the same for triple 16in guns. This modification caused much concern within the USN since the ship was now unbalanced – the size of the main battery guns was greater than its scale of protection.

Protection

The protection scheme was designed to defend against 14in shells. Total weight of armor was 41 percent of the ships' displacement. The "all or

North Carolina photographed in June 1942 before joining the Pacific Fleet. All USN fast battleships had their aviation facilities on the stern, consisting of a crane, two catapults, and room for three aircraft, like the OS2U Kingfishers in this view. (Naval History and Heritage Command)

THESE VIEWS DEPICT *North Carolina* as it appeared in August 1942 during the Battle of the Eastern Solomons. The ship projects a graceful and powerful appearance with its main battery of nine 16in guns arranged in three triple turrets and a secondary battery of ten twin 5in/38cal mounts. (Artwork by Peter Bull, © Osprey Publishing)

nothing' principle was employed, with the protected section of the ship extending from just forward of Turret 1 to just aft of Turret 3; this area included the magazines and machinery spaces. The main belt was 12in thick, was inclined at 15 degrees, and tapered to 6in on the lower edge of the belt. The conning tower received between 16in and 14.7in; the barbettes were similarly protected. The main gun turrets were well protected with 16in of face armor and 7in on the top.

Horizontal protection featured three armored decks. The first deck of 1.45in was designed to cause delay-fuzed projectiles to detonate; the second deck of 5in protected the ships' internals; and the third deck of .62in was designed to prevent shell splinters from damaging internal areas.

Underwater protection was also extensive. In total, it was 18.5ft deep and designed to withstand up to 700lb of TNT. Side protection was provided by five compartments divided by torpedo bulkheads. Two were filled with liquid, and the others left empty. Outboard of these was a large bulge that covered the same area as the main belt. The final protective layer was a triple bottom 5.75ft deep.

Propulsion

The requirement for high speed was made possible by technology in the form of new lightweight geared turbines and high-temperature, high-pressure boilers. The turbines and boilers were combined in four machinery rooms, rather than in separate engine and boiler rooms, to provide greater survivability in the case of a torpedo hit. To meet the design requirement of 27 knots the propulsion system was designed to supply 115,000shp, but the new technologies increased this output to 121,000shp. When commissioned, the ships had a top speed of 28 knots, but by 1945 after the addition of additional weight, speed was reduced to just under 27 knots. Speed was an issue when the battleships operated with the Fast Carrier Task Force since the carriers could steam at 33 knots. When commissioned, both ships experienced significant shaft vibration to the extent that it adversely affected

North Carolina at sea during the Gilberts operation in November 1943. The beam view shows the primary features of this powerful warship; note the three 16in triple gun turrets, large superstructure, two stacks, and secondary battery of five 5in/38cal twin turrets. (Naval History and Heritage Command)

fire-control instruments. This took several return trips to the shipyard to rectify. The new machinery was also economical and provided an outstanding range of 17,450nm at 15 knots.

North Carolina Class Construction					
Ship	Built at	Laid down	Launched	Commissioned	Fate
North Carolina (BB 55)	Brooklyn Navy Yard	10/27/37	6/13/40	4/9/41	Preserved as museum ship in Wilmington, NC
Washington (BB 56)	Philadelphia Navy Yard	6/14/38	6/1/40	5/15/41	Scrapped 1961

Armament and Service Modifications

The main battery consisted of nine 16in/45cal guns in three triple turrets. This gun proved reliable in service. For the first time on a USN battleship, the secondary battery used the excellent 5in/38cal dual-propose gun. Twenty of these guns were carried in ten twin turrets. Both the main and secondary batteries were unchanged during the ships' careers.

Original antiaircraft protection was inadequate with only four 1.1in quadruple mounts and 12 .50cal machine guns. The antiaircraft battery was dramatically increased as the war progressed. As soon as production problems were overcome, 40mm quadruple mounts replaced the 1.1in weapons. Both ships eventually carried 15 of the 40mm quadruple mounts. The machine guns were also quickly replaced by 20mm single mounts. Since both ships had the room to handle large numbers of these weapons, their numbers continued to grow until *North Carolina* embarked 48 in November 1944. By 1945, the ship carried 36 20mm guns in eight twin and 20 single mounts.

North Carolina Class Specifications (as built)	
Displacement	Standard 37,200 tons; full 45,500 tons
Dimensions	Length 728ft 9in; beam 108ft 4in; draft 35ft 6in
Propulsion	8 boilers and 4 geared turbines generating 121,000shp on 4 shafts; maximum speed 28 knots
Range	17,450nm at 15 knots
Crew	1,900

South Dakota Class

Design of the South Dakota class commenced in 1937. The principal objective facing the designers was to increase the level of armored protection to defeat 16in shells, thus making the ship balanced. At the same time, the main battery of nine 16in guns and a speed requirement for 27 knots was retained. Fitting this into a ship that adhered to the 35,000-ton treaty restriction was a challenge. The principal method used to save weight was to reduce the hull by 47ft. The new design was approved in January 1938, and two of the ships were ordered in April 1938. Congress authorized two more in June 1938.

South Dakota operating off the US East Coast in August 1943. This view gives a good impression of the compact but powerful appearance of the class. Clearly visible is the shorter bow area that allowed the designers to meet the 35,000-ton limit. Note that *South Dakota* only carried four 5in/38cal twin mounts on each beam, the only ship of its class with this configuration. (Naval History and Heritage Command)

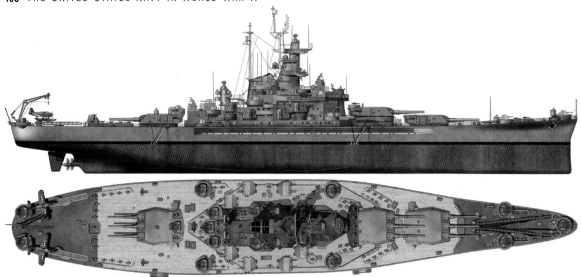

THESE VIEWS DEPICT *South Dakota* in its final appearance. The South Dakota class was 47ft shorter than the preceding North Carolina class, and its compact appearance is clear in these views. *South Dakota* was the only ship of its class to mount 16 (as opposed to 20) 5in/38cal guns. Its powerful antiaircraft battery of 17 40mm quadruple mounts is also evident, along with many single 20mm guns. (Artwork by Peter Bull, © Osprey Publishing)

South Dakota Class Construction					
Ship	Built at	Laid down	Launched	Commissioned	Fate
South Dakota (BB 57)	New York Shipbuilding, Camden	7/5/39	6/7/41	3/20/42	Scrapped 1962
Indiana (BB 58)	Newport News, Virginia	9/20/39	11/21/41	4/30/42	Scrapped 1963
Massachusetts (BB 59)	Bethlehem, Quincy	7/20/39	9/23/41	5/12/42	Preserved as museum ship in Fall River, MA
Alabama (BB 60)	Norfolk Navy Yard	2/1/40	2/16/42	8/16/42	Preserved as museum ship in Mobile, AL

Protection

The principal difference from the North Carolina class was an improved level of protection. To achieve the desired protection against 16in shells, the main belt was slightly thicker (12.2in), but it was inclined 19 degrees internally. This inclination improved the main belt's effective thickness to 17.3in against a shell from 19,000 yards. Other protection was slightly improved. The conning tower received a maximum of 16in of armor; the barbettes were provided with a maximum of 17.3in of armor. The main gun turrets were protected with 18in of face armor. Horizontal protection was provided by three armored decks, all of which were slightly increased from the North Carolina class. The first deck consisted of 1.5in; the second deck added between 5.75in and 6.05in; and the third deck another .62 to 1in.

Underwater protection was also improved. Towards the end of the design process for the North Carolina class, the possibility of ships sustaining underwater hull damage from steeply diving heavy shells that fell short of the ship was assessed to be important. However, as the design was so advanced, only supplemental protection for the magazines could be added. For the South Dakota class, the danger from underwater shell hits was fully addressed and measures taken to protect both magazine and machinery spaces. The inward-sloping main armor belt was continued down to the inner bottom plates. The extension of the armored belt down to the triple bottom caused problems because of the rigidity of the armor that could cause leakage into adjoining compartments. This problem was discovered in 1939 and addressed with additional reinforcement of the joint between the belt and the ship's bottom and an alteration that filled the four compartments in the bulge with fluid. Additionally, the strength of the outer and inner bottom plates and other internal longitudinal plates was increased relative to the North Carolina class. The internal bulge system was 17.9ft deep with the potential to withstand up to 700lb of TNT.

Alabama photographed in an early-war camouflage scheme in Casco Bay, Maine during its shakedown period in December 1942. The ship saw service with the RN's Home Fleet before being sent to the Pacific for the remainder of the war. (Naval History and Heritage Command)

Propulsion

The reduced length of the hull created challenges if the ship's design speed was going to be realized. One of the principles of ship design is that a longer hull results in greater maximum speed; to reach the same speed as the North Carolina class, greater propulsive power was needed. The design speed itself was also a matter of controversy. The original design speed called for only 22.5 knots, but this was clearly inadequate when intelligence confirmed that the most powerful IJN battleships of the period were capable of 26 knots. The General Board decided on a design speed of 27 knots fully loaded. To fit the increased engine power in a shorter hull required

Massachusetts maneuvering off Casablanca, Morocco, during the invasion of North Africa on November 8, 1942. On this day, the battleship performed well by knocking out the immobile French battleship *Jean Bart,* severely damaging a docked destroyer in Casablanca, and hitting three other French ships at sea. *Massachusetts* avoided torpedoes from a French submarine but was hit once by a French shore battery. (Naval History and Heritage Command)

positioning sets of evaporators and distilling equipment into the four machinery rooms, along with the boilers and turbines, rather than into their own separate compartments. The boilers within the machinery spaces were raised one deck for the propeller shaft to run beneath them and thereby reduce the space required for machinery. The turbines fitted were of an improved design. When the ships were completed, speed trials were not run; however, in March 1945 *Alabama* did conduct speed trials and generated just over 133,000shp, good for just over 27 knots in fully loaded condition.

Armament and Service Modifications

The main battery consisted of nine 16in/45cal guns in three triple turrets, which was identical to the North Carolina class. The secondary battery was different among the four ships in the class. The lead ship, *South Dakota*, was designed to accommodate a fleet staff. This required making the conning tower taller and adding command space. As a result, the ship could only carry four twin 5in/38cal gun mounts on each beam. The other three ships of the class carried a total of 20 5in/38cal guns arranged in ten twin gun mounts, five per beam.

Original antiaircraft protection was again inadequate with four 1.1in quadruple mounts and eight .50cal machine guns. As soon as production problems were overcome, 40mm quadruple mounts replaced the 1.1in weapons. By the end of the war, 18 of these were fitted. The machine guns were replaced by 20mm single mounts. Each ship carried a different number of these weapons at different points of the war. Top weight became an issue with the proliferation of antiaircraft weapons. As the 40mm gun was more effective, it got priority. As more of these were added, the numbers of 20mm guns were reduced. For example, *Massachusetts* had a high of 52 20mm guns in June 1944, but by the end of the war this was reduced to 32 single, one twin, and one quadruple mount.

South Dakota Class Specifications (as built)	
Displacement	Standard 35,562 tons; full 45,233 tons (1942)
Dimensions	Length 680ft; beam 108ft 2in; draft 36ft 2in
Propulsion	8 boilers and 4 geared turbines generating 130,000shp on 4 shafts; maximum speed 27.5kt
Range	15,000nm at 15kt
Crew	Design 1,793; wartime as many as 2,634

Iowa Class

The North Carolina class was assessed as unbalanced since it had insufficient armor relative to its main armament. The South Dakota class carried adequate armor, but with a top speed of 27 knots was not considered fast enough for a full array of missions. The Iowa class corrected the design shortcomings of both the North Carolina and South Dakota classes. As Japan became increasingly secretive about its naval construction program, on March 31, 1938, the United States, Great Britain, and France invoked the escalation clause to raise the displacement limit to 45,000 tons. With this increased displacement, the USN could fulfil its desire to build a battleship with the speed to force the Japanese fleet into battle, including the IJN's Kongo class which the USN assumed had a top speed of 26 knots. The USN was already beginning to think in terms of creating an independent force consisting of fast battleships with carriers acting in a supporting role. The Iowa class was fast enough to operate in this capacity.

Wisconsin tied up outboard of the hulk of *Oklahoma* at the Pearl Harbor Navy Yard on November 11, 1944. The size and obvious power and speed of the Iowa-class battleship provides a dramatic contrast with *Oklahoma* and its design dating from 1912. (Naval History and Heritage Command)

Iowa pictured during its shakedown cruise. This class was the epitome of USN battleship design with its combination of protection, speed, and firepower. (Naval History and Heritage Command)

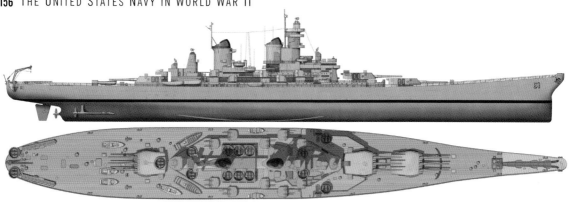

THESE VIEWS SHOW the lead ship of the USN's last class of battleships, the Iowa class. The ship projects an image of power and speed with its sweeping lines and massive superstructure that is faired into the forward stack. The ship carries a main battery of nine 16in/50cal guns and a secondary battery of 20 5in/38cal dual purpose guns. (Artwork by Peter Bull, © Osprey Publishing)

The increase of 10,000 tons displacement provided the General Board with the opportunity to consider either increasing the armament from nine to 12 16in guns and maintaining the top speed at 27 knots, or increasing the top speed of the new battleship to over 30 knots. In March 1938, President Roosevelt played a major role in this consideration by strongly suggesting there should be an increased top speed plus an extensive cruising range for the new battleship. Following President Roosevelt's suggestion, the General Board requested a battleship design with 33 knots top speed.

The first two ships were ordered on July 1, 1939 and were followed by a second pair on June 12, 1940. Two more ships, *Illinois* and *Kentucky*, were ordered on September 9, 1940. Work progressed slowly on these last two ships, and by the end of the war they were far from finished so both were canceled.

Iowa Class Construction					
Ship	Built at	Laid down	Launched	Commissioned	Fate
Iowa (BB 61)	Brooklyn Navy Yard	6/27/40	8/27/42	2/22/43	Preserved as museum ship in Los Angeles, CA
New Jersey (BB 62)	Philadelphia Navy Yard	9/16/40	12/7/42	5/23/43	Preserved as museum ship in Camden, NJ
Missouri (BB 63)	Brooklyn Navy Yard	1/6/41	1/29/44	6/1/44	Preserved as museum ship in Pearl Harbor, HI
Wisconsin (BB 64)	Philadelphia Navy Yard	1/25/41	12/7/43	4/16/44	Preserved as museum ship in Norfolk, VA
Illinois (BB 65)	Philadelphia Navy Yard	12/6/42	Never	Never	Scrapped 1958
Kentucky (BB 66)	Norfolk Navy Yard	3/7/42	Never	Never	Scrapped 1959

OPPOSITE This is a bow-on photograph of *New Jersey* in September 1943. Much of the ship's secondary battery and 40mm quadruple mounts are visible in the view. (Naval History and Heritage Command)

The design for the Iowa class drew heavily upon the South Dakota class for the form and structure of its armor protection, and the North Carolina class for its bow and hull shape. The required speed of 33 knots needed

230,000shp. The machinery layout of boilers and turbines in one machinery room, as in the North Carolina and South Dakota classes, was a concern since a torpedo hit at the juncture of two machinery rooms would produce massive flooding. Designers reverted to separate boiler and engine rooms on an alternating basis and cut the size of the spaces in half to 32ft. The machinery generated an amazing 230,000shp and was efficient enough to allow a maximum range of 18,000nm at 12 knots.

Armor protection covered 464ft of the hull, starting with an armored transverse bulkhead ahead of Turret 1, and ending with another armored transverse bulkhead aft of Turret 3. The main belt consisted of 11.3in on the first two ships and was increased to 14.5in on *Missouri* and *Wisconsin*. The main armor belt sloped inwards at 19 degrees to present an acute angle to diving shells. The conning tower received a maximum of 17.3in of armor; the barbettes were provided with a maximum of 17.3in of armor. The main gun turrets were protected by 19.5in of face armor. Horizontal protection was provided by three decks: the first deck of 1.5in, the main armored deck with an additional 6in, and the splinter deck of .625in. The magazines received extra protection with the splinter deck being replaced by a third armored deck with 1in of armor. Antitorpedo protection was based on the design fitted on the South Dakota class, but with several improvements. These included spacing the transverse bulkheads in the bulge closer together, increasing the volume of the bulge, and adding more armor to the lower belt where it joined with the joint of the triple bottom.

Armament and Service Modifications

After speed was selected as a priority, the main battery remained as nine 16in guns. However, the caliber of the nine guns increased from 45 to 50. The increase in barrel length and a heavier powder charge produced a muzzle velocity of

2,500ft/sec, compared to 2,300ft/sec for the 16in/45cal gun. This greater muzzle velocity resulted in a longer maximum range of 42,345 yards and superior armor-penetrating capability. The Iowas were equipped with a secondary battery of 20 5in/38cal dual-purpose guns fitted in ten twin gun mounts.

The light antiaircraft battery was extensive. The standard fit for the class was 20 quadruple 40mm mounts. *Iowa*, built as a fleet flagship, had an enlarged conning tower. Consequently, the quadruple 40mm mount on Turret 2 was omitted to avoid blocking the sight lines from the lower level of the conning tower. The 20mm battery was also heavy with a total of 49–52 single mounts, depending on the ship.

Iowa Class Specifications (as built)	
Displacement	Standard 48,592 tons; full 58,460 tons
Dimensions	Length 887ft 3in; beam 108ft 2in; draft 37ft 2in
Propulsion	8 boilers and 4 geared turbines generating 230,000shp on 4 shafts; maximum speed 33 knots
Range	18,000nm at 12 knots
Crew	1,921 (2,753 1945)

The Fast Battleships – an Assessment

The war in the Pacific became a carrier war on the first day of the conflict. When they reached the Pacific, beginning in mid-1942, the fast battleships were called on to perform a role they were never designed for – direct antiaircraft support for fleet carriers. Even though the North Carolina and South Dakota classes possessed a top speed deficit of 6 knots compared to the carriers, they were fast enough to integrate into carrier task forces. Their powerful secondary armament of 20 5in/38cal guns was able to break up Japanese dive-bomber formations at the carrier battles of Eastern Solomons in August and Santa Cruz in October 1942. Losses at Santa Cruz, many at the hands of *South Dakota*, were crippling to the Japanese. For the remainder of the war, the fast battleships provided outstanding antiaircraft support to the carriers.

Even though the main duty of the fast battleships was escorting carriers, the USN continually sought opportunities to employ its fast battleships in their primary role. These opportunities were few. The only time during the war when a fast battleship encountered a Japanese battleship was at the Second Naval Battle of Guadalcanal. On this occasion, *Washington* faced Kongo-class battleship *Kirishima*. This was far from being a fair fight given *Washington's*

superior protection, heavier guns, and radar-guided fire-control systems. Firing 75 16in shells in five and a half minutes at *Kirishima* as it was approaching on an opposing course, with *Washington*'s gun turrets training at 20 degrees per minute, as both ships were closing at a combined speed of 54 knots, with a rapid change of course by *Kirishima*, all at night, *Washington* hit its target 20 times, achieving an accuracy rate of 27 percent. This was the best example of accurate battleship gunfire during the dreadnought era.

The South Dakota class was probably the best of the treaty battleships. These ships possessed the best balance of firepower, protection, and speed of any design facing the 35,000-ton limit. Added to this was the class' superior antiaircraft protection and superior fire-control systems.

The Iowa class never got near a Japanese battleship. The only time during the war these ships engaged a surface target was on February 17, 1944 during the raid on Truk Atoll. *Iowa* and *New Jersey* engaged a Japanese destroyer using radar at ranges up to 39,000 yards – the longest distance ever that a USN battleship engaged a surface target. The target was straddled but managed to escape. On several other occasions, the fast battleships were pulled out of the Fast Carrier Task Force to form a battle line in anticipation of a surface engagement. On no occasion did this come to pass. Given the dominance of carrier aircraft over even the most heavily armored battleship, the fast battleships ended up being expensive luxuries that only the USN could afford.

CHAPTER 5
HEAVY CRUISERS

The USN built 18 heavy cruisers in the interwar period. All these ships were built under limitations resulting from a series of naval treaties, and thus were also known as "treaty cruisers." These ships gave valuable service during World War II and saw action in all the major battles in the Pacific. In addition to its prewar-built fleet of heavy cruisers, the USN also carried out a massive program of wartime cruiser construction. This included the largest class of heavy cruisers ever built, the 14-ship Baltimore class. Of these, only seven were commissioned in time to see service during World War II. The USN's extensive wartime cruiser construction program also included provisions for large cruisers to counter any supercruisers thought to be under construction by the Axis powers. Two of these ships were completed and saw service during the war. As predicted by many at the time, these proved to be white elephants.

PART 1: THE TREATY CRUISERS

The term "heavy cruiser" came into use in 1920 to distinguish it from a light cruiser in terms of size and importance. In 1931, the use of the term was clarified and used for any cruiser with 8in guns. Traditionally, American cruisers were seen primarily as scouting ships in support of the main battle fleet and were tasked to counter enemy scouting forces and screen the battle fleet. Their speed and range also made them well suited as commerce raiders or for protecting shipping lanes against enemy raiders. The Washington Naval Treaty magnified the importance of heavy cruisers. Since the treaty placed limits on

Pensacola pictured soon after completion in early 1930. The two ships of this class are easily identified by their four 8in gunhouses and their two large masts. (NARA)

the number of battleships the USN could operate but not on heavy cruisers, the latter became a substitute for the battleship. The smaller number of battleships meant that they were less likely to be risked, especially on secondary missions. Heavy cruisers were often used as substitutes.

Before the Pacific War, heavy cruisers were assigned to the Fleet Scouting Force, which reflected their primary mission. In addition to their scouting mission in support of the battle fleet, heavy cruisers were assigned as escorts to the Pacific Fleet's carriers. This was a natural fit, since they had the speed and endurance to keep up with the carriers, but it was also seen as necessary to protect the carriers from Japanese cruisers or battlecruisers. The heavy cruiser also possessed a relatively heavy antiaircraft fit that could help protect the carrier from air attack.

At the start of the Pacific War, the importance of the cruiser was immediately elevated. The attack on Pearl Harbor reduced the strength of the USN's battle line. It also demonstrated that the war would not be fought between opposing battle fleets and that carrier aviation would be dominant. The USN's older battleships lacked the speed to operate with the carriers. As the carrier became the center of American naval operations, the heavy

The two cruisers to the left are the first-generation treaty cruisers *Salt Lake City* and *Pensacola*. Inboard of them is the third-generation *New Orleans*. This photograph from 1943 shows the differences between the generations. The low freeboard of the first-generation ships is obvious, as is their top-heavy appearance with the large tripod foremasts. (Naval History and Heritage Command)

cruiser became an integral part of carrier task forces. Cruisers were the primary escorts for the carriers during the early-war carrier raids between February and April 1942, and during the first two carrier battles in the Coral Sea in May and at Midway in June.

When the focus of operations in the Pacific shifted to the South Pacific beginning in August 1942, the heavy cruiser assumed another role as the leading element of surface task forces committed to engage the IJN at night in the waters around Guadalcanal. From August until November, there were five major battles against the Japanese, with American heavy cruisers being the centerpiece of the American task forces in all but one. Against the well-drilled IJN, which had spent considerable time and resources developing and practicing night-fighting doctrine and equipment, the American heavy cruisers suffered severely. The extent of the carnage is shown by the fact that of the 14 heavy cruisers active during the campaign for Guadalcanal, five were sunk and another seven damaged.

After the struggle for Guadalcanal concluded with an American victory in February 1943, USN heavy cruisers continued to take a prominent role in the advance to Japan. Given additional antiaircraft weaponry, they continued to perform admirably as carrier escorts. They showed their versatility in shore bombardment missions and by engaging Japanese surface units when the opportunity was presented. Heavy cruisers were also active in the European theater in convoy escort and shore bombardment roles. By the end of the war, seven of the 18 treaty heavy cruisers had been sunk, but victory had been secured.

The Impact of the Washington and London Naval Treaties

The USN planned a massive expansion after World War I. Part of this was the construction of cruisers to screen the battle line and the battlecruiser force, and to form forces dedicated to scouting and providing protection from enemy scouting forces. Originally, the cruiser design to fill these needs was based on the Omaha-class scout cruiser; a 7,100 ton ship armed with 12 6in guns and a top speed of 35 knots. This changed with the ratification of the Washington Naval Treaty in February 1922. Because it thought a larger cruiser was required for the expanses of the Pacific, the USN was happy with the limitations on cruisers contained in the treaty, which were set at 10,000 tons with a gun no greater than 8in. While there were limits on individual ships, there was no limit set on the overall tonnage or number

USN Heavy Cruiser Weapons

The 8in gun was accepted without debate as the primary heavy cruiser weapon. It had a longer range than the 6in gun mounted on existing American and British large cruisers, so it was assumed that any 8in gun-armed ship would possess an advantage. The 8in gun also possessed greater striking power against heavily armored targets, and a greater range.

The Alaska-class large cruiser required a bigger main gun to successfully conduct its mission of destroying enemy heavy cruisers. To support this requirement, the USN developed a new 12in gun especially for the class. This entered service as the 12in/50cal Mark 8/0. It fired a 1,140lb armor-piercing shell at a maximum range of over 38,000 yards, giving it a theoretical range advantage of some 6,000 yards over Japanese heavy cruisers. The "superheavy" projectiles gave better armor penetration performance between 20,000 and 30,000 yards than the larger 14in guns mounted on prewar battleships.

USN Heavy Cruiser Main Guns				
Gun	Muzzle Velocity (ft/sec)	Max Range (yd)	Rate of fire (rpm)	Fitted on
8in/55 Mk 9 and 14	2,800	31,860	2–3	Pensacola, Northampton, Portland classes, 3 ships of New Orleans class
8in/55 Mk 12 and 15	2,500	30,050	3–4	4 ships of the New Orleans class, *Wichita*, Baltimore class
12in/50 Mk 8/0	2,500	38,573	2–3	Alaska class

Unlike Japanese heavy cruisers which were designed with a substantial torpedo armament, the USN considered its heavy cruisers to be primarily gun platforms. Originally, the Pensacola and Northampton classes carried two triple banks of 21in torpedoes, but by 1935 the USN had removed torpedoes from its heavy cruisers. The thinking was that actions would be fought at ranges that would never allow cruisers to use their torpedoes. This turned out to be a questionable decision considering the short-range actions fought at night against the Japanese in 1942, but it probably did not matter given the poor performance and reliability of American torpedoes during that time.

This fine view of *Augusta* shows its main battery trained to engage a target to starboard. The three triple mounts became the standard for all future American heavy cruiser designs. (Naval History and Heritage Command)

of cruisers that each power could build. For the USN, the upper limit of cruiser size became the standard design size for all. Since the Americans did not want to build ships with inferior armament to foreign contemporaries, 8in main batteries also became the norm.

Since the treaty set limits on battleship tonnage for the world's five largest navies, and none were set for cruisers, a cruiser building spree quickly ensued. In late 1922, the USN planned to finish the construction of the ten planned Omaha-class cruisers and 16 new 8in cruisers. However, Congress was reluctant to fund what it saw as excessive requests and, during the interwar period, the USN was tardy building up to its allowed limits. With evidence of Japanese heavy cruiser construction, Congress approved eight cruisers in late 1924, but only funded two. The other six were not funded until 1926 and 1927.

The first American heavy cruiser designs under the Washington Treaty favored firepower and speed over protection. The first generation of treaty cruisers were called "Tinclads" because of their sparse armor. These ships of the Pensacola and Northampton classes were well under the 10,000-ton treaty limitation, and therefore were not well-balanced designs. After a transitional design of the two ships of the Portland class, American designers hit their stride with the much more successful New Orleans class. These seven ships were well protected and maintained a high speed and powerful main and secondary batteries.

Since the Washington Naval Treaty imposed no limit on the numbers of cruisers that could be built, the primary goal of the London Naval Conference, opened in January 1930, was to place a cap on cruiser construction. With the Americans and British open to this notion, negotiations yielded an agreement to create two different types of cruisers and to limit the tonnage for each. Type A cruisers were those armed with guns of 6.1in or more (i.e. heavy cruisers), and the maximum 10,000-ton limit from the Washington Naval Treaty remained in place. The USN was allotted 180,000 tons of Type A cruisers, which easily translated into 18 10,000-ton ships. The Americans agreed not to build to their 18-ship limit immediately. Assuming 15 cruisers were completed by 1935, the USN was not allowed to start construction on the 16th ship until 1933 (being commissioned in 1936), with the final two ships begun at yearly intervals after that. This affected the construction of the last two units of the New Orleans class and the unique *Wichita*, which was the 18th and last treaty heavy cruiser built.

The system of naval treaties in place between the wars meant that all 18 USN heavy cruisers built during this period were designed with a series of compromises in mind. It was only after the expiration of those treaties that a heavy cruiser was designed that could fully incorporate the competing requirements of firepower, speed, and protection. This became the Baltimore class, which was the finest heavy cruiser design of the war.

Pensacola Class

The Pensacola class was begun after other contemporary treaty cruisers, but even with this potential advantage did not compare well with foreign rivals. The primary design consideration was to mount a heavy armament. The main battery had to match Japanese heavy cruisers which were known to carry ten 8in guns. The Pensacola class carried its ten 8in guns in only four turrets which avoided the problem of having a turret with a reduced arc of fire and meant that the hull could be shorter, which was a significant weight-saving measure. Another weight-saving measure was to provide less protection and less powerful machinery. This meant the Pensacola class was less well armored and had a slightly slower maximum speed than the IJN's first-generation Myoko-class treaty cruisers.

Another weight-saving feature was a flush deck hull and a low freeboard. The designers relied on a pronounced flare and sheer to keep the ships dry. Their two tripod masts and large fighting tops gave them a top-heavy appearance; in fact, they were top-heavy and prone to roll heavily even in moderate seas. This roll affected the fire-control equipment and thus gunnery accuracy.

Pensacola Class Construction					
Ship	Built at	Laid down	Launched	Commissioned	Fate
Pensacola (CA 24)	Brooklyn Navy Yard	10/27/26	4/25/29	2/6/30	Sunk as a target 1948
Salt Lake City (CA 25)	New York Shipbuilding, Camden	6/9/27	1/23/29	12/11/29	Sunk as a target 1948

Every treaty cruiser design struggled to combine a balance of firepower, speed, and protection. For the Pensacola class, the first two were achieved at the expense of the latter. Protection accounted for only 6 percent of the total design weight, giving a clear indication that armor was relatively sparse. The main belt was only 3in thick over the machinery spaces and 4in over the forward magazines, with the belt extending 5ft below the waterline. No armor covered the aft magazine because it was bizarrely assumed that any action would occur forward of the beam. The main armored deck was 1in and augmented to 1.75in over the magazines. The 8in mounts were more gun houses than armored turrets with 2.5in of frontal armor, 1.5in on the sides, and .75in on the rear. Turret barbettes received only .75in. The conning tower was protected by 1.25in of armor.

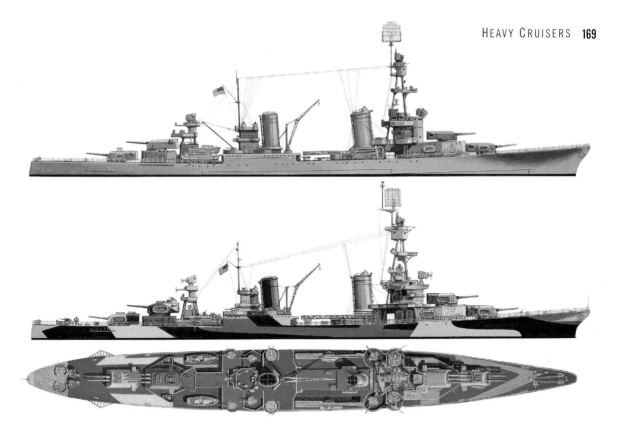

Since heavy cruisers were thought to be primarily scouting platforms, it was deemed very important to carry aircraft. On the Pensacola class, two catapults were fitted port and starboard just aft of the forward stack. In the space between the two stacks, four aircraft could be stored. No hangar was provided.

American designers were so successful in saving weight that the Pensacolas came in at only 9,100 tons. All considered, however, this was not a successful design and was inferior to the IJN's first-generation treaty heavy cruisers. The USN admitted as much by only building two ships before going to an improved design.

Armament and Service Modifications

The Pensacola class featured an unusual ten-gun main battery arrangement, in which a pair of twin and triple mounts were fitted forward and aft. The heavier triple mount was placed in a superfiring position over the twin mount. Placing the triple mounts this high on the ship, necessary because the barbette of the triple mounts could not be placed on the sleek hull, contributed to the top-heavy problem of the class. This made the Pensacola class the only class of USN heavy cruiser to carry ten 8in guns. The Pensacola class was fitted with two triple torpedo mounts placed on the upper deck abreast the aft stack. The secondary armament was restricted

THE TOP VIEW SHOWS *Pensacola* in its early-war configuration. Clearly visible are the four 8in gunhouses, making this class the only USN heavy cruiser class to carry its main armament in this arrangement. The 5in battery is situated in two groups, one near the forward superstructure and the other abaft the aft stack. Note aircraft-handling facilities amidships. The ship carries a CXAM radar on the foremast. **THE SECOND AND THIRD VIEWS ARE OF** *Salt Lake City* in its 1944 appearance. The ship's main and secondary armament remains unchanged, but both the forward and aft superstructures have been reduced to save top weight. An SK radar is fitted on top of the lowered foremast, and a SP radar on the new pole mast aft. There is also a profusion of antiaircraft guns with six 40mm quadruple mounts and 19 20mm single guns being visible. (Artwork by Paul Wright, © Osprey Publishing)

This is a view of *Pensacola* in August 1945 showing the cruiser in its late-war configuration. Both tripod masts have been removed and replaced with much smaller pole masts. Another weight-saving measure was to reduce the size of the fore and aft superstructures. The antiaircraft fit has been greatly expanded with an array of 40mm and 20mm mounts. (Naval History and Heritage Command)

to four 5in/25cal single mounts. A battery of eight 5in guns was deemed necessary for effective antiaircraft protection, but only four mounts were fitted to save weight.

Before the war, both ships received major modifications. By 1935, the torpedo mounts were removed from both ships. In their place, four additional 5in/25cal single mounts were added abreast the bridge structure. Also, just before the war, 1.1in quadruple mounts began to enter service, and each ship received two.

After the war began, all heavy cruisers received modifications focused on improving their antiaircraft and radar fits. To compensate for this, measures were also taken to compensate by reducing top weight. In 1942, antiaircraft fit was increased to four 1.1in quadruple and eight single 20mm guns. By 1943, the 1.1in mounts were replaced by quadruple 40mm mounts, and additional 20mm single mounts were added. To compensate, the mainmast was removed, the aircraft complement was reduced to two, and the starboard catapult was deleted. In 1945, *Pensacola* was thoroughly modernized and received a final fit of seven quadruple 40mm mounts and nine twin 20mm mounts. *Salt Lake City*'s final fit in 1945 was six quadruple 40mm and 19 single 20mm mounts.

Pensacola Class Specifications (as built)	
Displacement	Standard 9,097 tons; full 11,512 tons
Dimensions	Length: 585ft 8in; beam 65ft 3in; draft 19ft 6in
Propulsion	8 boilers and 4 geared turbines generating 107,000shp on 4 shafts; maximum speed 32.5kt
Range	10,000nm at 15kts
Crew	631

Northampton Class

Design work for what was to become the Northampton class began immediately after the Pensacola design was finalized. For the second class of USN treaty cruisers, the designers intended to incorporate a number of improvements in the areas of seaworthiness, survivability, and aircraft-handling arrangements. The six ships in the class were authorized in 1924, but not funded until 1927, and were finally laid down in 1928.

The new class was provided with a raised forecastle and increased freeboard. The added length, some 14ft, also improved seakeeping. Nevertheless, excessive rolling was still a problem and bilge keels were fitted. The ships remained lively in any kind of sea, and this affected gunnery accuracy.

It was apparent that the Pensacola class came in under weight. The obvious answer was to use this margin to provide extra armor to increase the level of protection for the Northampton class. The ideal protection scheme

This view of *Northampton* was taken shortly after its completion in 1930. The primary difference between this class and the preceding Pensacola class, the absence of the fourth 8in gun house aft, can readily be seen. Note that this early configuration included only four 5in guns and a bank of torpedo tubes, which can be seen abaft the rear stack. (Naval History and Heritage Command)

This April 1935 view of *Houston* shows a Northampton-class cruiser in its prewar configuration. The class is easily recognized by its two large tripod masts and widely spaced stacks. Beyond *Houston* is a New Orleans-class cruiser that can be identified by its two pole masts and tightly spaced stacks. (Naval History and Heritage Command)

would have provided protection against 8in shellfire from opposing enemy cruisers, but this was impossible on a 10,000-ton ship. After several schemes were considered, it was decided to improve splinter protection to the magazine and keep the remainder of the extra weight as a design reserve. Despite this, the final design came in at almost 1,000 tons under the treaty limit. Protection amounted to only 3in of armor in the main belt. Deck armor was 1in thick. Magazine protection was increased to 3.75in on the side and 2in overhead. The 8in gun houses had 2.5in on the front plate and 2in on the roof. Total weight of armor was 1,057 tons.

Northampton Class Construction					
Ship	Built at	Laid down	Launched	Commissioned	Fate
Northampton (CA 26)	Bethlehem, Ship Building, Quincy	4/12/28	9/5/30	5/17/30	Sunk 11/30/42
Chester (CA 27)	New York Shipbuilding, Camden	3/6/28	7/3/29	6/24/30	Scrapped 1959
Louisville (CA 28)	Bremerton Navy Yard	7/4/28	9/1/30	1/15/31	Scrapped 1959
Chicago (CA 29)	Mare Island Navy Yard	9/10/28	4/10/30	3/9/31	Sunk 1/30/43
Houston (CA 30)	Newport News, Virginia	5/1/28	9/7/29	6/17/30	Sunk 3/1/42
Augusta (CA 31)	Newport News, Virginia	7/2/28	2/1/30	1/30/31	Scrapped 1959

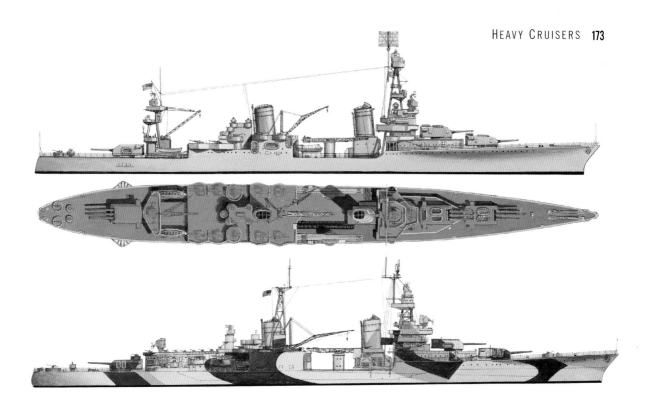

Aircraft facilities were much improved with a hangar being built aft of the stack that could accommodate four aircraft. The large hangar meant that aircraft were no longer stored and worked on in the open and they gained some measure of blast protection from the ship's main armament. Another two aircraft could be stored on the two catapults, but in practice only four aircraft were carried.

The six ships were all envisioned as flagships. The last three ships had the raised forecastle deck extended aft near the catapults, which allowed for extra accommodation spaces and suitability as a fleet flagship. The other three ships were intended to be used as squadron flagships.

Armament and Service Modifications

The ten-gun main battery of the Pensacola class was not repeated. During the design phase, there was considerable debate whether to adopt an eight-gun arrangement as on European heavy cruisers or to move to a nine-gun arrangement with three triple turrets. The triple-turret arrangement was adopted, which allowed the hull to be shorter. This adoption of a nine-gun main battery proved successful and was the preferred arrangement for every other USN heavy cruiser ever built. Otherwise, the armament was the same as the Pensacola class, with an identical torpedo battery and an inadequate secondary battery of four 5in/25cal guns. The only light weapons were a few .50cal machine guns.

THE TOP TWO PROFILES SHOW *Northampton* as it appeared during the Battle of Midway. The primary differences between *Northampton* and the earlier Pensacola class are the presence of only three 8in gunhouses and the more compact placement of the 5in battery. **THE BOTTOM PROFILE DEPICTS** *Louisville*, presenting a very different appearance in this October 1944 view. The forward superstructure has been reduced and the mainmast has been entirely removed and a new lattice mast built around the aft stack. The modified area aft now contains many single 20mm mounts. Note the heavy 40mm armament with four quadruple and four twin mounts. (Artwork by Paul Wright, © Osprey Publishing)

This May 1945 view of *Louisville* shows a Northampton-class cruiser in its late-war configuration. Both the forward and aft superstructures have been extensively reduced, and both tripod masts are gone. In their place is a lighter pole mast abaft the forward superstructure and a new tower built around the aft stack. The enhanced antiaircraft gun fit is visible with five 40mm quadruple mounts, four 40mm twin mounts (all located aft), and 13 twin 20mm guns, most mounted aft. (Naval History and Heritage Command)

As on the Pensacola-class ships, the torpedo tubes were removed by 1935 and before the war an additional four single 5in/25cal guns were fitted. Because of the shortage of the new 1.1in quadruple mount, four 3in/50cal single guns were substituted instead. The shortage of guns meant that there was no standard fit for the six Northampton-class ships. In 1942, the 3in/50cal single mounts were replaced with four 1.1in quadruple mounts and the machine guns were replaced with 20mm single guns. This was the basic configuration that *Northampton*, *Chicago* and *Houston* exhibited when they were lost. In 1943, the 40mm quadruple mounts replaced the 1.1in mounts and the number of 20mm guns was increased. As the air threat increased in the form of kamikazes, the final antiaircraft fit was further increased to four quadruple and two twin 40mm mounts, and up to 13 twin 20mm mounts.

Chester shown in May 1945 in its late-war configuration. Its 1945 radar fit is visible with an SK and SG radar on the new forward pole mast and an SP radar on the tower built around the aft stack. The Mark 34 directors both have a cylinder-shaped Mark 13 radar fitted on top of them. The other two prominent devices are Mark 33 fire-control directors used for the secondary battery, each equipped with the Mark 28 radar. (Naval History and Heritage Command)

Northampton Class Specifications (as built)	
Displacement	Standard 9,006 tons; full 11,420 tons
Dimensions	Length: 600ft 3in; beam 66ft 1in; draft 19ft 5in
Propulsion	8 boilers and 4 geared turbines generating 107,000shp on 4 shafts; maximum speed 32.5kt
Range	10,000nm at 15kt
Crew	617

Portland Class

Because the design of the next class of treaty cruiser was begun before the ships of the preceding class were even running trials, the extent to which the first two classes were underweight was not immediately understood. When this finally sank in, much criticism was leveled against the Pensacolas and Northamptons for being underprotected. They picked up the nickname of "Tinclads" as a result. With as much as 1,000 tons to work with, the designers of the next generation of treaty cruisers were determined to come up with a better-balanced design.

The desire to modify the design was upset by the existing authorization and funding scheme. In 1929, 15 additional heavy cruisers had been authorized and were planned to be built in three groups of five for the years 1929 through 1931. The first group was intended to be a repeat of the previous Northampton class, but criticism of the design prompted a move to re-cast it. Because of contractual issues this could only be done with the three ships planning to be built in Navy yards. The other two ships were contracted out to private builders; to re-cast their design at this late stage would have been exorbitantly expensive.

Portland returning to Pearl Harbor on June 14, 1942, after the Battle of Midway. The ship is little changed from the start of the war aside from the addition of light antiaircraft guns and the placement of an SC radar on the foremast. (Naval History and Heritage Command)

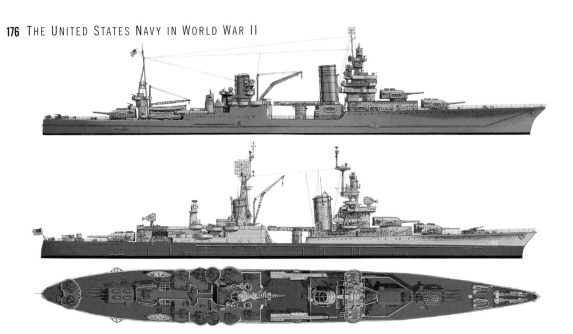

THE TOP PROFILE IS OF *Portland* as it appeared during 1942. The ship retains its large foremast, on top of which an SC radar has been fitted. The antiaircraft fit has been strengthened and includes a pair of 1.1in quadruple mounts abreast the bridge and another pair located aft in the middle of the 5in secondary battery. At this point only 12 20mm guns were fitted. THE NEXT TWO PROFILES SHOW *Indianapolis* in July 1945, just before its loss to submarine torpedoes. The ship has just received significant antiaircraft modifications, which include an SK radar on the new lattice mast built around the aft stack, six 40mm quadruple mounts, and eight twin 20mm mounts. Much top weight, primarily the forward and aft superstructures, has been removed or reduced to allow these late-war modifications. (Artwork by Paul Wright, © Osprey Publishing)

The result was a two-ship class built to a hybrid design combining features of the first generation of treaty cruisers with the upgrades of the planned second generation. The layout of the ship was largely identical to the Northampton class. The ships were 10ft longer, and the major difference in appearance was a shortened foremast and a much smaller mainmast aft. This reduced top-heaviness and therefore contributed to stability. Machinery was identical except for replacing the White-Forster boilers with ones designed by Yarrow.

The Portland-class design did make improvements in protection. The extra weight was converted to armor and the main belt was increased to 5.75in over the magazines, while remaining 3in over the machinery. The armor on top of the magazines was slightly increased to 2.125in. The deck armor was increased from a paltry 1in on the Northampton class to 2.5in.

As with the final three ships of the Northampton class, both ships of the Portland class were fitted to act as fleet flagships.

Portland Class Construction					
Ship	Built at	Laid down	Launched	Commissioned	Fate
Portland (CA 33)	Bethlehem, Quincy	2/17/30	5/21/32	2/23/33	Scrapped 1959
Indianapolis (CA 34)	New York Shipbuilding, Camden	3/31/30	11/7/31	11/15/32	Sunk 7/30/45

Armament and Service Modifications

The Portland class retained a main battery of nine 8in guns in three triple turrets. The torpedo tubes were deleted from the design and were not aboard

the ships when they were completed. The standard four-gun 5in/25cal secondary battery was increased to eight guns when completed.

Modifications early in the war centered on strengthening the ships' antiaircraft defenses. In early 1942, four quadruple 1.1in mounts were fitted, as well as 12 single 20mm guns on *Indianapolis* and 17 on *Portland*. In May 1943 both ships underwent further modification. The 1.1in mounts were replaced by 40mm quadruple mounts. By 1944, *Portland* had four quadruple and four twin 40mm mounts and 17 20mm guns. *Indianapolis* had six quadruple mounts and 19 20mm single mounts.

The appearance of the ships also changed when, in 1943, the front of the bridge was extended, the size of the aft superstructure reduced, and a lattice tripod mast was built around the aft stack. To reduce top weight, the starboard catapult was removed in both ships. Aircraft capacity was reduced to two on *Portland* and three on *Indianapolis*.

In May 1944, *Indianapolis* emerged from an overhaul with four quadruple 40mm and two twin 40mm mounts, 19 single 20mm, and a SK radar in new mast built around the aft stack, which was unique to this ship. *Indianapolis* underwent a final modernization in mid-July 1945; when the cruiser was sunk the same year, it was carrying six 40mm quadruple mounts and eight twin 20mm mounts.

This is *Indianapolis* in May 1943. Note the mainmast has been removed and a tripod mast built around the aft stack to mount the SK radar. The forward superstructure has been reduced and a growing profusion of antiaircraft guns is becoming evident. (NARA)

Portland Class Specifications (as built)	
Displacement	Standard 10,258 tons; full 12,775 tons
Dimensions	Length: 610ft; beam 66ft; draft 21ft
Propulsion	8 boilers and 4 geared turbines generating 107,000shp on 4 shafts; maximum speed 32.5kt
Range	10,000nm at 15kt
Crew	807

New Orleans Class

The New Orleans class was the second generation of American treaty cruisers; it was undoubtedly the best USN treaty cruiser and, overall, one of the best-balanced treaty cruisers produced by any nation. The ships were much better designed than the earlier Northamptons because they used the full permitted 10,000 tons.

Originally it was envisioned that 15 of these ships would be built, but this did not occur due to the parsimony of Congress and the overall tonnage restrictions on heavy cruisers introduced by the London Naval Treaty of 1930. In the end, only seven ships were built. The first three were from the 1929 budget, and the next three were funded in 1930, but the last ship in this group was not started until 1933. The London Naval Treaty prevented the final ship from being started until 1934. Because the construction of these ships was spread out over several years, there were actually three sub-groups of ships with slight differences in appearance and armament.

BELOW *New Orleans* photographed before the war. This class was readily distinguished from earlier treaty cruisers by the two stacks placed close together and the position of the aircraft-handling facilities abaft them. The lead ship of the class entered service in early 1934 and constituted a great improvement in American treaty cruiser design. (NARA)

RIGHT *Quincy* in May 1940, showing the placement of the secondary battery and the aircraft-handling facilities. The portion of the ship between the aft stack and the aft 8in turret was devoted to aircraft handling with the hangar, two cranes, and two catapults all being visible. (Naval History and Heritage Command)

The key difference in this class was the design emphasis placed on protection. This was accomplished by converting the unused 1,000 tons of displacement into armor and by reducing the hull by 14ft at the waterline compared to the Portland class and the beam by some 4ft. The reduction in the hull length was made possible by adopting a new arrangement in the machinery spaces that reduced the length of each engine room by 4ft. Of the design displacement, 15 percent was used for armor. The shorter hull meant the armor belt was shorter, and this weight saving was converted into additional thickness of the belt. The maximum belt thickness was increased to 5in, tapered to 3in on its lower part. The magazines received another 3–4.7in of additional side protection internally. Deck protection was 2.5in over the magazines and 1.125in elsewhere. The turret barbette received 5in of armor and the conning tower 2.5in. The turrets were much more heavily armored and made proof in some areas against 8in gunfire. Turret faces were protected with 8in of armor, 2.75in on the roof, and 1.5in on the sides and rear.

The same machinery was fitted as on the Portland class. The difference was that the unit arrangement was not employed, which meant that all boiler rooms were placed together forward of the engine rooms, creating the risk of all propulsive power being destroyed by a single well-placed torpedo. The class also had a reduced bunkerage, which meant that range was reduced to 7,600nm.

The provision of aircraft remained an important consideration. Aircraft arrangements were like those on the Portland class. Two catapults were fitted, serviced by two cranes, and stowage space was available for four aircraft. Since the two stacks were placed forward, all the aircraft-handling

Tuscaloosa shown just after being commissioned in mid-1934. The higher freeboard and absence of large superstructures and masts made this class more stable than earlier treaty cruisers and allowed a greater percentage of displacement to be devoted to protection. The New Orleans class was considered one of the USN's most attractive designs. (Naval History and Heritage Command)

facilities were abaft the aft stack. These were the best aircraft-handling facilities of any preceding treaty cruiser, since the well deck and the hangar gave ample room for handling and stowage.

New Orleans Class Construction					
Ship	Built at	Laid down	Launched	Commissioned	Fate
New Orleans (CA 32)	Brooklyn Navy Yard	3/14/31	4/12/33	2/15/34	Scrapped 1959
Astoria (CA 34)	Bremerton Navy Yard	9/1/30	12/16/33	4/28/34	Sunk 8/9/42
Minneapolis (CA 36)	Philadelphia Navy Yard	6/27/31	9/6/33	5/19/34	Scrapped 1959
Tuscaloosa (CA 37)	New York Shipbuilding, Camden	9/3/31	11/15/33	8/17/34	Scrapped 1959
San Francisco (CA 38)	Mare Island Navy Yard	9/9/31	3/9/33	2/10/34	Scrapped 1959
Quincy (CA 39)	Bethlehem, Quincy	11/15/33	6/19/35	6/9/36	Sunk 8/9/42
Vincennes (CA 44)	Bethlehem, Quincy	1/2/34	5/21/36	2/24/37	Sunk 8/9/42

There were subtle differences in appearance among the seven ships. The first three ships had the top of their turret face rounded, and the last four featured a flat face. Most different was the signal bridge (located above the navigation bridge), which was open on three ships and covered on the other four. The last two ships built, *Vincennes* and *Quincy*, were of the same appearance, but differed from the rest of the class. They had flat faces on the 8in turrets, their signal bridges were open, and these were the only two ships that had their barbette for Turret 2 exposed, since the forward turret was moved 9ft back as a cost-saving measure to reduce the length of the armor belt. Another minor difference was the placement of the third and fourth pairs of 5in guns (some were indented, and some were not).

Armament and Service Modifications

The main battery remained nine 8in guns arranged in three triple turrets. The seven ships in the class had three different types of 8in guns. From the onset, they were completed with a secondary battery of eight single 5in/25cal guns. Light antiaircraft armament was restricted to eight .50cal machine guns.

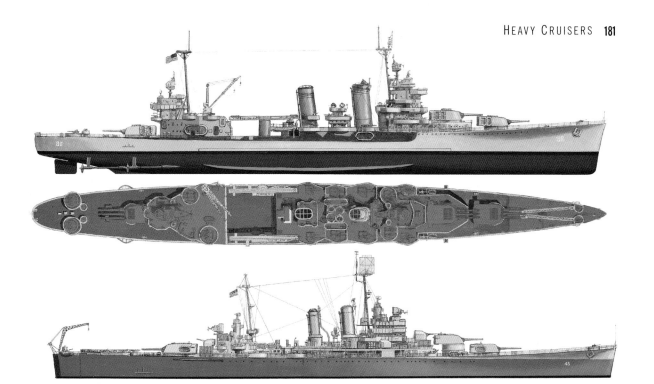

Prior to the war, the 5in guns were provided with splinter shields. By April 1942, each ship received four 1.1in quadruple mounts. The machine guns were also replaced by single 20mm mounts as soon as possible. By 1942 the prescribed number was 12, and these were placed in groups on the forward superstructure, on top of the hangar, and on the aft superstructure. *Astoria*, *Quincy*, and *Vincennes* were all lost in this configuration.

IN THE FIRST TWO PROFILES *Minneapolis* is shown in its late-war configuration. As opposed to early-war New Orleans-class ships, the forward superstructure has been reduced and an SK radar placed on the foremast. The 1.1in quadruple mounts have been replaced by 40mm quads, and another pair added on top of the hangar. Up to 25 single 20mm mounts can be seen. **THE THIRD PROFILE IS** *Wichita*, which had a unique appearance among all treaty heavy cruisers. The two stacks are tightly spaced and the aircraft-handling facilities have been moved to the fantail. Note the placement of the secondary battery is also much different, with two mounts placed on the centerline fore and aft of the superstructure. (Artwork by Paul Wright, © Osprey Publishing)

This view of *New Orleans* shows the cruiser in July 1943 after it had completed repairs from the Battle of Tassafaronga. The forward superstructure has been modified and the antiaircraft fit has been greatly expanded, with two 40mm quadruple mounts on the quarterdeck and two more abreast the forward superstructure. Positions for the 28 20mm single guns are also evident and are concentrated between the stacks and the aft superstructure. (Naval History and Heritage Command)

Three of the surviving four ships had been seriously damaged in the Guadalcanal campaign, so when they returned to the US for repair, they were also modernized. This changed their appearance markedly. Both the forward and aft superstructures were rebuilt. The new superstructures were more compact and lighter and were slightly different on each of the four ships. This was important since the ships were already at the limit of their weight allowances; any increase in antiaircraft weaponry had to be compensated for by the removal of other top weight. The new design also gave the new weapons greater arcs of fire. These allowed for a dramatic improvement of the antiaircraft fit in 1943. The 1.1in mounts were replaced by 40mm quadruple mounts, and another pair was added on top on the hanger, bringing the total to six. The number of single 20mm mounts was also increased; this was accomplished primarily by altering the searchlight tower between the stacks and adding a platform around the aft stack. Another weight-saving measure was to remove one of the catapults and to reduce the number of aircraft usually embarked to two. By the end of the war, the antiaircraft fit had been increased to between 16–28 single 20mm mounts; *Minneapolis* carried nine twin 20mm mounts.

New Orleans Class Specifications (as built)	
Displacement	Standard 10,136 tons; full 12,493 tons
Dimensions	Length: 588ft; beam 61ft 9in; draft 22ft 9in
Propulsion	8 boilers and 4 geared turbines generating 107,000shp on 4 shafts; maximum speed 32.7kt
Range	7,600nm at 15kt
Crew	868

Wichita Class

Wichita was originally intended as the eighth New Orleans-class ship, but this was altered by the London Naval Treaty. In accordance with the treaty, the final of 18 heavy cruisers would be started in 1935, but by that time the USN already had in hand a highly successful 10,000-ton light cruiser design, the Brooklyn class. In several respects, this was a more advanced design than the treaty heavy cruiser, so it was decided to use the Brooklyn design as the basis for the final USN treaty heavy cruiser. After issues were resolved on fitting the 8in gun battery onto a light cruiser hull, construction was begun in late 1935. The new design featured several important improvements. These included a better secondary battery layout, improved placement of aircraft-handling facilities, a higher freeboard for better seakeeping and greater range created by more bunkerage. The ships were also the best protected of the American treaty cruisers. This ship had the least design margin in terms of overall weight, so excessive topside weight was a problem for its entire life. After sea trials, more ballasting was added to address this issue.

Wichita Class Construction					
Ship	Built at	Laid down	Launched	Commissioned	Fate
Wichita (CA 45)	Philadelphia Navy Yard	10/28/35	11/16/37	2/16/39	Scrapped 1959

Wichita photographed in May 1940 while operating in the Atlantic. This overhead view shows its unique appearance among treaty heavy cruisers. Note the placement of the secondary battery, with four in covered gun mounts and four in open mounts. For the first time on a treaty heavy cruiser, two are on the centerline. The aircraft-handling facilities were moved to the stern, as seen in this overhead view. (Naval History and Heritage Command)

Machinery was comparable to the New Orleans class but with the substitution of Parsons geared turbines. These developed 100,000shp, which was sufficient to propel the ship at a top speed of 33 knots.

Protection was better than the New Orleans class. The main belt was 4in on the ends and a maximum of 6in with 2.25in of horizontal protection. The turret barbettes were covered by 7in of armor and the conning tower by 6in.

For the first time on an American cruiser, the aircraft-handling facilities were moved from their customary position amidships to the ship's fantail. This was a major improvement since it removed a major source of battle damage from fire to the less vulnerable rear of the ship. It also provided better arcs of fire for the antiaircraft weapons situated amidships. One large crane on the fantail serviced the two catapults. Stowage space on a blow-deck hangar, covered by a large siding hatch, could accommodate four aircraft.

Armament and Service Modifications

The armament of the new class was also substantially enhanced. The main battery remained the customary nine 8in guns in three triple turrets, but the guns were placed in new mountings. This turret featured a greater separation of the gun barrels, which corrected the problem with dispersion. The turret was also heavily armored with 8in of face armor, 3.75in on the sides and 2.75in on the roof. The mounting also featured better training and elevating speeds.

Wichita in 1943 in Northern Pacific waters. This design served as the departure point for all subsequent classes of USN heavy cruisers. (Naval History and Heritage Command)

For the secondary battery, the move was made from the cruiser-standard 5in/25cal gun to the newer 5in/38cal gun. The layout of the secondary armament was also enhanced with two of the guns placed on the centerline, which provided fore and aft coverage. Because of top-weight considerations, the 5in guns were placed in single, not twin, mounts. Four of these were enclosed, marking the first time an American cruiser received an enclosed 5in mount. *Wichita* was completed with the totally inadequate light antiaircraft armament of only eight .50cal machine guns.

Wichita's first modifications were to increase the ship's antiaircraft fit. By 1942, two quadruple 1.1in mounts were added, and the machine guns replaced by 20mm single guns. The number of 20mm guns increased to 22 by 1944 but was lowered to 18 in 1945 as top weight became critical. In late 1943, it underwent a three-month overhaul in Bremerton. During this period, its appearance was altered by the construction of a smaller forward superstructure to reduce top weight and to provide better arcs of fire for the much-increased antiaircraft suite. In addition to the 20mm single mounts, four quadruple 40mm and two twin 40mm mounts were included. Later in the war, two further twin 40mm mounts were added on the stern in response to the kamikaze threat.

Wichita Class Specifications (as built)	
Displacement	Standard 10,589 tons; full 13,015 tons
Dimensions	Length: 608ft 4in; beam 61ft 9in; draft 23ft 9in
Propulsion	8 boilers and 4 geared turbines generating 100,000shp on 4 shafts; maximum speed 33kt
Range	8,800nm at 15kt
Crew	863 (rising to 1,343 by 1945)

USN Treaty Cruisers – an Analysis

The first generation of USN treaty cruisers were generally regarded as unsuccessful designs, especially in comparison to their IJN contemporaries. The second class of first-generation ships (the Northampton class) featured incremental improvements, but the ships were still underweight and inadequately protected. Once American designers realized that they had an extra 1,000 tons to work with, the second generation of treaty cruisers was much improved. These were balanced designs that were much better protected, while still maintaining a heavy armament. The Wichita class was a mostly successful prototype for subsequent cruiser designs. The new 8in turret proved effective and was standard on the highly successful Baltimore class that followed. The layout of the secondary armament was much better, but still the design was constrained by the overall tonnage limitation. The main problems of this design, trying to jam too much onto too small a hull and the inadequate secondary armament, were not remedied until designers were freed from tonnage limitations.

The war record of USN treaty cruisers presents a mixed picture. This was particularly true of the supposedly better-protected New Orleans class, which saw three ships class sunk in a single night. In this case, the destruction of these ships was not due to any design problem, but to a general lack of battle readiness shared by all USN ships at this point in the war. Each of the three ships was subjected to a storm of accurate 8in shellfire from close range that no cruiser could have survived. Two of the ships were also torpedoed, ensuring their destruction. The remaining New Orleans-class ships served throughout the war in several roles and were highly successful. On occasion, they showed themselves able to take considerable damage and survive.

The primary shortcoming levied against USN treaty cruisers was indeed their inability to take damage and survive. This seems overblown since, in most instances where a ship was lost, the level of damage would have been fatal to any cruiser. Of the seven ships sunk, five fell into this category. The other two, *Northampton* and *Indianapolis*, succumbed to two torpedoes; on the other hand, *Minneapolis* survived after taking two torpedo hits. On five other occasions, a treaty cruiser took a single torpedo hit and survived.

The natural inclination is to compare American treaty cruisers to their Japanese counterparts. Both were powerfully armed, but in this regard the only real difference was that the Japanese ships retained a heavy torpedo battery. This was especially significant since the Japanese torpedo was the powerful Type 93. These torpedoes played important and even decisive roles in the battles of Java Sea and Savo Island. However, it is important to point out that the inclusion of torpedoes on their cruisers was a double-edged sword for the Japanese. The loss of three IJN heavy cruisers was directly attributable to the explosions of their own on-board torpedoes, and another two were severely damaged in this manner.

Ultimately, Japanese heavy cruisers were exposed to have a fatal flaw – vulnerability to air attack. Despite a growing number of light antiaircraft guns, this vulnerability increased as the war went on. In contrast, American treaty cruisers possessed a higher degree of protection from air attack by virtue of better fire-control systems and the development of a successful medium antiaircraft gun, which the Japanese never had. To be fair, though,

American cruisers were never subjected to the scale of air attack that Japanese cruisers were later in the war. Thus, it is impossible to judge whether American treaty cruisers would have been significantly better in defending themselves against heavy air attack.

Even comparing USN and IJN treaty cruisers at all is unfair on a certain level. While the Americans were using every possible weight-saving measure, the Japanese were not as diligent and came in with designs that were considerably overweight. This became practice, resulting in larger ships that had a greater capacity to take damage and the additional displacement to carry both a large gun and torpedo armament. On balance, American treaty cruisers must be judged as successful ships. They performed well in their intended roles and were instrumental in turning the tide against the Japanese. For this, six were sunk in 1942, joined by one other just days before the end of the war.

PART 2: THE WAR-BUILT CRUISERS

The last of the treaty heavy cruisers was the unique *Wichita*. It was based on the 10,000-ton light cruisers of the Brooklyn class, but equipped with an 8in main battery. In general, the USN considered *Wichita* to be successful, but the 10,000-ton limit caused the design to be cramped and to exhibit stability problems. Nevertheless, it was successful enough to be used as the template for the next three classes of heavy cruisers.

The primary reason for the development of the heavy cruiser was to get a main battery of 8in guns to sea. The USN had a love–hate relationship with the 8in gun. The treaty cruisers were given an 8in main battery because this was the largest gun allowed per treaty restrictions, and because the heavier gun gave a longer range and greater penetrative power against armored targets than a 6in gun. Even before World War II there was concern with the performance of the 8in gun based on gunnery trials. More importantly, wartime experience showed that against surface targets the 8in gun had an inadequate rate of fire, mainly because it used bagged powder charges, which made for a longer reload cycle. Rate of fire was also decreased by the time required to move the barrel to a loading angle and then back to the proper angle to fire. The rate of fire for treaty cruisers was 3 or 4rpm, which was too slow to engage fast-moving targets even with the use of radar. This was demonstrated during the Guadalcanal campaign when heavy cruisers were employed to engage Japanese destroyers, usually unsuccessfully, and they often suffered in the process. As a result, the heavy cruisers (those

The Baltimore-class heavy cruisers were the most powerful ships of their type in the world when they began to reach fleet service in mid-1943. This July 1, 1943 view of the lead ship gives an impression of its capabilities with a powerful main battery, bristling antiaircraft battery, and a full electronics suite. (NARA)

that survived) were moved out of the Solomons in 1943 and employed in Aleutian waters or on fast carrier escort duties. In their place, the Brooklyn and Cleveland-class cruisers with their fast-firing 6in guns (8–10rpm) were employed in the Solomons.

The full extent of the issue with the 8in gun was unknown as the USN was formulating its future cruiser construction plans. However, the worth of the heavy cruiser in the mind of American admirals relative to the light cruiser can be judged by the fact that many more Cleveland-class light cruisers were completed during the war than Baltimore-class heavy cruisers. Nevertheless, the construction of the Baltimore class had a prominent place in the wartime cruiser construction program. Since it was basically an enlarged version of *Wichita*, designers were able to address the stability problem and leave room for future growth. The scale of protection for these ships was also increased. Ironically, in the end this meant the heavy cruiser had a much longer life than the light cruiser, which was too cramped to sustain the addition of postwar electronics and in some cases batteries of large antiair missiles.

The Alaska-class large cruisers were an anomaly, since they were built for a mission that did not exist. Entering the war in its last few months, they were never used in their intended role, and never had their cruiser-like protection tested by enemy shells, torpedoes, or bombs. The fact that they were even built speaks more to the profligacy of the USN's wartime construction program than anything else.

Baltimore Class

The Baltimore class was the largest class of heavy cruisers ever built. The light cruiser contemporary of the Baltimore was the Cleveland class, which was the largest class of light cruisers ever built. This was no accident and reflects the USN's grandiose plans in the build-up to America's entry into World War II. To get these huge numbers of cruisers into service as quickly as possible, existing designs were used as a basis for the new ships. Both the Baltimore and Cleveland classes can trace their origins back to the Brooklyn class light cruiser designed when treaty restrictions were in place.

The programmatic origin of the Baltimore class began in late 1939 when the General Board proposed an improved Wichita-class design of 12,000 tons as part of the list of designs to augment cruiser numbers. The Fiscal Year (FY) 1941 building program was augmented by the Two-Ocean Navy Act, with the result that eight of the new Baltimore-class heavy cruisers were funded. Even this was quickly seen as inadequate for wartime requirements. A plan considering actual US ship-building capabilities and the needs of the Navy was formulated in early 1942 and approved in August 1942. This added an additional 16 heavy cruisers. Of these, four were built to a modified design (the Oregon City class), six were completed to the original Baltimore-class design, and another six Oregon City-class units were canceled in August 1945.

Boston seen in late November 1944 entering dry dock at an advanced base. The ship's camouflage scheme is heavily worn, reflecting the fact that the cruiser had been operating virtually non-stop since January 1944. *Boston* was the most heavily decorated Baltimore-class ship of the war. (NARA)

The first four Baltimore-class ships were ordered on July 1, 1940. Even after construction had begun, the General Board continued to push for more protection, but this was rejected for fear that any design modification would slow production. The second batch of four ships was ordered from the same yard in Quincy, Massachusetts on September 9, 1940.

Baltimore Class Construction					
Ship	Built at	Laid down	Launched	Commissioned	Fate
Baltimore (CA 68)	Bethlehem, Quincy	5/26/41	7/28/42	4/15/43	Scrapped 1972
Boston (CA 69)	Bethlehem, Quincy	6/31/41	8/26/42	6/30/43	Scrapped 1975
Canberra (CA 70)	Bethlehem, Quincy	9/3/41	4/19/43	8/14/43	Scrapped 1980
Quincy (CA 71)	Bethlehem, Quincy	10/9/41	6/23/43	12/15/43	Scrapped 1974
Pittsburgh (CA 72)	Bethlehem, Quincy	2/3/43	2/22/44	10/10/44	Scrapped 1974
St. Paul (CA 73)	Bethlehem, Quincy	2/3/43	9/16/44	2/17/45	Scrapped 1980
Columbus (CA 74)	Bethlehem, Quincy	6/28/43	11/30/44	6/8/45	Scrapped 1977
Helena (CA 75)	Bethlehem, Quincy	9/9/43	4/28/45	9/4/45	Scrapped 1975
Bremerton (CA 130)	New York Shipbuilding, Camden	2/1/43	7/2/44	4/29/45	Scrapped 1974
Fall River (CA 131)	New York Shipbuilding, Camden	4/12/43	8/13/44	7/1/45	Scrapped 1972
Macon (CA 132)	New York Shipbuilding, Camden	6/14/43	10/15/44	8/26/45	Scrapped 1973
Toledo (CA 133)	New York Shipbuilding, Camden	9/13/43	5/5/45	10/27/46	Scrapped 1974
Los Angeles (CA 135)	Philadelphia Navy Yard	7/28/43	8/20/44	7/22/45	Scrapped 1975
Chicago (CA 136)	Philadelphia Navy Yard	7/28/43	8/20/44	1/10/45	Scrapped 1991

The design of the new class of heavy cruiser was the subject of some debate. Because the hull had a light-cruiser ancestry, the ship had a basic light cruiser arrangement like that on the Cleveland class. The General Board considered other larger and more complex designs for the new heavy cruiser, but these were rejected in favor of the modified Wichita-class design, which was deemed easier to produce. However, the General Board did insist on an increase in protection. The Board also recommended that displacement be increased by 500 tons to a total of 12,500 tons. The final selection of the design was made on December 15, 1939. The displacement continued to grow, even after approval of the design. By the middle of 1940, the displacement had grown to 13,300 tons and length to 664ft, with the extra weight due to a longer main belt and additional splinter protection topside.

The principal problem with the Wichita class was its poor stability, which was directly attributable to the 10,000-ton treaty limit. While the Baltimore-class ships retained the basic layout and protective scheme of the *Wichita*, the new design was much larger. To address the stability problem, the hull was lengthened by some 65ft and the beam was increased by 9ft. Overall design displacement was increased from *Wichita*'s treaty-derived 10,000 tons to 13,600 tons.

The arrangement of the machinery spaces reflected that of the Cleveland class. The four boilers generated 120,000shp giving the ship a top speed of 33 knots, which was just below the design speed of 34 knots. There were four boiler rooms instead of two in the original design, and this required another 16ft added to the overall length and another 500 tons of displacement. Each boiler was placed in its own compartment. The forward pair of boilers was separated from the aft pair by the forward turbine compartment so that a single critical hit could not knock out all propulsive power. The ship also received two diesel generators, which could provide back-up power in a damage-control scenario.

Protection was broadly like that provided to *Wichita*. The main belt remained at a maximum of 6in but was extended forward to protect the plotting room and the central fire-control station from *Pittsburgh* on. The belt was tapered down to 4in on its lower edges. The armored deck was 2.5in in thickness, and the ends of the armored box were protected by bulkheads between 5in and 6in. Armor on the conning tower was removed from the first six ships to save weight and compensate for the growth of the antiaircraft battery. From *Columbus* on, the conning tower received 6.5in of armor on the sides and 3in on the top. The three 8in turrets were well protected with 8in of face armor, 3in on the roof, 3.25–1.5in on the side, and 1.5in on the rear. The six 5in/38cal mounts also received some armor – 1in on the face and 0.75in on the sides and roof. The barbettes to the main battery received 6.3in of armor. Overall, the weight of armor was 1,790 tons, which equated to 12.9 percent of standard displacement.

THESE TWO PROFILES SHOW *Pittsburgh* in its late-war November 1944 configuration. Note the secondary battery of 12 5in/38cal guns in six twin gun mounts, the heavy 40mm battery, and the numerous 20mm single mounts. The only difference from the early ships in the class is the single crane on the fantail. (Artwork by Paul Wright, © Osprey Publishing)

OPPOSITE *Canberra* entering a floating dry dock for maintenance in February 1944 before it joined the Fast Carrier Task Force. (NARA)

RIGHT *Quincy* off Portland, Maine on April 14, 1944 during workups. The twin aircraft cranes on its fantail mark it as one of the first four ships of the class. Shortly after this photo was taken, it departed for Europe and its first combat action off Normandy. (NARA)

BELOW *Chicago* was commissioned in time to get into action for the last few months of the war. (NARA)

This indicated that the protective scheme of the Baltimore design did not receive as much additional protection as might be expected on a much larger hull compared to earlier heavy cruiser designs.

For spotting and reconnaissance duties, it was still considered important to equip cruisers with aircraft. *Wichita* had its aircraft-handling facilities on the stern. This was favored for damage-control considerations and ease of operation, so the practice was continued on the Baltimore class. Two catapults were provided, and on the first four ships two aircraft cranes were placed on the fantail. After the first four ships, one of the cranes was landed, and the remaining one placed on the centerline on the fantail. There was also a small hangar on the stern, which could accommodate two aircraft. In total, four aircraft could be carried.

Armament and Service Modifications

The main battery consisted of nine 8in Mark 12/15 guns placed into three triple turrets. As was now the custom on American heavy cruisers, two were placed forward with one in a superfiring position, and the third placed aft.

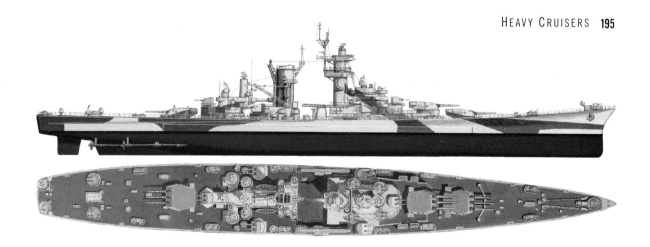

in favor of using available steel for the construction of destroyer escorts. In May 1943, the construction of four Cleveland-class light cruisers was canceled and the deferred *Hawaii* was reinstated. At the same time, the last three Alaska-class ships were canceled. The third ship in Alaska class, *Hawaii*, was never finished. When the war ended, it was 84 percent completed, but construction was suspended. Its size and speed made it a candidate for conversion into a command ship or as a platform for guided missiles, but nothing ever came to fruition. It was finally sold for scrap in 1959.

The names of the class give an indication of its intermediate position between heavy cruisers and battleships. They were named after territories, not states as in the case of battleships, or cities in the case of cruisers. The ships were designated CB, or large cruiser. They were not battlecruisers, as many writers have taken the CB to mean.

THESE VIEWS SHOW *Alaska* as it appeared in 1944 after joining the Pacific Fleet for the final drive on Japan. The ship maintains its basic cruiser configuration with the main battery in three triple turrets and six 5in/38cal mounts. The heavy antiaircraft armament includes 14 40mm quadruple mounts. (Artwork by Paul Wright, © Osprey Publishing)

Alaska Class Construction					
Ship	Built at	Laid down	Launched	Commissioned	Fate
Alaska (CB 1)	New York Shipbuilding, Camden	12/17/41	8/15/43	6/17/44	Scrapped 1961
Guam (CB 2)	New York Shipbuilding, Camden	2/2/42	11/12/43	9/17/44	Scrapped 1961
Hawaii (CB 3)	New York Shipbuilding, Camden	12/20/43	11/3/45	Never	Scrapped 1960
Philippines (CB 4), *Puerto Rico* (CB 5), and *Samoa* (CB 6) were never laid down; all were canceled June 24, 1943.					

The Alaska design was not limited or influenced in any way by treaty restrictions. This allowed designers to pay particular attention to improving protection. The resulting scale of protection was impressive for a cruiser, but not comparable to a fast battleship (which is what the battlecruiser had turned into). The main belt was 9.5in thick and was inclined at 10 degrees,

This view of *Guam* was taken while the ship was working up near Trinidad shortly after being commissioned in September 1944. It arrived in the Pacific in February 1945 and began combat operations the next month. (NARA)

which was unusual for a cruiser. The belt tapered down to 5in on its bottom edge. This was adequate to protect the machinery and magazine spaces from 12in shells at extended ranges. Horizontal protection was also impressive, with a bomb deck of 1.4in and a main armored deck of between 2.8in inboard and 3.25in outboard. The armored bulkhead on each end of the armored box was 10.6in thick. The 12in turrets received 12.8in of armor on their face, 5in on their roof, between 6in and 5.25in on the sides, and 5.25in in the rear. The barbette was protected with between 11in and 13in of armor. The conning tower was also armored and received a maximum of 9in. The total weight of armor was 4,720 tons, which amounted to some 16.4 percent of displacement. This was again comparable to a cruiser's level of protection, but far from that of a fast battleship. Because of its cruiser hull, no torpedo bulges were fitted, making the ships potentially vulnerable to torpedo damage.

The aircraft-handling facilities were moved from the fantail to amidships. This had the advantage of increasing the height of the catapult, thus allowing aircraft to be launched in heavier weather, and it also moved the aircraft out of the blast of the ship's own guns. The location of the aircraft-handling facilities clearly showed the cruiser heritage of the design.

On trials in November 1944, *Alaska* recorded 32.7 knots on 154,846shp. This was disappointing since it was several knots below its design speed, and it meant that the ships had no potential speed advantage over an enemy cruiser.

Armament

The main battery consisted of the new 12in/50cal gun developed specifically for this class. The ship was fitted with three triple turrets, giving it a broadside of nine 12in guns. The fire-control director for the main battery had to be mounted higher than on the 8in gun cruisers to fully exploit the range of the 12in guns. Accordingly, the Mark 34 director was placed on top of the forward superstructure, in the style of USN battleships.

Secondary armament was identical to the modern heavy cruisers with six twin 5in/38cal mounts with two on each beam and two on the centerline. The light antiaircraft armament was considerably augmented before completion. Originally, six quadruple 1.1in mounts were envisioned. This was converted to six 40mm quadruple mounts in May 1941. By August 1945, the light antiaircraft fit had been scaled up to 14 40mm quadruple mounts and 34 single 20mm guns.

Alaska Class Specifications	
Displacement	Standard 29,779 tons; full 34,253 tons
Dimensions	Length: 808ft 6in; beam 91ft 1in; draft 31ft 10in
Propulsion	8 boilers and 4 steam turbines generating 150,000shp on 4 shafts; maximum speed 33kt
Range	12,000nm at 15kt
Crew	1,517

USN War-built Cruisers – an Analysis

The Baltimore class was the finest class of heavy cruiser that saw action during World War II. American designers had taken a good but imperfect design and made it into a well-balanced ship with good stability, good habitability for its expanded wartime crews, and room for wartime upgrades in antiaircraft weaponry and electronics. Most of all, the Baltimore-class ships possessed superior protection to any other wartime cruiser, as well as superior fighting power. The radar-guided 8in guns firing a heavy shell with

This view is from *Boston* as it blasted Japanese steel production facilities at Kamaishi on the home island of Honshu on August 9, 1945. *Boston* and the other ships in its class never had an opportunity to engage surface targets during the war but did conduct shore bombardment on several occasions. (NARA)

good penetrative characteristics made the Baltimore class the most powerful heavy cruiser afloat. Their level of antiaircraft protection was clearly superior to that of any other wartime cruiser.

However, these advantages remained theoretical, not proven, since these fine ships never had an opportunity to show their full potential in combat. Given their speed, modern radar, and antiaircraft fits, the new Baltimore-class heavy cruisers were always assigned to carrier-screening duties. On no occasion did they engage Japanese naval units. Only one Baltimore-class unit saw action in the Atlantic theater where it conducted shore bombardment in support of amphibious landings.

The protection of these ships was also never severely tested since they came to the Pacific late in the war. The most severe instance of damage due to combat was when *Canberra* was hit by a single Japanese aircraft-launched torpedo on October 13, 1944. This flooded the two aft boiler rooms and both engine rooms, but the ship did not lose power in the two forward boiler rooms. The large size of the ship proved adequate to save it, but this was not unusual since treaty cruisers also showed the ability to take a single torpedo hit, but usually sank when hit by two.

The Alaska class never had a clear purpose since the ships they were built to counter – large Japanese cruisers – did not exist. Arriving in the Pacific in the last phases of the war, the only role for them was as an antiaircraft escort for the fast carriers. Though they were fine ships in this role, they were essentially no better than any of the modern heavy cruisers. They were, in fact, a white elephant with no clear mission. If anything, they were a testament to the profligacy of the USN and its extravagant wartime construction plans.

They were designed for a very narrow mission: chasing down Japanese heavy cruisers. Had the Japanese ever employed their heavy cruisers independently, and had the *Alaska* ever come across one, it would certainly have overpowered it with its 12in guns and superior protection. However, just as the British had been tempted to use their early battlecruisers as capital ships in the battle line, it is much more likely that had the IJN posed a serious surface threat in 1945 when the Alaska-class ships entered service, the USN would have used its impressive large cruisers in a main fleet action. Though the Alaska-class ships were well protected for cruisers, the scale and the arrangement of their armor was still based on cruiser principles, and they would not have fared well against a real battleship.

They were expensive to build ($70 million in 1945 dollars), had an enormous wartime crew of 2,200, and consumed fuel at an alarming rate. Their maneuverability was the worst of any large USN ship save the two Lexington-class carriers. The ships possessed poor compartmentation, and, most glaringly, had no dedicated antitorpedo protection. This made it clear that they were not battlecruisers.

The Alaska-class large cruisers were beautiful and powerful ships which had no real purpose. Though larger than any heavy cruisers, their cruiser lines are still discernable; this precluded carrying heavy armor, thus it is impossible to consider them as true battlecruisers. This fine port bow view of *Alaska* is from November 1944 while the ship was on trials. (NARA)

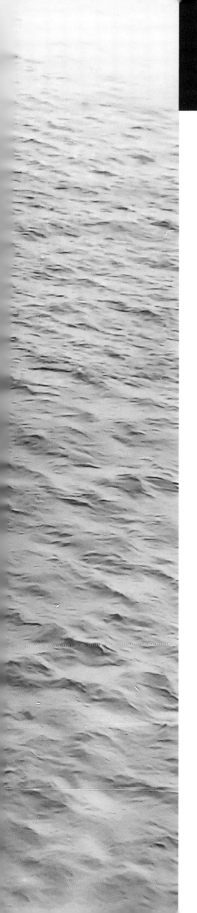

CHAPTER 6
LIGHT CRUISERS

Before World War II, the USN debated whether to focus on light or heavy cruisers. Large cruisers with 8in guns were initially favored by the USN since their guns had greater penetrative power. However, a smaller (light) cruiser with 6in guns had several favorable attributes. Light cruisers were cheaper which meant more could be built. The 6in gun had a greater rate of fire which meant it was better suited to deal with enemy destroyer attacks. Six-inch cruisers were also thought to be the right size for commerce protection. The ambivalence the USN had between the 6in and 8in guns was shown after the collapse of the naval treaty system. When the USN no longer faced tonnage restrictions for cruisers, it began an immense cruiser-building program that included large cruisers (the Alaska class, often referred to incorrectly as battlecruisers), three classes of heavy cruisers, and four classes of light cruisers. It is important to note that the preponderance of wartime cruiser building was of light cruisers, which the USN had come to believe was the more effective type of cruiser.

Either directly or indirectly, naval treaties in the 1920s and 1930s shaped all classes of USN light cruisers. Following the Washington Naval Treaty, a building spree for 10,000-ton cruisers promptly ensued. The USN, which faced interwar parsimony from Congress for shipbuilding budgets, elected to spend its limited funds on building the largest cruisers possible under treaty limitations. At the London Conference of 1930, the USN wanted to stick to construction of large 8in cruisers since they had the range to operate in the Pacific and had equivalent firepower to existing IJN cruisers. Despite USN and RN differences, an agreement was reached to extend tonnage limitations to cruisers. Cruisers were divided into two clear types: heavy cruisers limited to 10,000 tons with guns no

This bow view from January 1943 of *Denver* shows the rounded bridge which was a recognition feature of the early ships in the class. The centerline placement of the forward 5in/38cal twin mount is also evident. (Naval History and Heritage Command)

larger than 8in and light cruisers with guns 6.1in or less. Total cruiser tonnage for the USN was set at 323,500 tons, which included the previously permitted 18 heavy cruisers. The remaining 143,500 tons for light cruisers consisted of 70,500 tons for the ten Omaha-class ships and some 73,000 tons for new construction. The London Treaty thus allowed the construction of seven Brooklyn-class light cruisers, each of almost 10,000 tons. The treaty's provision to replace aging ships, combined with some weight savings from the first seven ships, also allowed the construction of two more modified Brooklyns.

The decision to build large 10,000-ton light cruisers instead of a greater number of smaller ships was contentious. The Brooklyn class endorsed the concept that a large ship was preferable since it could be properly protected. Some studies suggested that it could be better protected than the heavy cruisers already in service. Another key design factor was the requirement for great endurance for Pacific operations. In this regard, 10,000nm at 15 knots was the minimum. A larger ship would also possess better seakeeping characteristics. Finally, a large cruiser would be big enough to mount the required four triple 6in gun turrets. The prevailing view was that the necessary combination of endurance, protection, and firepower could not be designed into a ship any less than 8,500 tons.

The next USN cruiser design, the Atlanta class, was affected indirectly by the 8,000-ton limit for new cruisers agreed at the 1936 London Conference. The USN's first thought was to build a smaller version of the Brooklyn class on the 8,000-ton hull which would have a main battery of 6in guns and an antiaircraft battery of 5in guns. This proved impossible given the 8,000-ton limit, and a concept to develop a dual-purpose 6in mount to solve this problem also proved impossible. These problems led to the adoption of a new ship of only 6,000 tons fitted with a battery of the successful 5in/38cal dual-purpose gun. The Cleveland class, a modified Brooklyn design, was adopted from an existing design since there was not enough time to create a new design better suited to prevailing requirements. The Cleveland class was part of the dramatic expansion of American sea power funded in 1938 and 1940 and became the largest class of light cruisers in history.

OMAHA CLASS

Before World War I, the USN had only three modern scouting cruisers. Requests for additional scout cruisers had been rejected by Congress every year from 1905. By 1915, with war raging in Europe, the need for a balanced fleet could no longer be delayed, so Congress finally approved funding in

August 1916. It provided for ten battleships, six battlecruisers and ten scout cruisers over fiscal years 1917–19. The scout cruisers became the Omaha class; four were planned to be built in 1917, followed by three in each of the next two years.

To perform scouting duties, the new class had to have high speed, good endurance, and good seakeeping abilities. This new class had to act as both a strategic and a tactical scout, so a larger ship was required to create the necessary endurance. After much debate, the Secretary of the Navy approved a 7,100-ton design that carried a heavy battery of 6in guns, light protection, and a high speed of 35 knots. This made them the fastest cruisers of their day. What finally emerged was a unique-looking cruiser with four tall, thin stacks on a narrow beam with fore and aft clusters of 6in guns.

Omaha Class Construction					
Ship	Built at	Laid down	Launched	Commissioned	Fate
Omaha (CL 4)	Todd, Tacoma,	12/6/18	12/14/20	2/24/23	Scrapped 1946
Milwaukee (CL 5)	Todd, Tacoma	12/13/18	3/24/21	6/20/23	Returned from USSR in 1949 and scrapped
Cincinnati (CL 6)	Todd, Tacoma	5/15/20	5/23/21	1/1/24	Scrapped 1946
Raleigh (CL 7)	Bethlehem, Quincy	8/16/20	10/25/22	2/6/24	Scrapped 1946
Detroit (CL 8)	Bethlehem, Quincy	11/10/20	6/29/22	7/31/23	Scrapped 1946
Richmond (CL 9)	Cramp, Philadelphia	2/16/20	9/29/21	7/2/23	Scrapped 1947
Concord (CL 10)	Cramp, Philadelphia	3/29/20	12/15/21	11/3/23	Scrapped 1947
Trenton (CL 11)	Cramp, Philadelphia	8/18/20	4/16/23	4/19/24	Scrapped 1947
Marblehead (CL 12)	Cramp, Philadelphia	8/4/20	10/9/23	9/8/24	Scrapped 1946
Memphis (CL 13)	Cramp, Philadelphia	10/14/20	4/17/24	2/4/25	Scrapped 1947

To gain the desired high speed, a very high length-to-beam ratio of 10:1 was employed and machinery capable of producing 93,000shp fitted. This required 12 boilers driving four steam turbines. The widely spaced boilers

This view of *Marblehead* in 1933 shows the prewar configuration of the Omaha-class cruisers. The narrow beam of these cruisers is evident, as well as their tall stacks and masts. Note the forward cluster of six 6in guns. (Naval History and Heritage Command)

required four stacks that gave the ships their distinctive appearance. Endurance was designed as 9,000nm at 15 knots, but in service proved to be only 8,460nm at 10 knots.

Protection was light, as would be expected of a fast ship built for scouting. A 3in main belt was fitted at the waterline. Compartmentation was as extensive as possible to make up for the lack of hull protection. There was only 1.5in of deck armor, and the conning tower had 1.2in of protection. The 6in turrets and gun houses were provided with 1in of armor.

Another important requirement to perform scouting duties was the capability to carry aircraft. By World War II, the ships carried two catapults located forward of the aft superstructure which swung outboard to launch aircraft. Two aircraft were carried.

The design had several problems. The ship ended up being overloaded and the narrow beam made it very cramped. Seakeeping was generally good, but the lower aft casemate 6in guns were unusable at high speed or in heavy seas due to wetness; the lower torpedo tubes were also affected. The twin 6in gun mount was cramped which reduced its rate of fire. The cruisers were insufficiently insulated which made them too hot for the tropics and too cold for northern waters. There was no wood deck, making the steel decks too hot. The crew suffered from inadequate toilet facilities and the lightly built hulls leaked. In the final analysis, the Omaha class was not a success. The ships were incapable of strategic scouting, so this mission was assigned to the fleet's heavy cruisers. When they first entered service, they were assigned as destroyer flotilla leaders to provide them with the firepower

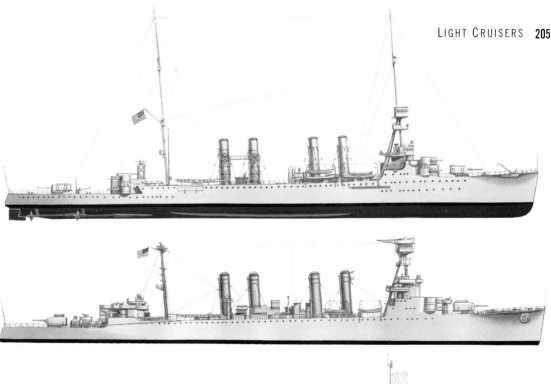

necessary to repel a destroyer attack. By the start of the war, other more modern ships were employed in this capacity, so the Omaha-class cruisers were relegated to secondary duties and theaters.

Armament and Service Modifications

For their size, the ships were adequately armed, but the arrangement of the main armament was archaic. The main battery was maximized for end-on fire which resulted in the vertical pair of casemate guns – these remained the trademark of the class throughout its career. Two twin turrets were fitted fore and aft for a total of 12 6in guns. The lower casemate guns aft were soon removed, bringing the main battery to ten 6in guns.

A heavy 21in torpedo battery was originally fitted. After the removal of the two twin torpedo mounts on the main deck, this left two triple mounts fitted on the forecastle deck. Mine rails were

THE TOP PROFILE DEPICTS *Omaha* as it was completed. The ship's appearance was distinctive because of its tall masts, four slim stacks, and forward and aft clusters of 6in guns. The set of hull-mounted torpedo tubes and the bottom casemate gun in the aft superstructure were found to be unworkable and were soon removed. **IN THE MIDDLE PROFILE,** *Raleigh* is shown as it appeared at the time of the Pearl Harbor raid. The ship retains its distinctive and archaic appearance but has received an enhanced antiaircraft battery of 3in guns and eight heavy machine guns. **THE BOTTOM PROFILE DEPICTS** *Detroit* in the late-war configuration of this class. A full radar suite of an SK set on the foremast and two SG sets on the top of both masts are evident. The antiaircraft battery has been augmented to eight 3in guns and five twin 40mm mounts, with 12 20mm single mounts. (Artwork by Paul Wright, © Osprey Publishing)

Raleigh in May 1944 after completing its refit and modernization period. This view shows the ship's modified forward superstructure with a new bridge. Note the 40mm twin mount abaft the forward twin 6in mount. Much of the ship's electronics suite is on display including an SK air-search radar on the foremast, an SG surface-search radar on top of the pole mast, and a Mark 3 fire-control radar for the main battery located just forward of the SK. (Naval History and Heritage Command)

also originally fitted with a capacity to carry 224 mines but were removed early in their careers to save weight.

When designed, antiaircraft armament was a secondary concern. As built, the cruisers were limited to two 3in/50cal guns on each side. After refit in the 1930s, the antiaircraft battery was brought up to six 3in/50cal single mounts amidships and one each fore and aft for a total of eight. Also, four .50cal machine guns were fitted in the foremast tub and four more on the aft superstructure to provide defense against dive-bombers.

The ability of these ships to accommodate significant modernization was greatly limited by their already overcrowded and overweight condition. When the war began, the ship's antiaircraft and electronics suites were modernized. To compensate for this extra topside weight, the conning tower was removed, and the bridge structure simplified. Beginning in March 1942, the antiaircraft suite was augmented with a 1.1in quadruple mount fore and aft. Single 20mm mounts were added in groups of four on the bridge and on the aft superstructure.

In the mid-war period, the 1.1in quadruple mounts were replaced by twin 40mm mounts and a third twin 40mm mount replaced a 3in/50cal mount on the centerline. The two centerline 3in/50cal mounts were moved amidships making the 3in/50cal battery eight guns. The number of 20mm single mounts rose to ten or 12. Radars were modernized with the addition of the SG for surface search, one on each mast, and the SK radar fitted on the mainmast for air search. The final standard antiaircraft fit in 1945 was eight 3in/50cal single guns, three 40mm twin mounts and 12 20mm single mounts; however, three ships had different fits. Some ships had their torpedo tubes removed to save weight.

Omaha Class Specifications	
Displacement	Standard 7,100 tons; full 8,960 tons (by 1944 10,243 tons full load)
Dimensions	Length 555ft 6in; beam 55ft 4in; draft 15ft
Propulsion	12 boilers and 4 geared turbines generating 90,000shp on 4 shafts; maximum speed 35kt
Range	8,460nm at 10kt
Crew	458

BROOKLYN CLASS

The Brooklyn class was a direct result of the London Naval Treaty of 1930 and was also the most important USN cruiser design leading up to World War II. The new class was clearly the best cruiser design produced by the USN to date, including all treaty heavy cruisers, and it introduced several new features which were continued on almost all USN light and heavy cruisers. The Brooklyns were the basis for the last treaty heavy cruiser, the single-ship Wichita class, which was the basis for the Baltimore class of heavy cruisers, the largest class of heavy cruisers ever built. The Brooklyns

A fine starboard bow view of *Honolulu* in February 1939. This prewar view of a Brooklyn-class cruiser shows no search or fire-control radars, a closed bridge, and a total absence of 20mm or 40mm guns. (Naval History and Heritage Command)

were also the design basis for the next class of light cruisers, the Cleveland class, which was the largest class of light cruiser ever built.

Brooklyn Class Construction					
Ship	Built at	Laid down	Launched	Commissioned	Fate
Brooklyn (CL 40)	Brooklyn Navy Yard	3/12/35	11/30/36	9/30/37	Sold to Chile in 1951 and renamed O'Higgins; scrapped 1992
Philadelphia (CL 41)	Philadelphia Navy Yard	5/28/35	11/17/36	9/23/37	Sold to Brazil in 1951 and renamed Barroso; scrapped 1974
Savannah (CL 42)	New York Shipbuilding, Camden	5/31/34	5/8/37	3/10/38	Scrapped 1966
Nashville (CL 43)	New York Shipbuilding, Camden	1/24/35	10/2/37	6/6/38	Sold to Chile in 1951 and renamed Capitan Prat and later Chacabuco; scrapped 1985
Phoenix (CL 44)	New York Shipbuilding	4/15/35	3/13/38	10/3/38	Sold to Argentina in 1951 and renamed Desiete de Octubre and later General Belgrano; sunk by RN submarine Conqueror on 5/3/82
Boise (CL 47)	Newport News, Virginia	4/1/35	12/3/36	8/12/38	Sold to Argentina in 1951 and renamed Nueve de Julio; scrapped 1983
Honolulu (CL 48)	Brooklyn Navy Yard	9/10/35	8/26/37	6/15/38	Scrapped 1959
St. Louis (CL 49)	Newport News, Virginia	12/10/36	4/15/38	5/19/39	Sold to Brazil in 1951 and renamed Tamandare; sank 1980 on way to breakers
Helena (CL 50)	Brooklyn Navy Yard	12/9/36	8/27/38	9/18/39	Sunk 7/6/43

Design work began in the fall of 1930. Several schemes were considered and in June 1931 a design of 9,600 tons was approved. Because funding from Congress was not available to start construction, design development continued. Early in 1933, the IJN announced the characteristics of its new Mogami-class light cruiser with a main battery of 15 6.1in guns. The USN was now forced to re-cast the Brooklyn design to match this. The previous 12-gun design was a balanced design, but to match the 15-gun Japanese design, some compromises had to be made in protection. The USN's desire for enough armor to withstand 8in shells at specific ranges was now impossible, and it was forced to settle for a cruiser armored against 6in gunfire. The final design was a good balance of offensive power, protection, and speed. The main battery was comprised of 15 6in guns with an antiaircraft battery of eight 5in guns. Protection was assessed to be adequate against 6in gunfire, and the maximum speed of 32.5 knots was adequate for all fleet duties.

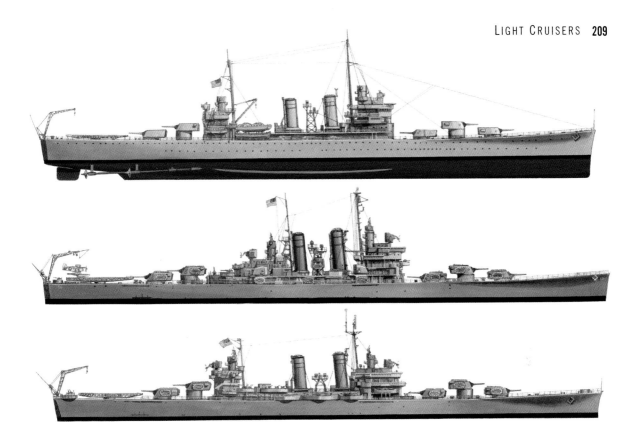

The design speed was achieved by four shafts driven by four turbines with power from eight boilers. The boilers were grouped ahead of the engine room. More effective would have been an arrangement in which the placement of boilers and turbines was alternated so that a single hit could not knock out all propulsive power. The system provided a total of 100,000shp. The protection scheme was superior to other light cruisers of the period. The main belt was 5.63in, with armored bulkheads of 2–5in at the end of the belt. Internal protection of the magazines included a 2in longitudinal belt. Horizontal protection was comprised of a 2in thick armored deck; the turret barbettes received 6in. The 6in turrets received 6.5in on their faces and 2in on their roofs. The conning tower was protected by 5in of armor. The total weight of armor was 1,798 tons, or 15 percent of the design standard displacement.

The Brooklyn class introduced the aft placement of aviation facilities. This had the effect of making it easier to recover aircraft, not interfering with the placement of guns amidships, and improving resistance to battle damage since the aircraft and their fuel were located away from vulnerable areas. Two catapults were fitted aft, supported by a single crane on the fantail, and up to four aircraft could be stored in the hangar which was below deck.

THE TOP PROFILE DEPICTS *Honolulu* in its early-war configuration. The Brooklyn class was a powerful and balanced design, as can be seen here, with a heavy main battery of 15 6in guns in five triple turrets. For the first time on a USN cruiser, the aircraft facilities were moved aft. **THE MIDDLE PROFILE SHOWS** *Helena* at the time of its loss in July 1943. *Helena* was one of the two ships of a sub-class of the Brooklyn class with the primary difference being the adoption of twin 5in/38cal mounts for the 5in/25cal single mounts. By mid-war, light cruisers had search and fire-control radars as evident on *Helena*. The antiaircraft battery has also been upgraded with four 40mm quadruple mounts and single 20mm single guns. **THE BOTTOM PROFILE DEPICTS** *Nashville*. This is a Brooklyn-class cruiser in its late-war configuration. The ship retains its 5in/25cal battery but shows the final Brooklyn-class fit of four quadruple and six twin 40mm mounts. (Artwork by Paul Wright, © Osprey Publishing)

Brooklyn photographed in May 1942. By the end of the year, it would be in action off North Africa. The cruiser spent its entire wartime career in the Mediterranean and the Atlantic. (Naval History and Heritage Command)

The last two ships in the class, *St. Louis* and *Helena*, were built to a modified design. The most important and obvious difference was the substitution of the 5in/38cal gun for the 5in/25cal. As early as 1936, the USN was convinced of the superiority of the .38cal gun and sought to add it to the later Brooklyn-class ships despite the additional weight of the newer weapon. The last two ships also had different internal machinery arrangements. There were two engine rooms and two boiler rooms; this increased compartmentation increased the ships' resistance to battle damage and was made possible by the adoption of smaller boilers which took up less space.

Armament and Service Modifications

The Brooklyn class introduced one of the USN's most successful guns in its history, the 6in/47cal. The USN long debated the effectiveness of the 6in gun compared to the 8in gun. The 8in gun had several advantages, but in comparison, the 6in gun had the advantage of a faster rate of fire. In prewar exercises, a rate of up to ten rounds per gun per minute was achieved. With its battery of 15 6in guns, a Brooklyn-class cruiser could smother a target in a rain of shells. The range advantage of the 8in gun was minimized by the likely effects of weather and light which made it unlikely that engagements would be conducted at extended ranges. In an engagement against surface targets, the USN came to see the 6in gun as superior. The effectiveness of the 6in/47cal was greatly enhanced by its excellent fire-control systems. The Brooklyn class introduced the Mark 34 director that was a great improvement on earlier systems. During the war, the Mark 34 was coupled with the

Mark 3 fire-control radar, and then the improved Mark 8 or Mark 13 radars. These systems allowed the 6in batteries to engage targets quickly in any light or weather conditions.

The antiaircraft battery was eight 5in/25cal single mounts and eight .50cal machine guns for protection against dive-bombers. The final two ships substituted eight 5in/38cal guns in twin mounts for the eight single 5in/25cal mounts.

Before the war, it was intended to augment the ships with four quadruple 1.1in mounts. This proved impossible because of shortages, so the plan was adjusted to two quadruple 1.1in mounts and two 3in guns. Only *Helena* was given these before the war. Once fitted, the 3in guns remained on some ships well into the war. Early-war modifications were limited to a few additional 20mm guns. In the mid-war period, all surviving ships had their

St. Louis in its late-war configuration in October 1944. The forward superstructure has been rebuilt. Details are obscured by the dazzle camouflage scheme, but two quadruple and two twin 40mm mounts can be seen on the starboard side. An SK-2 radar is fitted on the foremast and SG sets are on top of both pole masts. (Naval History and Heritage Command)

bridges radically altered. The bridge was cut down a level and a new open bridge built on top as a fire-control platform. This also served to reduce top weight, as did the removal of the armored conning tower. A pair of twin 40mm guns was fitted on the new forward superstructure and another pair placed forward on the main deck abeam the new conning tower. In late 1942, the standard Brooklyn-class antiaircraft battery was set at four twin and four quadruple 40mm mounts.

Savannah was extensively reconstructed after being struck by a German guided bomb in 1943. Its hull was blistered up to the main deck and the ship's appearance changed with a simplified bridge. The single 5in/25cal guns were removed, and four twin 5in/38cal mounts added. Four quadruple 40mm mounts were placed on towers amidships, and six twin 40mm mounts placed abreast the bridge, the aft superstructure, and on the fantail. This modification was planned for all the Brooklyns but proved impossible. *Brooklyn*, *Philadelphia*, and *Honolulu* were blistered, but not re-armed. By end of the war, all ships except *Honolulu* were fitted with four quadruple and six twin 40mm mounts and ten twin 20mm mounts (*Nashville* had nine), but all but *St. Louis* and *Savannah* retained single 5in/25cal guns.

Brooklyn Class Specifications (as built)	
Displacement	Standard 9,767 tons; full 12,207 tons
Dimensions	Length 608ft 4in; beam 61ft 9in; draft 22ft 9in
Propulsion	8 boilers and 4 geared turbines generating 100,000shp on 4 shafts; maximum speed 32.5kt
Range	10,000nm at 15kt
Crew	868

ATLANTA CLASS

Under the 8,000-ton restriction of the 1936 London Naval Treaty, several different designs were considered for the USN's new small cruiser. When it was apparent that a 6-inch dual-purpose mount would not be ready in time, this left a design centered on the existing twin 5-inch/38 mount. The preliminary design for the new cruiser was completed in July 1938 and resulted in a 6,000-ton ship. The first four ships were ordered in April 1939 and the second group ordered in September 1940. Because of the modifications made to the second and third groups, these are often referred to as the Oakland and Juneau classes.

Atlanta Class Construction					
Ship	Built at	Laid down	Launched	Commissioned	Fate
Atlanta (CL 51)	Federal, Kearny	4/22/40	9/6/41	12/24/41	Sunk 11/13/42
Juneau (CL 52)	Federal, Kearny	5/27/40	10/25/41	2/14/42	Sunk 11/13/42
San Diego (CL 53)	Bethlehem, Quincy	3/27/40	7/26/41	1/10/42	Scrapped 1960
San Juan (CL 54)	Bethlehem, Quincy	5/15/40	9/6/41	2/28/42	Scrapped 1962
Oakland (CL 95)	Bethlehem, San Francisco	7/13/41	10/23/42	7/17/43	Scrapped 1960
Reno (CL 96)	Bethlehem, San Francisco	8/1/41	12/3/42	12/28/43	Scrapped 1962
Flint (CL 97)	Bethlehem, San Francisco	10/23/42	1/25/44	8/31/44	Scrapped 1966
Tucson (CL 98)	Bethlehem, San Francisco	12/23/42	9/3/44	2/3/45	Scrapped 1971
Juneau (CL 119)	Federal, Kearny	9/15/44	7/15/45	2/15/46	Scrapped 1962
Spokane (CL 120)	Federal, Kearny	11/15/44	9/22/45	5/17/46	Scrapped 1973
Fresno (CL 121)	Federal, Kearny	2/12/45	3/5/46	11/27/46	Scrapped 1966

This is *Atlanta* as it was completed in December 1941. The graceful appearance of the class is evident with its symmetrical main battery and two evenly spaced stacks. Note the waist 5in/38cal mounts. The ship is devoid of radar and carries only three 1.1in quadruple mounts for close-range antiaircraft protection. (Naval History and Heritage Command)

Protection was light and totaled only 585.5 tons of armor. The main belt was a maximum of 3.75in over the machinery spaces and more shallow forward and aft over the magazines. The belt was closed off by 3.75in armored bulkheads. The armored deck was a thin 1.25in, and 2.5in of armor were devoted to the conning tower. The gun houses and handling rooms were provided with 1.25in of armor.

The design speed of 32.5 knots was achieved with a power plant capable of producing 75,000shp. The cruisers were fitted with high-pressure/high-temperature steam plants with alternating boiler and engine rooms. On sea trials, *Atlanta* made 33.67 knots. Other ships made only 31 knots in wartime conditions.

The second group introduced modifications to the ships' armament. The primary difference was the removal of the two 5in/38cal twin waist mounts. The final group of three ships incorporated war experience. By this point,

their mission as antiaircraft cruisers was clear, so they were maximized for this role. The design was badly overweight, so measures were taken to improve stability by reducing the height of the main battery and simplifying and lowering the forward superstructure.

Armament and Service Modifications

The first four units were given a main battery of eight 5in/38cal twin mounts arranged in six on the centerline and two on the waist aft. The antiaircraft battery was originally set at three 1.1in quadruple mounts and eight 20mm single guns. Two quadruple torpedo tube mounts were fitted aft. Uniquely for a USN cruiser, antisubmarine equipment was also added including a hull-mounted sonar and two removable depth charge tracks. Later, six depth charge throwers were also fitted. In practice, even a small cruiser was not maneuverable enough to effectively employ these weapons against submarines and all were removed by late 1944.

The second group (the Oakland class) was fitted with eight 40mm twin mounts in addition to its main battery of 12 5in/38cal guns. These ships also received 18 20mm single mounts. The third group (the Juneau class) was completed after the war so received all the upgrades given to earlier ships. These ships were fitted with the definitive armament of the class which totaled six 5in/38cal twin mounts, six quadruple and six twin 40mm mounts, and eight twin 20mm guns. These ships were completed without torpedo tubes.

The first four units were completed with a rounded and closed bridge. The lack of an open bridge was a major disadvantage because it inhibited control of the antiaircraft guns against air attack. An extemporized open bridge was fitted, and as the ships went into overhaul they were given a true open bridge. All later ships were completed with square, open bridges. To save weight, later ships had their conning tower removed, as were the boat crane and all ship's boats.

The two surviving ships from the first group (*San Juan* and *San Diego*) were refitted in late 1943. A 40mm quadruple mount was placed on the fantail, and the three 1.1in quadruple mounts replaced with 40mm twin mounts. The 20mm battery had been increased to 13 in October 1942. In 1945, these ships had 16 5in guns, one quadruple and five twin 40mm mounts, nine 20mm guns, and their torpedo tubes. In 1945, it was planned to give all ships in the second group modifications to deal with the kamikaze threat. The torpedo tubes and twin 40mm mounts located aft were removed and replaced by 40mm quadruple mounts. Another 40mm quadruple mount was placed on the aft superstructure in place of the twin 40mm mount already there and the 40mm quadruple mount on the stern remained. This translated to a final armament of 12 5in/38cal guns, four quadruple and four twin 40mm mounts, and 16 20mm

A fine beam shot of *Oakland* showing the basic configuration of the second group of Atlanta-class ships. The waist 5in/38cal mounts have been removed, and the number of twin 40mm mounts increased to eight. The quadruple torpedo mounts aft have been retained. (Naval History and Heritage Command)

guns in eight twin mounts. Only *Oakland* received this refit before the end of the war. In January 1945, approval was given to remove the torpedo mounts; by the end of the war, only *Flint* retained them.

Atlanta Class Specifications (as built)	
Displacement	Standard 6,718 tons; full 8,340 tons
Dimensions	Length 541ft 6in; beam 53ft 2in; draft 20ft 6in
Propulsion	4 boilers and 2 geared turbines generating 75,000shp on 2 shafts; maximum speed 32.5kt
Range	8,500nm at 15kt
Crew	623

CLEVELAND CLASS

The need for cruisers called for immediate production of existing designs. The design genesis of the Cleveland class was the *Helena* with two 5in/38cal mounts placed on the centerline replacing one triple 6in turret. To address stability concerns, the new class had its beam increased by 2ft and weight reduced by 230 tons. The new design was quickly completed and approved in October 1939. A total of 39 ships were planned, but of these only 26 were completed as light cruisers, which still made this the largest class of light cruisers ever by a wide margin. Additionally, another was completed in 1958 as a guided-missile cruiser, nine were completed as light carriers of the highly successful Independence class, and three others were canceled. A further 13 ships were ordered to an improved design using the benefit of war experience. These improved ships were given a new class name after the lead ship *Fargo*, but only two were commissioned after the war.

Cleveland Class Construction					
Ship	Built at	Laid down	Launched	Commissioned	Fate
Cleveland (CL 55)	New York Shipbuilding	6/1/40	11/1/41	6/15/42	Scrapped 1960
Columbia (CL 56)	New York Shipbuilding	8/19/40	12/17/41	7/29/42	Scrapped 1959
Montpelier (CL 57)	New York Shipbuilding	12/2/40	2/12/42	9/9/42	Scrapped 1960
Denver (CL 58)	New York Shipbuilding	12/26/40	4/4/42	10/15/42	Scrapped 1960
Amsterdam (CL 59)	New York Shipbuilding	5/1/41			Completed as light carrier *Independence*
Santa Fe (CL 60)	New York Shipbuilding	6/7/41	6/10/42	11/24/42	Scrapped 1960
Tallahassee (CL 61)	New York Shipbuilding	6/2/41			Completed as light carrier *Princeton*

Birmingham (CL 62)	Newport News, Virginia	2/17/41	3/20/42	1/29/43	Scrapped 1959
Mobile (CL 63)	Newport News, Virginia	4/14/41	5/15/42	3/24/43	Scrapped 1960
Vincennes (CL 64)	Bethlehem, Quincy	5/7/42	7/17/43	1/21/44	Sunk as target 1969
Pasadena (CL 65)	Bethlehem, Quincy	2/6/43	12/28/43	6/8/44	Scrapped 1972
Springfield (CL 66)	Bethlehem, Quincy	2/13/43	3/9/44	9/9/44	Converted into guided-missile cruiser in 1960; scrapped 1980
Topeka (CL 67)	Bethlehem, Quincy	4/21/43	8/19/44	12/23/44	Converted into guided-missile cruiser in 1960; scrapped 1975
New Haven (CL 76)	New York Shipbuilding	8/1/41			Completed as light carrier *Belleau Wood*
Huntington (CL 77)	New York Shipbuilding	11/17/41			Completed as light carrier *Cowpens*
Dayton (CL 78)	New York Shipbuilding	12/29/41			Completed as light carrier *Monterey*
Wilmington (CL 79)	New York Shipbuilding	3/16/42			Completed as light carrier *Cabot*
Biloxi (CL 80)	Newport News, Virginia	7/9/41	2/23/43	8/31/43	Scrapped 1962
Houston (CL 81)	Newport News, Virginia	8/4/41	6/19/43	12/20/43	Scrapped 1960
Providence (CL 82)	Bethlehem, Quincy	7/27/43	12/28/44	5/15/44	Converted into guided-missile cruiser 1959; scrapped 1980
Manchester (CL 83)	Bethlehem, Quincy	9/25/44	3/5/46	10/29/46	Scrapped 1961
Buffalo (CL 84)	Federal, Kearny	Never			Canceled Dec 1940
Fargo (CL 85)	New York Shipbuilding	4/11/42			Completed as light carrier *Langley*
Vicksburg (CL 86)	Newport News, Virginia	10/26/42	12/14/43	6/12/44	Scrapped 1964
Duluth (CL 87)	Newport News, Virginia	11/9/42	1/13, 1944	9/18, 1944	Scrapped 1960
Unnamed (CL 88)	Federal, Kearny	Never			Canceled December 1940
Miami (CL 89)	Cramp, Philadelphia	8/2/41	12/8/42	12/28/43	Scrapped 1962
Astoria (CL 90)	Cramp, Philadelphia	9/6/41	3/6/43	5/17/44	Scrapped 1971
Oklahoma City (CL 91)	Cramp, Philadelphia	12/8/42	2/20/44	12/22/44	Converted into guided-missile cruiser 1960; sunk as target 1999
Little Rock (CL 92)	Cramp, Philadelphia	3/6/43	8/27/44	6/17/45	Converted into guided-missile cruiser 1960; preserved as museum ship in Buffalo, NY
Galveston (CL 93)	Cramp, Philadelphia	2/20/44	4/22/45	5/28/58	Converted into guided-missile cruiser 1958; scrapped 1975
Youngstown (CL 94)	Cramp, Philadelphia	9/4/44	Never		Canceled Aug 1945
Buffalo (CL 99)	New York Shipbuilding	8/31/42			Completed as light carrier *Bataan*
Newark (CL 100)	New York Shipbuilding	10/26/42			Completed as light carrier *St. Jacinto*
Amsterdam (CL 101)	Newport News, Virginia	3/3/43	4/2/1944	1/8/45	Scrapped 1971
Portsmouth (CL 102)	Newport News, Virginia	6/28/43	9/20/44	6/25/45	Scrapped 1971
Wilkes-Barre (CL 103)	New York Shipbuilding	12/14/42	12/24/43	6/1/44	Scuttled 1972
Atlanta (CL 104)	New York Shipbuilding	1/25/43	2/6/44	12/3/44	Scuttled 1970
Dayton (CL 105)	New York Shipbuilding	3/8/43	3/19/44	1/7/45	Scrapped 1962

ABOVE This is *Cleveland* at the Philadelphia Navy Yard in 1942 in its early-war configuration. No radars or smaller antiaircraft guns have yet been fitted. (Naval History and Heritage Command)

The design possessed a small margin in stability. However, the requirement to add 40mm and 20mm guns for air defense, while not reducing the 12-gun 5in/38cal battery, was paramount. Stability was maintained by adding ballast and using a hull redesign which moved the belt from sloping inward to sloping outward, giving the hull a slight tumblehome appearance. These ships faced critical stability issues throughout their lives which were continually worsened with the addition of more antiaircraft guns and electronics.

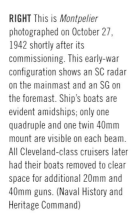

RIGHT This is *Montpelier* photographed on October 27, 1942 shortly after its commissioning. This early-war configuration shows an SC radar on the mainmast and an SG on the foremast. Ship's boats are evident amidships; only one quadruple and one twin 40mm mount are visible on each beam. All Cleveland-class cruisers later had their boats removed to clear space for additional 20mm and 40mm guns. (Naval History and Heritage Command)

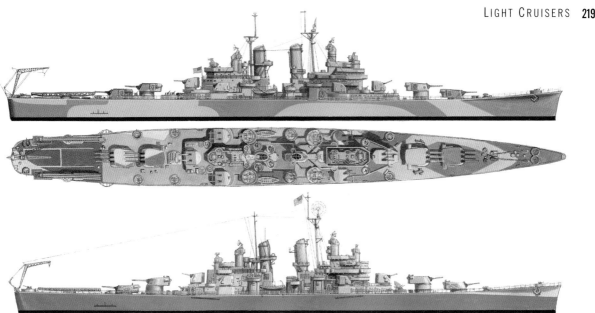

Protection was like that of the Brooklyn class with a main belt of a maximum of 5in of armor; horizontal protection was provided by a 2in armored deck. The turret barbettes received 6in; the four 6in turrets had 6.5in of face armor and 3in on the tops and sides. The conning tower was protected by 5in. The total weight of armor was 1,468 tons.

The same engineering plant as used on the Atlanta class was adopted. High-pressure boilers were retained which were more efficient and weighed less, and the unit principle which separated the boiler and engineering spaces was again employed. The propulsion system generated 100,000shp that was sufficient to drive the ship at its design speed of 32.5 knots, though in service 30 knots was more common. The ship's aviation facilities were retained aft. Two catapults were fitted, supported by a crane on the fantail. Four aircraft could be carried.

Armament and Service Modifications

The 6in/47cal Mark 16 gun was retained as the main battery for the Cleveland class. Twelve guns were carried in four triple turrets with fire control provided by two Mark 34 directors. The antiaircraft battery included 12 5in/38cal guns fitted in six twin mounts. Two of these were fitted on the centerline for the first time on a USN light cruiser. Two Mark 37 directors were fitted to provide fire control. The original light antiaircraft suite was limited to machine guns which was clearly inadequate. The stability issue presented a persistent problem to upgrading the antiaircraft suite throughout the war. *Cleveland* was

THE TOP AND MIDDLE PROFILES SHOW *Houston* in a mid-war configuration. The electronics fit includes an SK radar on the foremast and SGs on both masts; the Mark 34 and 37 directors are also both radar equipped. The antiaircraft fit has not reached its final limit, but already four quadruple and two twin 40mm mounts are evident. In addition, 20 single 20mm guns were fitted onboard. **THE BOTTOM PROFILE SHOWS** *Vincennes* in late-war configuration. An SK-2 radar has been placed on the platform on the foremast. The antiaircraft battery has reached its final configuration with four quadruple and six twin 40mm mounts. The 20mm fit has been reduced to ten single mounts. (Artwork by Paul Wright, © Osprey Publishing)

Vincennes was the first ship to be built with a square bridge, which is evident in this view. The ship carries one twin and two quadruple 40mm mounts on each beam and approximately 20 single 20mm guns. (Naval History and Heritage Command)

completed with four twin 40mm mounts and 15 20mm singles. The second ship, *Columbia*, was completed with two quadruple and two twin 40mm mounts and a similar number of single 20mm guns.

The first seven ships were completed with round bridges. Starting with *Vincennes*, all units received a square open bridge. *Vincennes* was also the first ship with a full Combat Information Center upon completion. Major modifications were limited by the need to produce ships quickly and the stability problem. Despite efforts to limit the weight growth, *Cleveland* showed an increase in 480 tons comprised mainly of top weight that made the stability issues worse.

Despite this, the antiaircraft battery grew throughout the war. Four more positions for 40mm guns were found on the main deck between the centerline 5in/38cal mounts and the superfiring 6in turrets. By May 1944, the uniform 40mm battery was set at four quadruple and six twin mounts for all ships. The 20mm suite varied during the war rising to as many as 21 on some ships without the full 40mm fit but was reduced to ten by late war. To compensate, one of the catapults was eliminated in 1945. Later units were also completed with no conning tower.

Cleveland Class Specifications	
Displacement	Standard 11,744 tons; full 14,131 tons
Dimensions	Length 610ft 1in; beam 66ft 4in; draft 24ft 6in
Propulsion	4 boilers and 4 geared turbines generating 100,000shp on 4 shafts; maximum speed 32.5kt
Range	11,000nm at 15kt
Crew	1,285

USN LIGHT CRUISERS – AN ANALYSIS

The Omahas were not a successful design. Accordingly, they were not committed to high-threat areas during the war. When exposed to damage they fared poorly. *Raleigh* was torpedoed and hit by an aircraft bomb at Pearl Harbor, and clearly would have sunk had it not been moored in harbor where aggressive damage control measures could be employed. During the NEI campaign, *Marblehead* was hit by two 220lb aircraft bombs and suffered another near miss, and it nearly succumbed to flooding and fires.

The Brooklyn class proved to be powerful warships. *Boise* seemed destined for an early end since it was assigned to the Asiatic Fleet with its hopeless mission of defending the NEI but the cruiser ran aground and was sent home for repairs. *Helena* was damaged at Pearl Harbor. That left three Brooklyns in the Pacific during the early-war period, soon to be joined by *Nashville*. In the fierce night battles in the Solomons they performed well. The ships were handicapped by USN night-fighting doctrine and the limitations of early radar, but even so were clearly superior to IJN light cruisers.

The four ships which spent their careers in the Atlantic were used almost exclusively in a shore bombardment role. In this capacity, they were very successful since their rapid-fire 6in shells could flood a troop concentration with high explosives. At the landings at Gela, Sicily on July 10 and 11, 1943, *Boise*'s and *Savannah*'s fires were instrumental in repelling Italian and German armored attacks. At Salerno in southern Italy, the story was repeated from September 9–15 as American troops battled to establish a beachhead, defeat German counterattacks, and then break out. At Anzio during January 1944, *Brooklyn* provided sustained fire support, and *Philadelphia* supported the breakout from the beachhead in May.

Several Brooklyns were damaged, proving they could take a beating. *Savannah* and *Philadelphia* were the targets of German guided-bomb attacks and *Savannah* was nearly sunk when a bomb penetrated the ship's armor to hit a magazine. This was the largest bomb to hit a USN ship during the entire war, but *Savannah* survived, though was under repairs for most of the remainder of the war. In the Pacific, the main threat was torpedoes, and these ships proved able to survive a single hit, especially in a non-critical area. *Helena* was the only ship of its class lost, but no light cruiser could be expected to deal with the damage wrought by three torpedoes.

The Atlantas were graceful ships and were probably the best-looking USN light cruiser. However, they were very cramped which grew worse as the numbers of antiaircraft guns increased and the electronics fit became more complex. When used to lead destroyers in the fierce night battle off Guadalcanal in November 1942, the lightly protected cruisers fared poorly and the USN did not repeat this mistake again. They performed well as carrier-screening units. They were more superdestroyers than true cruisers with their 5in main battery, antisubmarine equipment, and lack of aviation facilities.

The Clevelands were a hurried design which did not consider war experience from Europe. The USN had calculated that a single torpedo hit could sink these cruisers, but not one was lost during the war. *Houston* provided proof they could take heavy damage and survive when it was hit twice by torpedoes. No other Cleveland-class ship was this heavily damaged, and several survived a single torpedo hit with no danger of sinking. Despite their chronic stability problems, they mounted strong antiaircraft and electronic suites.

Most importantly, USN 6in gun cruisers possessed unrivalled offensive capabilities for a light cruiser. The rate of fire of these weapons was unmatched by any other navy. On several occasions in the Solomons, the 6in gun, combined with radar-guided fire control, proved itself as a ship-killer. When handled correctly, as at the Battle of Empress Augusta Bay, USN light cruisers were able to better 8in-gun IJN heavy cruisers. In many situations, it is hard to attribute the loss of specific IJN ships to a specific type of USN gun, but 6in/47cal guns aboard the Brooklyn and Cleveland classes were responsible for the destruction of more major Japanese ships (destroyer size and larger) than any other type of USN gun.

Among the last Cleveland-class cruisers commissioned was *Dayton*, shown here in April 1945. The ship was completed with all late-war modifications including an SK-2 radar on the foremast, Mark 13 radars on the Mark 34 directors, Mark 12/22 radars on the Mark 37 directors, and a full battery of 40mm guns. (Naval History and Heritage Command)

CHAPTER 7
DESTROYERS

It is well known that interwar naval treaties restricted construction of capital ships, but they also affected the construction of destroyers. The London Naval Treaty of 1930 placed limits on overall destroyer construction and restricted the maximum size of destroyers. With these restrictions in place, the USN faced a choice between a small number of larger destroyers with greater capabilities including heavier armament, greater endurance, and superior sea-keeping characteristics, or a larger number of smaller ships which were compromised in one or several of the areas mentioned above. This friction between optimal ship design and overall numbers was never resolved until treaty restrictions were cast aside, which in the case of the USN did not occur until the Fletcher class of 1940.

Between the wars, American naval strategy envisioned a decisive naval engagement somewhere in the western Pacific as the culmination of a steady naval advance toward Japan. In this construct, the decisive arm was the battle line composed of the fleet's battleships. However, destroyers had a key role to play. They had a list of missions, both offensive and defensive. Offensively, they were tasked to probe enemy formations to gauge their strength and then engage in torpedo attacks once the battle was joined. The primary target of these attacks was ideally enemy battleships since they were the central measure of naval power. This required a high tactical speed and a heavy torpedo armament. A heavy gun armament was also required to defend the destroyer from light enemy units as the destroyer closed for a torpedo attack.

There was a constant friction in American destroyer design over which to stress – gun or torpedo armament. Because of its relative lack of light cruisers, the USN expected its destroyers would play a major role in defeating Japanese destroyer attack against the battle line. This, and the need to carry a dual-purpose armament to defend against Japanese air attack from island bases as the USN advanced across the Pacific, mitigated for a strong gun armament.

Evans was a Wickes-class destroyer built at Bath Iron Works. Two of the ship's 4in guns are visible – one on the bow and one on the port platform abreast the four stacks. (Naval History and Heritage Command)

Nevertheless, torpedo armament could not be ignored since this was the only way a destroyer was able to inflict significant damage on heavy enemy units. Though the USN did not foresee many opportunities for a destroyer to use its torpedoes in a fleet engagement, destroyers had to carry a heavy torpedo armament because of the inability to replenish torpedoes at sea. This meant that three or four quadruple launchers were carried to ensure that sufficient torpedoes were carried for two fleet engagements.

Defensively, American destroyers were tasked to screen units of the battle line against the expected attacks by Japanese destroyers. Destroyers would also screen the battle line and other heavy fleet units from enemy submarines; this required effective antisubmarine armament. Also, during the period between the wars, the potential effect of enemy air power began to be appreciated, thus requiring that American destroyers possess some measure of defensive antiaircraft capability.

Given the requirement to operate in the Pacific where high endurance was a must, and the requirement for high speed and a heavy armament of guns and torpedoes, and some antisubmarine and antiaircraft weaponry, American designers favored large destroyer designs. The USN entered the war with many legacy destroyers from World War I and a mix of treaty destroyers. After the end of treaty restrictions, the USN began a huge destroyer building program. At the start of the war, these were just beginning to come into service.

PART 1: THE FLUSH-DECK DESTROYERS

A massive force of 273 Caldwell-, Wickes-, and Clemson-class destroyers was mass-produced during and after World War I. By 1941, 177 remained, including three converted to banana boats, and 50 transferred to the RN. The USN retained some as destroyers, but most were eventually converted into specialized roles and rendered outstanding service until the end of the war.

Wickes Class

When the United States entered World War I, the USN had an immediate need for a large number of destroyers. Only six Caldwell-class destroyers were authorized in 1916. To provide the numbers of destroyers necessary, the USN decided to mass produce destroyers to a design based on the Caldwell class even though this design was deficient in antiaircraft and antisubmarine capabilities. The Wickes class retained the same general arrangements as the Caldwell-class destroyers. To simplify construction, it reverted to a twin-screw arrangement. The design was standardized with four stacks. This feature, and the ships' flush deck, gave them a unique appearance, and the ships were referred to as "four-stackers" or flush-deck destroyers.

Most importantly, the ships were heavily armed with 12 torpedo tubes in four triple-tube mounts (two on each beam), and four 4in/50cal single guns. Two guns were mounted on the centerline and the other two on platforms, one on each beam. A single 3in/23cal gun was fitted for antiaircraft protection.

As the scope of the German submarine threat became more obvious in 1917–18 and the need for destroyers grew, additional Wickes-class destroyers were ordered. In all, 111 were eventually built. The last ship was finally commissioned in April 1921. By 1940, 32 of these ships had been retired. A further 22 were given that year to the RN. Of those remaining in service, six had been converted to high-speed transports and four to minelayers.

In December 1940, a program was begun to convert many of these ships into ASW escorts. This entailed removing the 4in guns and two torpedo mounts and replacing them with 3in dual-purpose guns. Additional depth charges were fitted; subsequent modifications involved the removal of the aft boiler in favor of additional fuel to increase endurance. Twelve other ships were modified into fast transports and nine converted into minesweepers.

Wickes Class Specifications (as built)	
Displacement	Standard 1,154 tons; full 1,247 tons
Dimensions	Length: 314ft 4in; beam 30ft 10in; draft 9ft 2in
Propulsion	4 boilers and 2 geared turbines generating 24,610shp on 2 shafts; maximum speed 35.3 knots
Range	2,500nm at 20kt (design)
Crew	100

Clemson Class

The Clemson class started as an effort to create an improved destroyer but ended as a slightly modified Wickes class. There were very few differences between the two classes. Antisubmarine armament was augmented with Y-gun depth-charge launchers that could launch depth charges broadside. Otherwise, the armament remained the same as for the Wickes class.

Reuben James in the early 1930s. The salient features of the USN's World War I destroyers, the four stacks and a flush deck, are clearly visible. (Naval History and Heritage Command)

The USN ordered 161 of this new class, but only 64 had been started when World War I ended. A total of 144 ships were eventually built with the final Clemson-class destroyer not being completed until August 1922. By the time the last ship was completed, the entire class was outdated. By the start of World War II, it was obsolete. In 1940–41, the USN began recommissioning laid-up flush-deck destroyers. These ships were little changed from their original configuration. Sonar had been added between the wars, and some carried more Y-guns. In December 1940, 37 of the ships were scheduled for the ASW modifications described above for the Wickes class. Only 27 were completed before the war started and the program ended.

By 1940, 14 had been converted to small seaplane tenders, four to minelayers and nine to minesweepers. Twenty were given to the Royal Navy in 1940. Almost all were eventually converted to other uses as more modern ASW ships entered service. In total, 22 flush-deck destroyers were converted to minelayers, 18 to minesweepers, 14 to seaplane tenders, and 36 to fast attack transports. Except for the seaplane tenders, which were later converted back to escorts or minesweepers, the old flush-deck destroyers proved useful in these specialized roles.

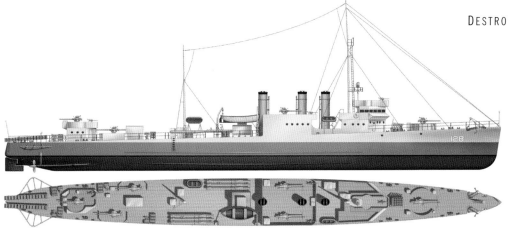

Clemson Class Specifications (as built)	
Displacement	Standard 1,190 tons; full 1,308 tons
Dimensions	Length: 314ft 4in; beam 30ft 10in; draft 9ft 2in
Propulsion	4 boilers and 2 geared turbines generating 27,000shp on 2 shafts; maximum speed 35.5kt
Range	2,500nm at 20kt
Crew	122

PART 2: THE PREWAR-BUILT DESTROYERS

The London Naval Treaty of 1930 extended individual ship and total tonnage limitations to destroyers. The USN's allocation was 150,000 tons, of which 16 percent could be comprised of ships up to 1,850 tons while the balance was not to exceed 1,500 tons. Before the treaty restrictions for destroyers came into effect, the USN had already begun to study new destroyer designs. In 1929, studies yielded a 1,440-ton ship intended to combine the long range and heavy armament needed to operate with a fleet fighting its way across the Pacific. In April 1931, the USN settled on a 1,500-ton ship with increased speed and seaworthiness compared to the flush-deckers.

When the USN decided to resume destroyer construction in 1930, only three private shipbuilders retained their own design departments (Bethlehem Shipbuilding Corporation in Quincy, Massachusetts; New York Shipbuilding in Camden, New Jersey; and Newport News Shipbuilding and Dry Dock Company in Virginia). All three were also licensed to fabricate turbines by Britain's long-time world leader, the Parsons Marine Steam Turbine Co., Ltd. For FY 1932, Congress funded five 1,500-ton destroyers; in June 1932, it funded three more for FY 1933 and then eight 1,850-tonners for FY 1934. Contracts for these 16 destroyers were awarded to two of the big three – Bethlehem for the 1,500-tonners and New York Shipbuilding for the 1,850-ton leaders.

In December 1940, the USN began to modernize its flush-deck destroyers to act as long-range ASW escorts. **THESE VIEWS SHOW** *Babbitt* in 1944 after all these modifications had been completed. The aft torpedo tubes, all four 4in/50cal guns, and the 3in/23cal antiaircraft gun have been removed and replaced with six 3in/50cal dual-purpose guns. In 1942–43, four 20mm guns replaced the machine guns, and the aft boiler and stack was removed to add more fuel. By 1944, a total of four K-guns had been added and a Hedgehog ASW mortar was fitted forward of the bridge. (Artwork by Johnny Shumate, © Osprey Publishing)

This December 1943 view of *Farragut* shows the basic layout of this class with its four single 5in/38cal mounts and two quadruple torpedo mounts. (Naval History and Heritage Command)

Treaty Classes: 1,500-ton Destroyers
Farragut Class

On September 20, 1932, three years into the Great Depression, as national unemployment climbed toward 25 percent, workers at Bethlehem Shipbuilding's nearly empty Fore River Yard in Quincy, Massachusetts, laid down the keel for the USN's first new destroyer since 1922. *Farragut* bore little resemblance to the flush-deckers. For improved strength, the hull was welded with longitudinal frames. Seakeeping was also improved by the incorporation of a raised forecastle, which gave it more than 4ft of additional freeboard at the bow, while amidships its reduced freeboard lowered its center of gravity. Above the bridge, a Mark 33 main battery director controlled the main battery of five 5in/38cal single guns. Two quadruple torpedo tube mounts were also fitted on its centerline abaft the No. 3 5in gun. Depth charges were not part of its original armament, though stern racks were added in 1936.

Farragut was commissioned in March 1934, less than a week before the first destroyers of the next 1,500-ton class were laid down. Bath Iron Works in Maine built two ships in the class while the other six were built at four Navy yards. All joined the fleet by April 1935: average time to launch was 15 months; commissioning took another five. Trials speed was 36.5 knots. Standard displacement turned out to be well under 1,500 tons, which left room for growth within treaty limits. The Farragut-class design set the template for future prewar American destroyer designs.

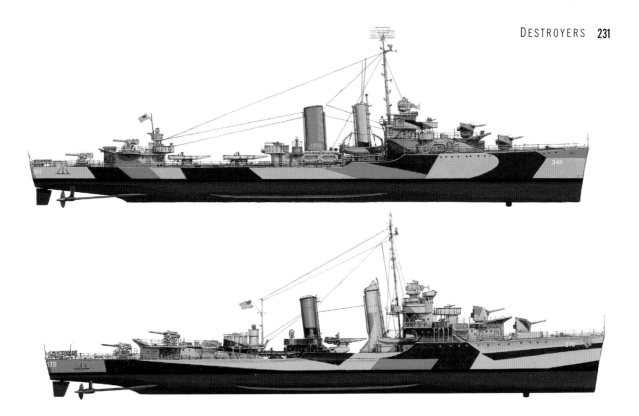

Farragut Class Specifications (as built)	
Displacement	Standard 1,395 tons; full 2,335 tons
Dimensions	Length: 341ft 3in; beam 34ft 3in; draft 8ft 10in
Propulsion	4 boilers and 2 geared turbines generating 42,800shp on 2 shafts; maximum speed 36.5 knots
Range	5,800nm at 15 knots
Crew	250

THE TOP VIEW IS OF *Dewey*, a member of the Farragut class commissioned in 1934. This is its appearance in December 1944. Note the ship retains only four 5in/38cal guns, but still has both its torpedo mounts. The ship carries an antiaircraft fit of two twin 40mm mounts and five single 20mm guns. **THE BOTTOM VIEW IS OF** *Smith*, also in 1944. *Smith* was a member of the Mahan class, considered to be the most successful 1,500-ton destroyer design. The ship retains four 5in/38cal guns and three banks of torpedoes; note the antiaircraft fit of two twin 40mm mounts and five single 20mm guns. (Artwork by Paul Wright, © Osprey Publishing)

Mahan Class

The second 1,500-ton class was the 18-ship Mahan class. The last two ships (*Dunlap* and *Fanning*) were modified slightly and are considered a sub class.

As a result of competitive bidding, contracts for six destroyers were awarded not to the "big three," but two each to Bath Iron Works, Federal Shipbuilding & Dry Dock Co., at Kearny, New Jersey, and United Shipyards, Inc. on Staten Island, New York. Lacking adequate design and drafting organizations of their own, the three chose the firm of Gibbs & Cox to be their design agent. The choice was controversial. the 11-year-old firm had no experience in designing warships. However, it had designed four passenger-cargo liners and fitted them with superheated steam boilers, high-speed turbines and double reduction gears – a propulsion system far more advanced than anything attempted by the USN.

This April 1942 photograph of *Mahan* shows the ship after an overhaul during which the No. 3 5in/38cal mount was removed. The ship still retains four single 5in/38cal guns and 12 torpedo tubes. (Naval History and Heritage Command)

Despite some opposition within the Navy, the Mahan class was the first to use the advanced machinery already developed by General Electric, Westinghouse, and Allis-Chalmers for municipal electric companies. The new propulsion system used superheated boilers and closed feedwater systems to achieve high thermodynamic efficiency. While pressure was kept at 400psi as in the Farraguts, temperature was planned for 850°F but then lowered to 700°F over concerns about the use of ordinary lubricating oil. High- and low-pressure turbine speeds were increased to 5,850rpm and 4,926rpm respectively, which required double reduction gears. Separate 10,000rpm cruising turbines were installed to maximize fuel economy over long distances. Carefully scaled mock-ups were used in planning the engineering spaces, which so impressed the USN that it began specifying them in future contracts. Construction included an increased use of welding.

The torpedo battery was increased to 12 tubes; one mount was placed on the centerline between the stacks and one mount on each beam. Five single 5in/38cal dual-purpose guns were also fitted even with the increase in torpedo armament. These were the best of the USN's 1,500-ton destroyer designs.

Mahan Class Specifications (as built)	
Displacement	Standard 1,488 tons; full 2,103 tons
Dimensions	Length: 341ft 4in; beam 35ft 5in; draft 12ft 4in
Propulsion	4 boilers and 2 geared turbines generating 49,000shp on 2 shafts; maximum speed 36.5kt
Range	6,500nm at 12kt
Crew	158

Gridley Class

Four ships were built to this design, two by Bethlehem Quincy laid down in 1935 and two more by Bethlehem San Francisco the following year. The design reflected pressures to increase the torpedo armament of American destroyers. This was accomplished by fitting four quadruple mounts, two on each beam. The cost for such a heavy battery was the loss of a 5in gun. The four remaining 5in/38cal guns were fitted in single mounts, two forward and two aft. Their appearance was marked with a single large stack. New high-pressure boilers raised the ships' top speed to 38.5 knots.

Gridley Class Specifications (as built)	
Displacement	Standard 1,590 tons; full 2,219 tons
Dimensions	Length: 340ft 10in; beam 35ft 10in; draft 12ft 9in
Propulsion	4 boilers and 2 geared turbines generating 50,000shp on 2 shafts; maximum speed 38.5kt
Range	6,500nm at 12kt
Crew	158

Gridley-class destroyer *Maury* photographed after its completion in mid-1938. These ships were equipped with a massive torpedo battery of four quadruple mounts. (Naval History and Heritage Command)

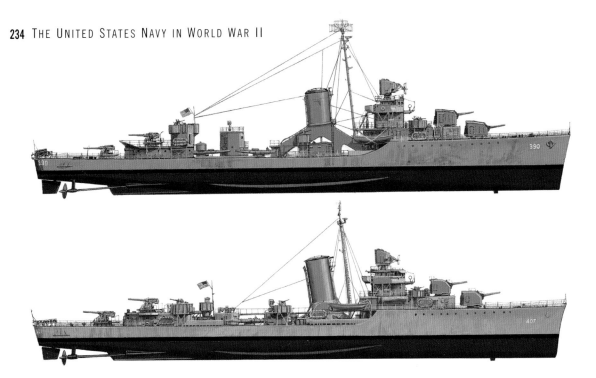

THE TOP PROFILE DEPICTS one of the eight Bagley-class destroyers, *Ralph Talbot*, in 1943. The ship retains its original four quadruple torpedo mounts and four-gun main battery. Six single 20mm guns constitute the ship's antiaircraft battery. Note the boiler uptakes trunked into a single stack. Ten Benham-class ships were commissioned in 1939 and early 1940. The design was an improvement of the Bagley class. **SHOWN IN THE BOTTOM PROFILE IS** *Sterett* in 1943. Two of the ship's torpedo mounts have been removed and replaced by two twin 40mm mounts. (Artwork by Paul Wright, © Osprey Publishing)

Bagley Class

Laid down in 1935 and built in four different Navy yards, the eight-ship Bagley class reverted to the machinery of the earlier Mahan class. Their appearance was similar to the Gridley class with their boiler uptakes trunked into a single stack. The Bagleys carried the same weapons fit as the Gridley class – 16 torpedo tubes in four quadruple mounts, two on each beam and a gun battery of four 5in/38cal guns in single mounts.

Bagley Class Specifications (as built)	
Displacement	Standard 1,646 tons; full 2,245 tons
Dimensions	Length: 341ft 4in; beam 35ft 6in; draft 12ft 10in
Propulsion	4 boilers and 2 geared turbines generating 49,000shp on 2 shafts; maximum speed 38.5kt
Range	6,500nm at 12kt
Crew	158

RIGHT The 12 units of the Bagley class were armed similarly to the Gridley class but carried different machinery. This is a prewar photograph of *Bagley*. (Naval History and Heritage Command)

Benham Class

Ten Benhams were built, three by Federal and seven divided among five Navy yards. Laid down in 1936–37, they commissioned in 1939. There were only small changes from the Bagley class. The new class continued the use of high-speed turbines and double reduction gears. Like the Mahans and successors, they were designed for 850°F but like the Gridleys the class operated at 600 psi and 700°F. With three rather than four boilers and machinery that weighed about 12 percent less, however, its fuel consumption at 12 knots fell by 22 percent compared with the Gridleys and its cruising radius at 15 knots rose by about the same amount. Topside, its more efficient fireroom arrangement paid off in a less congested main deck, differing from the Bagleys in a lack of prominent boiler uptakes. The weapons fit was the same as the Gridley class.

Benham Class Specifications (as built)	
Displacement	Standard 1,637 tons; full 2,250 tons
Dimensions	Length: 340ft 9in; beam 35ft 6in; draft 12ft 10in
Propulsion	3 boilers and 2 geared turbines generating 50,000shp on 2 shafts; maximum speed 38.5kt
Range	6,500nm at 12kt
Crew	184

Benham-class destroyer *Lang* in October 1943. The ship retains the usual four 5in/38cal mounts, but two of the original four torpedo mounts have been removed to provide for additional antiaircraft weaponry. (Naval History and Heritage Command)

Treaty Classes: 1,850-ton Destroyer Leaders

Unlike the RN, the USN had no tradition of destroyer leader designs and although sketches had been prepared in 1917 and 1927, it was only in response to the London Treaty that these ships were produced.

Porter Class

New York Shipbuilding prepared the design and laid keels for four ships in December 1933. Bethlehem Quincy laid down the other four the next year. The first USN destroyer leaders were handsome ships, 40ft longer than the Farraguts, with tripod mainmasts, aft superstructures, and a heavy main gun battery of eight single-purpose 5in/38cal guns in four twin mounts. The guns could only be elevated to a maximum of 35 degrees so could only engage surface targets. Two quadruple 1.1in mounts were fitted for antiaircraft defense. The class carried a torpedo battery of eight 21in tubes in two centerline mounts. They could also carry eight torpedo reloads in special containers abreast the after stack, although reloading under way was impracticable. The ships had space for an embarked staff.

The Porter class was the USN's first attempt to build a destroyer leader. This is the lead ship of the class in November 1941 showing its impressive main battery of four twin 5in/38cal gun mounts and a total of eight torpedo tubes. (Naval History and Heritage Command)

Porter Class Specifications (as built)	
Displacement	Standard 1,834 tons; full 2,597 tons
Dimensions	Length: 381ft 1in; beam 36ft 11in; draft 13ft
Propulsion	4 boilers and 2 geared turbines generating 50,000shp on 2 shafts; maximum speed 37kt
Range	6,500nm at 12kt
Crew	194

Somers Class

The Somers were intended as repeat Porters to fill out the treaty quota of 13 destroyer leaders. Two ships from Federal Shipbuilding, using Gibbs & Cox as its design agent, were funded in 1935 followed by three more from Bath the next year. The Somers machinery was designed to operate at 600psi and 850°F and the performance gains over the previous class were similar – about 22 percent better fuel consumption at 12 knots and 21 percent greater cruising radius at 15 knots compared with the Porters. *Somers'* internal arrangement also permitted trunking the boiler uptakes into a single stack, which made possible three centerline torpedo mounts. Aside from the extra bank of torpedoes, the Somers were armed as the Porter class.

Somers Class Specifications (as built)	
Displacement	Standard 2,047 tons; full 2,767 tons
Dimensions	Length: 381ft; beam 37ft 11in; draft 12ft 5in
Propulsion	4 boilers and 2 geared turbines generating 52,000shp on 2 shafts; maximum speed 37kt
Range	7,500nm at 15kt
Crew	294

Post-Treaty Classes

Sims Class

The expiration of the London Naval Treaty at the end of 1936 allowed American destroyer designers to increase the size of their ships and equip them with heavier weapons fits. The first attempt to do this was the 12-ship Sims class. These ships were laid down in 1937–38 at Bath, Federal, Newport News and four Navy yards. Six were commissioned in 1939 with the others following the next year.

The Sims class was also the first class to incorporate the new Mark 37 main battery director. It was fitted above the forward superstructure in a fully enclosed, armor-protected housing ready to accommodate future fire-control radar. The firing solution "computer" for the director was located below decks. As designed, the weapons fit mirrored the Mahan class' configuration with five 5in/38cals and three torpedo mounts. However, when the first Sims-class ships were completed, they were found to be overweight and exhibited stability problems. Several immediate measures were taken to compensate, including the removal of one of the beam torpedo mounts and moving the other beam mount to the centerline. The remaining uncompleted ships were finished in this configuration.

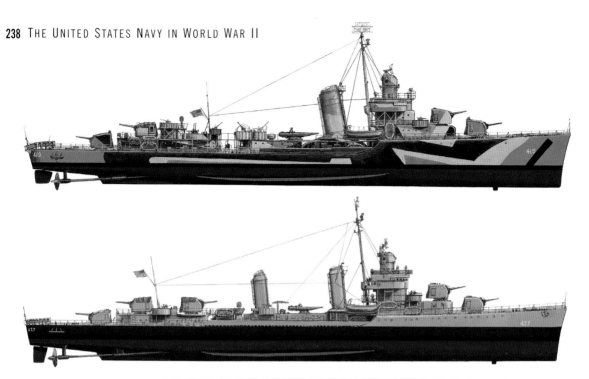

THE TOP PROFILE IS *Wainwright*, a member of the Sims class. By 1944, the ship had its antiaircraft fit reinforced to four twin 20mm mounts and four single 20mm guns. One of its torpedo mounts was removed to compensate for the extra top weight. The Benson class reverted to a two-stack arrangement due to the wide separation of its boiler rooms.

THE BOTTOM PROFILE IS *Hilary P. Jones* with all five of its 5in/38cal guns, but one of its quintuple torpedo mounts has already been removed. (Artwork by Paul Wright, © Osprey Publishing

ABOVE RIGHT This is *Sims* in 1940. The 12 ships of the Sims class were an effort to mount a heavy main battery of five 5in/38cal guns with 12 torpedo tubes. This made the ships dangerously top heavy, forcing the removal of one of the torpedo mounts. (Naval History and Heritage Command)

Sims Class Specifications (as built)	
Displacement	Standard 1,764 tons; full 2,313 tons
Dimensions	Length: 348ft 4in; beam 36ft; draft 12ft 10in
Propulsion	3 boilers and 2 geared turbines generating 50,000shp on 2 shafts; maximum speed 35kt
Range	6,500nm at 12kt
Crew	192

Benson Class

Twenty-four destroyers were funded in FYs 1938, 1939, and 1940, eight per year. Laid down mainly in pairs at Bethlehem, Bath, Federal, and Navy yards, the 24 ships all commissioned within a 12-month period, July 1940–July 1941. The class was intended to be an improved Sims design with the same heavy armament. The stability problems with the Sims class meant the Benson class was completed with the five 5in/38cal and two torpedo mount configuration. For the first time, a quintuple torpedo mount was adopted.

Improvements in boiler technology made it possible to divide the boilers and engines into two "split" plants. In this new arrangement, to minimize the likelihood that a single hit would disable a ship, the forward fireroom and engine room were placed together, as were the after fireroom and engine room. There were two different types of machinery used in the class. The six ships built to the Bethlehem design had round stacks and are often considered as a separate class named after *Gleaves*. The rest of the ships had flat-sided stacks. The ships were some 75 tons heavier than the Sims class due to heavier machinery and a stronger hull. This created ongoing concerns with stability which increased throughout the war.

Benson Class Specifications (as built)	
Displacement	Standard 1,839 tons; full 2,395 tons
Dimensions	Length: 348ft 4in; beam 36ft 1in; draft 13ft 2in
Propulsion	4 boilers and 2 geared turbines generating 50,000shp on 2 shafts; maximum speed 35kt
Range	6,500nm at 12kt
Crew	208

Gwin was one of 24 Benson-class units. It is shown in 1941 in its original configuration with five 5in/38cal guns and two quintuple torpedo mounts. (Naval History and Heritage Command)

Bristol Class

In 1940, with war looming, the USN was compelled to take immediate steps to increase its destroyer fleet. The easiest way to do this was to simply continue the construction of the Benson class. Eventually, 72 of the slightly modified Bristol class were ordered between 1940 and 42. Only a handful were completed before the entry of the United States into the war, and construction continued into August 1943 when the last ship in the class was completed. By the end of their production runs, the high-volume yards, Bethlehem Quincy and Federal, were completing new ships in as little as five months. To simplify construction and improve visibility, the last ten ships from both Federal and Seattle-Tacoma Shipbuilding incorporated "square" bridges. Federal was unusual in building Bristol-class ships alongside more capable Fletcher-class ships.

Because of the prolonged building period for this class, there were several different weapons fits, with many ships being completed with modifications already incorporated on previous ships. All ships carried four 5in/38cals in full gun houses. Until the 40mm became available, 24 of the ships mounted a 1.1in quadruple and five 20mm singles, but two 40mm twins and four 20mm single mounts was the standard early-war antiaircraft fit. The quintuple torpedo mounts were retained, but some ships sacrificed their after bank of torpedo tubes for a massively increased depth charge stowage capability and 6-8 K-gun depth charge projectors.

The 72 units of the Bristol class, like *Duncan* pictured here in October 1942, settled on a standard configuration of four fully enclosed 5in/38cal mounts and a single quintuple bank of torpedoes. (Naval History and Heritage Command)

Bristol Class Specifications (as built)	
Displacement	Standard 1,839 tons; full 2,395 tons
Dimensions	Length: 348ft 4in; beam 36ft 1in; draft 13ft 2in
Propulsion	4 boilers and 2 geared turbines generating 50,000shp on 2 shafts; maximum speed 35kt
Range	6,500nm at 12kt
Crew	208

Modifications to Prewar Destroyers

As American destroyer designers attempted to produce heavily armed and fast ships within treaty restrictions, each of the three design bureaus exceeded their original weight estimates. The result was that successive classes became increasingly top heavy. To compensate, destroyers were ballasted with lead. The Sims class had real problems in this regard as demonstrated in 1939 when one of the ships failed its inclining test, indicating a lack of reserve stability. Immediately, the several Sims that had been completed to their original design lost their No. 3 5in guns and wing torpedo tubes in favor of two centerline mounts. Additional fixes were accomplished by redistributing weight and substituting lighter materials but, as with all the 1,500-tonners before them, there was no substitute for eliminating top weight. Examples of saving top weight included ships being completed with a mix of their after 5in guns being completed with no gun houses or open-topped gun houses covered by canvas for protection against cold and ice. Eventually, any fitting that could not be justified was removed in the name of stability – even one of the anchors, with its hawse pipe plated over.

As built, all the prewar destroyers depended on lookouts stationed in a crow's nest fitted high on the mast for early warning. In 1941, the SC radar entered service and its ungainly stacked-dipole bedspring antenna was mounted atop the foremast. Next to be fitted was a microwave surface search radar, the highly successful SG, with its small rotating parabolic reflector that could be fitted below the SC antenna. Beginning in January 1942, a new gunfire-control radar (the FD, later referred to as the Mark 4), was fitted atop the Mark 37 director.

Competing with the persistent top weight issues on these destroyers was the requirement to improve their antiaircraft protection. When built, most ships carried only four Browning .50cal machine guns, with the quadruple 1.1in machine cannon initially fitted in the destroyer leaders. Both weapons were ineffective in their intended role. As soon as production allowed, the .50cal machine guns were replaced by 20mm guns in free-swinging mounts. Usually, six of these weapons were fitted early in the war. Since the 20mm gun lacked stopping power, the 40mm Bofors gun was preferred, especially after the advent of the kamikaze in October 1944. As early as mid-1942, the water-cooled 40mm twin mount replaced the 1.1in quad. With a Mark 51 director, the effective range of the 40mm was about 4,000 yards. Many ships landed their amidships 5in mount with its compromised arc of fire in exchange for more 20mm guns, which were later replaced by 40mm twin mounts. By 1945, when air attack was the predominant threat, some destroyers received a kamikaze refit. At the expense of all remaining torpedo tubes, many ships received as many as four 40mm twin mounts and four twin 20mm mounts. The USN preferred the quadruple 40mm mount for antiaircraft work, but due to its weight, only the destroyer leaders received one quadruple mount late in the war, as did a handful of 1,500-tonner ships. To increase the ASW capabilities of these ships, especially those operating in the Atlantic, the stern racks were modified to carry more depth charges and outboard-mounted K-gun depth charge projectors appeared at the end of 1941 to replace the centerline-mounted Y-gun.

PART 3: THE WAR-BUILT DESTROYERS

The USN's wartime destroyer construction program focused on three classes – the 2,100-ton Fletcher class and its larger Allen M. Sumner- and Gearing-class derivatives. American shipyards produced an enormous number of these ships, 287 (including an astounding 175 Fletchers making it the largest destroyer class ever built), doubling the USN's destroyer force. These ships were not just numerous, they were a fine balance of ruggedness and seaworthiness, armament, speed, and survivability.

Fletcher Class

This was the first class of American destroyer built completely free of treaty restrictions and its design took advantage of wartime lessons. The first ship was not ordered until mid-1940, and the first did not reach the Pacific until late 1942. The ship was much bigger than previous designs and therefore permitted the use of powerful machinery for a high maximum speed (38 knots), a strong gun and torpedo armament, and even some protective plating to key areas like the bridge, command, and machinery areas. The main battery was five 5in/38cal mounts able to conduct dual-purpose fire guided by the excellent Mark 37 director. The ships' increased size made them capable of accepting additional antiaircraft guns without sacrificing any of the 5in mounts or torpedoes. Torpedo armament was two quintuple mounts with no reloads.

Nicholas, shown here, made 36.43 knots on trials on May 28, 1942. This view gives a fine impression of the power of these ships. The ship was commissioned on June 4, 1942, and its radar has not yet been fitted. (Naval History and Heritage Command)

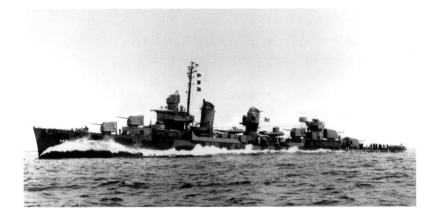

Johnston photographed on October 27, 1943 the same day it was commissioned after being completed at Seattle-Tacoma. Note the standard electronics fit comprised of an SC air search radar atop the mast, a SG surface search radar on a platform just below it, and a Mark 12 fire control radar atop the Mark 37 director. (Naval History and Heritage Command)

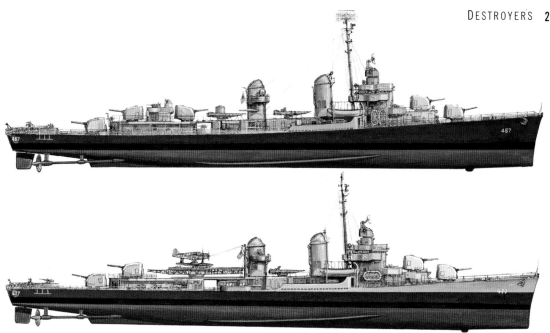

The design of the Fletcher class stemmed from the fact that Benson- and Bristol-class ships were top heavy and could not carry five 5in guns and ten torpedoes as designed. In October 1939, the General Board began internal hearings regarding design characteristics for a new destroyer to be funded in FY 1941. The result was an enlarged 2,050-ton design that could comfortably mount the Bensons' originally intended armament. On January 27, 1940, the design was approved by the Secretary of the Navy and soon the firm of Gibbs & Cox was selected as design agent. Alarming events in Europe led to Congress appropriating funds for the first 25 Fletchers in June, and as their delivery could not be expected for two years, Congress also authorized more destroyers of the preceding classes. In July, Congress passed the Two-Ocean Navy Act, the largest single naval building program in US history, which provided for 115 additional destroyers.

Not only was the Fletcher-class the best destroyer of World War II, but it was capable of being built in such numbers as to make it a war-winning weapon. Eleven shipyards built 175 Fletchers. Federal Shipbuilding & Dry Dock Company of Kearny, New Jersey, the lead yard, delivered 29. Bath Iron Works, the most prolific, completed 31 including the first one, *Nicholas*. The new destroyers were delivered at a rate of three per month in mid-1942, climbing to five in October, and ten or more in seven of the last eight months of 1943. The Charleston and Boston Navy yards were fastest to launch; two from the former took only 77 days. Excluding those from the Puget Sound Navy Yard and Gulf Shipbuilding, the average was 193 days and, excluding six ships set aside for an aborted floatplane catapult installation, the average from keel laying to commissioning was 331 days. All except two were delivered by the end of 1944.

THE TOP PROFILE DEPICTS *Strong*, the fourth Fletcher built at Bath Iron Works and the first fitted with a 40mm twin Bofors between the No. 3 and No. 4 5in mounts. The ship presents a graceful appearance with its widely spaced stacks, five-gun main battery, and two quintuple torpedo mounts. **THE BOTTOM PROFILE SHOWS** one of the six round-bridge Fletchers scheduled for modification during construction to take a floatplane catapult. *Pringle* and two others were completed with this arrangement, which *Pringle* used in January 1943 while escorting a convoy in the Atlantic. The catapult was not considered a success and was soon removed. (Artwork by Paul Wright, © Osprey Publishing)

Fletcher class	
Hull Numbers	**Names**
445–451	Fletcher,[A1] Radford,[A1] Jenkins,[A1] La Vallette,[A1] Nicholas,[A2] O'Bannon,[A2] Chevalier[A2]
465–475	Saufley,[A1] Waller,[A1] Strong,[A2] Taylor,[A2] De Haven,[A2] Bache,[A3] Beale,[A3] Guest,[A4] Bennett,[A4] Fullam,[A4] Hudson[A4]
476–481*	Hutchins,[A4] Pringle,[A5] Stanly,[A5] Stevens,[A5] Halford,[A6] Leutze[A6]
498–502	Philip,[A1] Renshaw,[A1] Ringgold,[A1] Schroeder,[A1] Sigsbee[A1]
507–522	Conway,[A2] Cony,[A2] Converse,[A2] Eaton,[A2] Foote,[A2] Spence,[A2] Terry,[A2] Thatcher,[A2] Anthony,[A2] Wadsworth,[A2] Walker,[A2] Brownson,[B3] Daly,[B3] Isherwood,[B3] Kimberly,[B3] Luce[B3]
526–541	Abner Read,[B7] Ammen,[B7] Mullany,[B7] Bush,[B7] Trathen,[B7] Hazelwood,[B7] Heermann,[B7] Hoel,[B7] McCord,[B7] Miller,[B7] Owen,[B7] The Sullivans,[B7] Stephen Potter,[B7] Tingey,[B7] Twining,[B7] Yarnall[B7]
544–547	Boyd,[B8] Bradford,[B8] Brown,[B8] Cowell[B8]
550–597	Capps,[A9] David W. Taylor,[A9] Evans,[A9] John D. Henley,[A9] Franks,[B10] Haggard,[B10] Hailey,[B10] Johnston,[B10] Laws,[B10] Longshaw,[B10] Morrison,[B10] Prichett,[B10] Robinson,[B10] Ross,[B10] Rowe,[B10] Smalley,[B10] Stoddard,[B10] Watts,[B10] Wren,[B10] Aulick,[A11] Charles Ausburne,[A11] Claxton,[A11] Dyson,[A11] Harrison,[A11] John Rodgers,[A11] McKee,[A11] Murray,[A11] Sproston,[A11] Wickes,[A11] William D. Porter,[A11] Young,[A11] Charrette,[B4] Conner,[B4] Hall,[B4] Halligan,[B4] Haraden,[B4] Newcomb,[B4] Bell,[B5] Burns,[B5] Izard,[B5] Paul Hamilton,[B5] Twiggs,[B5] Howorth,[A6] Killen,[A6] Hart,[B6] Metcalf,[B6] Shields,[B6] Wiley[B6]
629–631	Abbot,[B2] Braine,[B2] Erben[B2]
642–644	Hale,[B2] Sigourney,[B2] Stembel[B2]
649–691	Albert W. Grant,[B5] Caperton,[B2] Cogswell,[B2] Ingersoll,[B2] Knapp,[B2] Bearss,[B9] John Hood,[B9] Van Valkenburgh,[B9] Charles J. Badger,[B3] Colahan,[B3] Dashiell,[B1] Bullard,[B1] Kidd,[B1] Bennion,[B4] Heywood L. Edwards,[B4] Richard P. Leary,[B4] Bryant,[B5] Black,[B1] Chauncey,[B1] Clarence K. Bronson,[B1] Cotten,[B1] Dortch,[B1] Gatling,[B1] Healy,[B1] Hickox,[B1] Hunt,[B1] Lewis Hancock,[B1] Marshall,[B1] McDermut,[B1] McGowan,[B1] McNair,[B1] Melvin,[B1] Hopewell,[B8] Porterfield,[B8] Stockham,[B7] Wedderburn,[B7] Picking,[B3] Halsey Powell,[B3] Uhlmann,[B3] Remey,[B2] Wadleigh,[B2] Norman Scott,[B2] Mertz[B2]
792–804	Callaghan,[B8] Cassin Young,[B8] Irwin,[B8] Preston,[B8] Benham,[B3] Cushing,[B3] Monssen,[B3] Jarvis,[B10] Porter,[B10] Colhoun,[B10] Gregory,[B10] Little,[B10] Rooks[B10]

*Initially intended for a floatplane catapult [A] Round bridge [B] Square bridge

[1] Federal, Kearny [2] Bath Iron Works [3] Bethlehem, Staten Island [4] Boston NY [5] Charleston NY [6] Puget Sound NY [7] Bethlehem, San Francisco
[8] Bethlehem, San Pedro [9] Gulf, Chickasaw AL [10] Seattle-Tacoma [11] Consolidated, Orange TX

Freed from treaty restrictions, the designers came up with a destroyer much larger and more capable than any USN destroyer before it. Design for the "2,100-ton" class began with a flush-deck hull with increased draft amidships for greater strength. At 376.5ft, its overall length was 28.5ft (nearly 8 percent) greater than the Benson and Bristol classes.

The propulsion machinery was that newly standardized with the Bristol class – using high-pressure, high-temperature steam, which delivered 20 to 30 percent greater efficiency than contemporary foreign designs. Babcock & Wilcox or Foster Wheeler manufactured the boilers; General Electric, Westinghouse, or Allis-Chalmers produced the steam turbines, which were rated at 60,000 total shp, 20 percent more than the Bristol class. Design speed was 38 knots – 5 knots faster than the contemporary Essex-class carriers and Iowa-class battleships that the new destroyers would screen.

The ships' engineering spaces occupied the central third of the ship. Another third was devoted to fuel and ammunition, which left the final third for the crew. The general arrangement carried over the split powerplant pioneered in the Benhams. Immediately abaft the forward fireroom was the forward engine room, which drove the starboard shaft; the after fireroom and engine room formed a separate pair. All were isolated from the rest of the ship by watertight bulkheads and could be entered only via vertical ladders descending from scuttles in the main deck. The new destroyers proved unable of attaining their design speed of 38 knots. *Nicholas* reached 37.1 on trials at a moderate displacement and, while runs of 36 knots or more were occasionally logged under wartime conditions, 34 knots was generally regarded as their best formation speed.

The main gun battery consisted of five 5in/38cal dual-purpose guns. Four guns in single mounts were fitted fore and aft. A fifth gun was added amidships, where its arc of fire was restricted to 140 degrees on either side – less at low elevation. Controlling the 5in guns was a Mark 37 director mounted atop the bridge structure with an optical rangefinder plus its own fire-control radar. Through electrical connections to a computer in a plotting room below decks, the director could control the guns for both antiair and surface action.

This is *Spence* in its late-war appearance in October 1944. The ship was lost two months later in a typhoon. Note the addition of ECM equipment on a small pole mast above the aft deck house. (NARA)

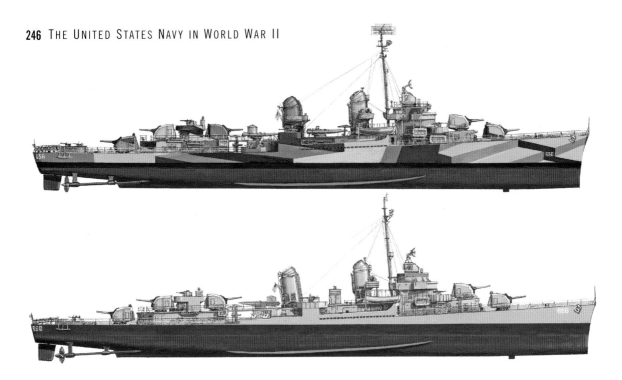

Complementing the main battery was a powerful torpedo battery of ten tubes, arranged in two quintuple mounts. The first was placed between the two stacks and the second abaft the aft stack. The standard torpedo was the Mark 15, which was 24ft long and weighed 3,850lb with an 825lb warhead. Depending on the speed setting, range was from 6,000 yards at 45 knots up to 15,000 yards at 26.5 knots. Running depth could be set from a torpedo director on the bridge or locally. The Mark 15 quickly proved to be unreliable – running too deep and exploding prematurely or not at all. These problems, which doubtless would have been corrected before the war had funds been available for adequate testing, proved difficult to find and fix during wartime. Only in 1943 did the Mark 15 come into its own as an effective weapon.

Antiaircraft protection became an increasingly important consideration as the war progressed. Most of the USN's 1,500-ton destroyers were completed with a light antiaircraft battery of four .50cal machine guns – clearly inadequate and inferior to foreign destroyers being built during the same period. Despite the larger size of the Fletchers, they were initially designed with only a single 1.1in quadruple mount and four machine guns for antiaircraft protection. Only a few ships were fitted with the 1.1in quadruple mount since by the time they were nearing completion, the 20mm Oerlikon and the 40mm Bofors guns were becoming available. By late 1941, the standard antiaircraft fit was one twin 40mm mount in place of the 1.1in mount and six single 20mm mounts. By the mid-war period, the standard antiaircraft fit was raised to five twin 40mm mounts (two abreast the bridge, two abreast the aft stack, and one aft) and seven 20mm guns. Late in the war, 57 Fletchers received the kamikaze refit to further enhance their air defenses. This entailed replacing the amidships twin 40mm mounts with two quadruple 40mm mounts equipped with the latest fire control to allow blind fire. The four single 20mm guns on the waist were replaced with twin mounts, raising the total to 11 20mm guns. To compensate, the forward torpedo mount was landed.

For ASW work, each Fletcher carried sonar. A heavy depth charge fit included two stern racks and six K-guns abreast the aft deckhouse.

One recognition feature differentiated the Fletchers from one another. Fifty-eight – one-third of the total – were completed with the round-faced bridge structure introduced in the Sims class; the remainder were built with a square-faced pilot house and a walkaround platform forward for improved all-around observation plus a lowered gun director for a reduced silhouette and improved stability.

The most unusual Fletcher variant was one equipped with a catapult and one aircraft. To fit the catapult, the No. 3 5in gun and the aft bank of torpedoes was removed. The cramped operating conditions made this arrangement impracticable, so only three of the six ships planned received a catapult, and they were soon removed from these three.

Fletcher Class Specifications (as built)	
Displacement	Standard 2,325 tons; full 2,924 tons
Dimensions	Length: 376ft 6in; beam 39ft 7in; draft 13ft 9in
Propulsion	4 boilers and 2 geared turbines generating 60,000shp on 2 shafts; maximum speed 38 knots
Range	6,500nm at 15 knots
Crew	273

Allen M. Sumner Class

The first Fletchers were still under construction when the General Board convened a new cycle of hearings in October 1941. These spawned a revised design in which three 5in/38cal twin mounts replaced the Fletchers' five single mounts. The Secretary of the Navy approved the new design in May 1942. Again, Federal was assigned the lead ship – *Allen M. Sumner* – and again Bath was first to lay a keel – *Barton* on May 24, 1943, a mere two weeks after completing its last Fletcher. To accommodate the twin turrets, designers widened the Fletcher hull by 14in and increased standard displacement by 200 tons. The length from the Fletchers remained

ABOVE This is Sumner-class destroyer *Barton* running trials on December 29, 1943. The similarity of the Sumner class to the preceding Fletcher class is apparent with the salient exceptions being the twin 5in/38cal mounts and the placement of the aft torpedo mount. (NARA)

BELOW This view shows *Allen M. Sumner* as completed with the enclosed "British-style" pilot house running trials on March 26, 1944. The Sumner class was the first to incorporate a built-in Combat Information Center. (Naval History and Heritage Command)

unchanged and the same machinery was planned. The extra displacement translated into a design speed of about one less knot, but in practice the actual loss was greater.

Nineteen early Sumners received a low bridge but complaints that it was very cramped resulted in a revised arrangement similar to that of the square-bridge Fletchers. Below the waterline, to reduce the Fletchers' wide turning radius, the Sumners were completed with twin rudders. Also added was a diesel generator capacity, a deckhouse that provided a passageway between the forward and after berthing quarters, and later adoption of four-bladed screws turning at reduced rpm to lessen cavitation.

The main battery was arranged in three twin mounts, two forward and one aft. Four guns could fire on forward bearings; in an unusual feature, the aft mount could fire over the mast to engage targets forward. As on the Fletchers, the new class carried two quintuple torpedo mounts. The original antiaircraft fit was limited to two twin 40mm mounts and four 20mm guns.

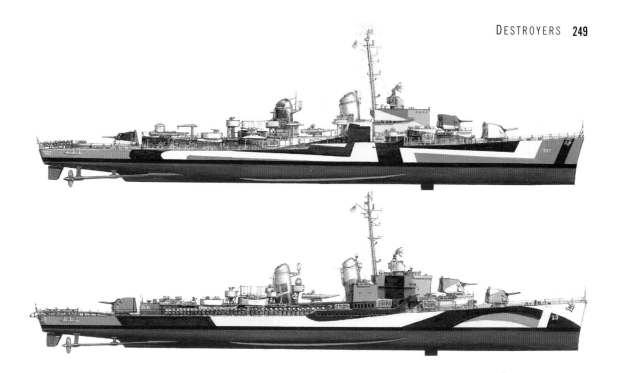

By the time most ships were completed, the antiaircraft suite had been greatly increased to two quadruple 40mm and two twin 40mm mounts, and ten single 20mm guns. By the end of the war, some ships had shed their aft torpedo mount in favor of a third quadruple 40mm mount and had ten twin 20mm replace the single 20mm mounts.

THE TOP VIEW SHOWS *De Haven* when completed in 1944. The Sumner class was built on the same size hull as the Fletcher class but had important differences. The main gun battery was increased to six 5in/38cals in three twin turrets and the ships carried a heavier antiaircraft battery. **THE BOTTOM PROFILE DEPICTS** *Robert H. Smith*, the lead ship of a class of 12 Sumner-class destroyers converted as high-speed minelayers. To carry up to 120 mines, the torpedo mounts and some antiaircraft guns had to be removed. None of these ships were used during the war in minelaying operations. (Artwork by Paul Wright, © Osprey Publishing)

Allen M. Sumner class	
Hull Numbers	**Names**
692–709	*Allen M. Sumner,*[1] *Moale,*[1] *Ingraham,*[1] *Cooper,*[1] *English,*[1] *Charles S. Sperry,*[1] *Ault,*[1] *Waldron,*[1] *Haynsworth,*[1] *John W. Weeks,*[1] *Hank,*[1] *Wallace L. Lind,*[1] *Borie,*[1] *Compton,*[1] *Gainard,*[1] *Soley,* [1] *Harlan R. Dickson,*[1] *Hugh Purvis*[1]
722–741	*Barton,*[2] *Walke,*[2] *Laffey,*[2] *O'Brien,*[2] *Meredith,*[2] *De Haven,*[2] *Mansfield,*[2] *Lyman K. Swenson,*[2] *Collett,*[2] *Maddox,*[2] *Hyman,*[2] *Mannert L. Abele,*[2] *Purdy,*[2] *Robert H. Smith,*[A2] *Thomas E. Fraser,*[A2] *Shannon,*[A2] *Harry F. Bauer,*[A2] *Adams,*[A2] *Tolman,*[A2] *Drexler*[2]
744–762	*Blue,*[3] *Brush,*[3] *Taussig,*[3] *Samuel N. Moore,*[3] *Harry E. Hubbard,*[3] *Henry A. Wiley,*[A3] *Shea,*[A3] *J. William Ditter,*[A3] *Alfred A. Cunningham,*[3] *John R. Pierce,*[3] *Frank E. Evans,*[3] *John A. Bole,*[3] *Beatty,*[3] *Putnam,*[4] *Strong,*[4] *Lofberg,*[4] *John W. Thomason,*[B4] *Buck,*[B4] *Henley*[B4]
770–781	*Lowry,*[5] *Lindsey,*[A5] *Gwin,*[A5] *Aaron Ward,*[A5] *Hugh W. Hadley,*[5] *Willard Keith,*[5] *James C. Owens,*[5] *Zellars,*[6] *Massey,*[6] *Douglas H. Fox,*[6] *Stormes,*[6] *Robert K. Huntington*[6]
857	*Bristol*[6]
[A] Destroyer–minelayer (DM 23–34) [B] Commissioned after World War II [1] Federal, Kearny [2] Bath Iron Works [3] Bethlehem, Staten Island [4] Bethlehem, San Francisco [5] Bethlehem, San Pedro [6] Todd, Tacoma	

This is *Robert H. Smith*, lead ship of a class of high-speed minelayers converted from Sumner-class destroyers. Note the two mine tracks that lead to its stern and the absence of torpedo mounts. (Naval History and Heritage Command)

Seventy Sumners were completed, beginning with *Barton* on December 30, 1943. All but three were commissioned during the war at an average time from keel laying of 266 days.

During construction, 12 Sumners were fitted with tracks for mines and designated fast minelayers, becoming known as the Robert H. Smith class. To carry up to 120 mines, these ships lost both torpedo mounts, three 20mm guns, and two depth charge launchers.

Allen M. Sumner Class Specifications (as built)	
Displacement	Standard 2,619 tons; full 3,218 tons
Dimensions	Length: 376ft 6in; beam 40ft 10in; draft 14ft 2in
Propulsion	4 boilers and 2 geared turbines generating 60,000shp on 2 shafts; maximum speed 36.5 knots
Range	3,300nm at 20 knots
Crew	336

Gearing Class

The Sumner class demonstrated a disappointing endurance in service. To remedy this, a production variant was approved with another 14ft added to increase fuel capacity by more than 40 percent. The new class was named after the lead ship, *Gearing*. Other than the extra space added between the two stacks, and an increase in displacement, the ships were virtually identical to the Sumners. One hundred and fifty-two Gearings were ordered. Federal

built the lead ship plus nine more at a new facility at Port Newark, New Jersey. Bath delivered the first two, *Frank Knox* and *Southerland*, in December 1944. Forty-five were completed before the end of the war, and the total of ships built to this design eventually reached 93.

In January 1945, considering experience with kamikaze tactics and the planned invasion of Japan, the first seven Gearings from Bath and the first five from Orange began undergoing conversion to radar picket destroyers. An additional 12 were also planned for conversion. However, only Bath's first five arrived in the Pacific by June 1945 in time to earn campaign medals. The radar picket conversion removed the forward torpedo mounts and the addition of a mast with an SP height-finding radar, and IFF and ECM equipment. The aft torpedo mount was also removed and replaced by a third quadruple 40mm mount.

ABOVE The Gearing class was a lengthened variant of the Sumner class. The difference between the two classes was an extra 14ft amidships. The Gearing class can be differentiated by the greater space between the two stacks. This view is of *Frank Knox* running trials in December 1944. (NARA)

LEFT This is *Chevalier*, one of five Gearings to see war service. It has completed the conversion to a radar picket as seen by the radar mast placed between the stacks. (NARA)

Gearing class	
Hull Numbers	**Names**
710–721	*Gearing,*[1] *Eugene A. Greene,*[1] *Gyatt,*[1] *Kenneth D. Bailey,*[1] *William R. Rush,*[A1] *William M. Wood,*[A1] *Wiltsie,*[A1] *Theodore E. Chandler,*[A1] *Hamner,*[A1] *Epperson*[A1]
742–743	*Frank Knox,*[2] *Southerland*[6]
763–765	*William C. Lawe,*[A3] *Lloyd Thomas,*[A3] *Keppler*[A3]
782–790	*Rowan,*[4] *Gurke,*[4] *McKean,*[4] *Henderson,*[4] *Richard B. Anderson,*[A4] *James E. Kyes,*[A4] *Hollister,*[A4] *Eversole,*[A4] *Shelton*[A4]
805–853	*Chevalier,*[2] *Higbee,*[2] *Benner,*[2] *Dennis J. Buckley,*[2] *Corry,*[A5] *New,*[A5] *Holder,*[A5] *Rich,*[A5] *Johnston,*[A5] *Robert H. McCard,*[A5] *Samuel B. Roberts,*[A5] *Basilone,*[A5] *Carpenter,*[A5] *Agerholm,*[A2] *Robert A. Owens,*[A2] *Timmerman,*[A2] *Myles C. Fox,*[2] *Everett F. Larson,*[2] *Goodrich,*[2] *Hanson,*[2] *Herbert J. Thomas,*[2] *Turner,*[2] *Charles P. Cecil,*[2] *George K. MacKenzie,*[2] *Sarsfield,*[2] *Ernest G. Small,*[2] *Power,*[A2] *Glennon,*[A2] *Noa,*[A2] *Fiske,*[A2] *Warrington,*[A2] *Perry,*[A2] *Baussell,*[A2] *Ozbourn,*[A2] *Robert L. Wilson,*[A2] *Witek,*[A2] *Richard E. Kraus,*[A2] *Joseph P. Kennedy, Jr.,*[A6] *Rupertus,*[A6] *Leonard F. Mason,*[A6] *Charles H. Roan*[A6]
858–890	*Fred T. Berry,*[A7] *Norris,*[7] *McCaffery,*[7] *Harwood,*[A7] *Vogelgesang,*[8] *Steinaker,*[8] *Harold J. Ellison,*[8] *Charles R. Ware,*[8] *Cone,*[8] *Stribling,*[A8] *Brownson,*[A8] *Arnold J. Isbell,*[A8] *Fechteler,*[A8] *Damato,*[A8] *Forrest Royal,*[A8] *Hawkins,*[5] *Duncan,*[5] *Henry W. Tucker,*[5] *Rogers,*[5] *Perkins,*[5] *Vesole,*[5] *Leary,*[5] *Dyess,*[5] *Bordelon,*[5] *Furse,*[5] *Newman K. Perry,*[5] *Floyd B. Parks,*[5] *John R. Craig,*[5] *Orleck,*[A5] *Brinkley Bass,*[A5] *Stickell,*[A5] *O'Hare,*[A5] *Meredith*[A5]
[A] Commissioned after World War II [1] Federal, Port Newark [2] Bath Iron Works [3] Bethlehem, San Francisco [4] Todd, Tacoma [5] Consolidated, Orange TX [6] Bethlehem, Quincy [7] Bethlehem, San Pedro [8] Bethlehem, Staten Island	

Gearing Class Specifications (as built)	
Displacement	Standard 2,616 tons; full 3,460 tons
Dimensions	Length: 390ft 6in; beam 40ft 10in; draft 14ft 4in
Propulsion	4 boilers and 2 geared turbines generating 60,000shp on 2 shafts; maximum speed 36.8 knots
Range	4,500nm at 20 knots
Crew	336

USN DESTROYERS – AN ANALYSIS

American destroyers were well-balanced ships that proved capable of performing many different missions requiring capabilities in all naval warfare areas. USN destroyers were designed primarily as platforms to attack other ships and were given formidable gun and torpedo batteries to accomplish this mission. Thrown into the surface battles around Guadalcanal, they performed poorly in this mission because of doctrinal and equipment faults. In 1942, destroyers were not used as independent strike platforms, but even if they had been, the problems with the Mark 15 torpedo would have curtailed their effectiveness. Once the faults with the Mark 15 were addressed and American admirals discovered the power of the torpedo in night combat, American

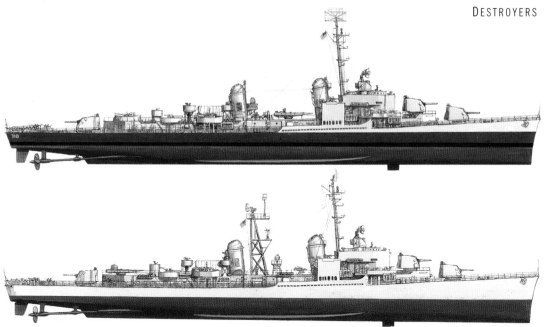

destroyers outperformed their vaunted Japanese counterparts in the latter part of the Solomons campaign in 1943 and for the remainder of the war.

American destroyers possessed superior antiaircraft capabilities compared to other navies by virtue of their excellent weaponry and superior fire-control systems. The ultimate test in this regard came during the Okinawa campaign when USN destroyers were deployed to unsupported radar picket stations and came under sustained kamikaze attack. Between February and May 1945, 38 percent of all kamikaze attacks selected destroyers for attack. Attacking destroyers was not the best choice for kamikazes since they possessed the firepower and maneuvering capability to defend themselves. The intensity of kamikaze attacks resulted in 13 destroyers being sunk and many others damaged, but by taking the brunt of these attacks USN destroyers absorbed the attention of many kamikazes that should have been devoted to other more valuable and vulnerable targets.

In addition to being good antiaircraft and eventually excellent antisurface platforms, USN destroyers were capable ASW platforms. In the Pacific, they sank or were the primary agent in sinking some 36 IJN submarines. In return, three American destroyers were lost to Japanese submarine attack during the war, and German U-boats only accounted for only six.

Compared to the destroyers of other navies, USN destroyers were the best all-around destroyers of the war. This was epitomized by the Fletcher class. Japanese destroyers also had a well-deserved reputation for excellence, but that was driven by their performance in one area – as torpedo boats. They proved very vulnerable to submarine and air attack as the war progressed.

THE TOP PROFILE DEPICTS the lead ship of the long-hull Sumner class was *Gearing*, which completed at Federal's new facility at Port Newark, New Jersey and commissioned on May 3, 1945, but did not see action in World War II. The ship has had its aft torpedo mount replaced with a 40mm quadruple mount. The ship's antiaircraft consisted of three 40mm quadruple mounts and 11 single 20mm guns.
IN THE BOTTOM VIEW *Southerland*, Bath's second Gearing, is shown in 1945. The ship has been converted into a radar picket destroyer with a radar mast replacing the forward bank of torpedo tubes. (Artwork by Paul Wright, © Osprey Publishing)

CHAPTER 8
SUBMARINES

When it entered the war in December 1941, the USN had 112 submarines in commission. Half of this impressive total consisted of boats dating back to just after World War I. When the USN began combat operations, it also had 65 submarines on order. These were Gato-class boats that would soon prove they were war-winning weapons.

PART 1: THE OLD CLASSES

The O, R, and S classes were commissioned from 1916 to 1924. Many were placed in reserve during the 1920s and 1930s but were brought back into service in 1941 as training boats. The S class was used in combat for the opening period of the war.

The O Class was a small coastal submarine of 529 tons with a crew of 29 commissioned from 1916 to 1918. Of the 16 built, one was lost in 1941 to an accident and seven remained in service until 1945 as training boats. Nineteen of the slightly larger R class were also retained for training duties until 1945. Three were transferred to the RN during the war and another was lost to operational reasons.

The much larger (51 boats) and more capable S class was commissioned from 1918 to 1924. Though not large and fast enough to be considered "fleet" boats (able to operate with the battle fleet), and though clearly obsolescent by 1941, they were kept in service and some were assigned to combat duties until replaced by newer designs in late 1943. All but nine survived until the end of the war in training commands. There were four variants of the S class, but in general they had a displacement of 840–870 tons, a length of 219–231ft, with a top surface speed of 15 knots from two diesel engines. Endurance was limited to 5,000nm at 10 knots, which was

The 12 boats of the Tambor class were the final maturation of the fleet boat design before the massive expansion of the submarine force with the Gato and Balao classes. Built to peacetime standards, they were probably the best USN submarines in terms of habitability. This is *Tambor* after a mid-war modification to its conning tower. (Naval History and Heritage Command)

ABOVE *S-39* photographed prewar still displaying its pendant number. Note the 4in deck gun forward. (Naval History and Heritage Command)

a major restriction in the immense Pacific. They were armed with four torpedo tubes (with a torpedo capacity of 12) and carried either a 3in or 4in deck gun.

PART 2: THE PREWAR CLASSES
The V-Boats

These nine boats, built from 1921 to 1934, were from five separate classes. Built with the numbers *V-1* through *V-9*, they were given names in 1931. Among them were the largest non-nuclear boats ever built by the USN. The example driving the construction of these large boats was the German U-cruisers from World War I. To operate as commerce raiders, the boats exchanged high speed for long endurance, a large number of torpedoes, and large-caliber deck guns.

The first three were commissioned between 1924 and 1926. The boats were not successful in service. Their machinery was unreliable and they failed to make their design speed either on the surface or submerged. They were also poor sea boats. After a few defensive war patrols, all three were relegated to training duties for the remainder of the war.

BELOW *Barracuda* (formerly *V-1*) was a large cruiser-type submarine commissioned in 1924. Note the large 5in/51cal deck gun in front of the conning tower. These submarines were decommissioned in 1937 but brought back into service during the war as transport submarines. The conversion was not successful. (Naval History and Heritage Command)

V-4, renamed *Argonaut*, was the largest of the V-boats and the only USN submarine designed as a minelayer. It and the three previous boats carried the largest deck guns on any USN submarine – two 6in/53cal single guns. As a minelayer, the boat was not a success because of its complex minelaying system. Able to carry 16 torpedoes, later increased to 20, with four (increased to six in 1942) torpedo tubes, it remained useful, but was too unwieldy for patrol duties. It was converted to a transport submarine able to carry 120 Marines and was employed successfully in that role.

V-4 Specifications (as built)	
Displacement	Standard 2,710 tons; submerged 4,164 tons
Dimensions	Length: 381ft; beam 33ft 10in
Propulsion	2 diesel engines generating 3,175shp for a maximum surface speed of 13.65kt; submerged speed 7.43kt
Operating depth	300ft
Range	18,000nm at 10kt; patrol endurance 90 days
Crew	86

Narwhal, shown here in 1932, was the USN's last attempt to create a large cruiser-type submarine. Note the two 6in/53cal deck guns, the largest ever carried by a USN submarine. Though used for patrols at the start of the war, *Narwhal* and its sister boat *Nautilus* proved more useful as transport submarines assigned to special missions. (Naval History and Heritage Command)

The next two V-boats, *V-5* and *V-6* – later renamed *Narwhal* and *Nautilus* – were essentially repeats of *V-4* but without the minelaying equipment. Instead the boats had a heavy torpedo armament of four bow and two stern tubes with a large torpedo load of up to 38–40 torpedoes (24–26 internal and another 12–16 stored externally). The size of these boats made them slow to dive and easy to spot both on the surface and at shallow depths. After the war began, both were modernized with more reliable diesel engines and four external torpedo tubes. Both ships conducted special missions for the duration of the war after being converted to transport submarines.

Dolphin (formerly *V-7*) shown under way in about 1932. Its resemblance to the fleet boats of World War II is obvious in this view; in fact, it was the forerunner of the fleet boat design series. (Naval History and Heritage Command)

V-5 Specifications (as built)	
Displacement	Standard 2,730 tons; submerged 4,040 tons
Dimensions	Length: 370ft 7in; beam 33ft 3in
Propulsion	2 diesel engines generating 5,633shp for a maximum surface speed of 17.44kt; submerged speed 8kt
Operating depth	300ft
Range	18,000nm at 10kt; patrol endurance 90 days
Crew	89

Commissioned in June 1932, *V-7* (later *Dolphin*) represented the USN's discontentment with the large and expensive cruiser-type submarines. *V-7* was a much smaller design more suitable for patrol operations and was the first of what became the fleet-type submarines. Its internal layout became the template for these vessels. Because of its smaller size, it carried a smaller torpedo load of 18 internally and three more externally. The boat was equipped with six torpedo tubes – four bow and two stern. Top speed was 17 knots with its German-designed diesels. By the start of the war, the boat was in a poor material condition. *Dolphin* made three war patrols before being transferred to training duties.

V-7 Specifications (as built)	
Displacement	Standard 1,560 tons; submerged 2,240 tons
Dimensions	Length: 319ft 3in; beam 27ft 11in
Propulsion	4 diesel engines (2 main and 2 generator) generating 4,086shp for a maximum surface speed of 17.3kt; submerged speed 8kt
Operating depth	250ft
Range	6,000nm at 10kt; patrol endurance 75 days
Crew	63

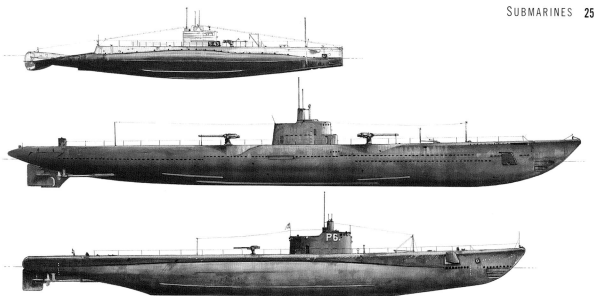

The final two boats of the V Class, later named *Cachalot* and *Cuttlefish*, continued the trend to smaller boats. Both were based on a German World War I design and featured savings in weight and space made possible by a new type of German-designed diesel engine. Another design advance was realized in *Cuttlefish* built by the Electric Boat Company in Groton, Connecticut. The yard made improvements to the boat's internal arrangements and was the first to make significant use of welding for the hull. *Cuttlefish* also received air conditioning and was the first boat fitted with the Mark 1 Torpedo Data Computer. Despite these advanced features, the class was not a success since its small size inhibited speed and endurance. After a few war patrols, they were used for training duties.

V-8 Specifications (as built)	
Displacement	Standard 1,130 tons; submerged 1,650 tons
Dimensions	Length: 271ft 11in; beam 24ft 11in (*V-8* 274ft; beam 24ft 9in)
Propulsion	2 diesel engines generating 3,070shp for a maximum surface speed of 16.5kt; submerged speed 8 knots
Operating depth	250ft
Range	11,000nm at 10kt; patrol endurance 75 days
Crew	45

USN Submarine Classes in the 1930s

Two different types made up the P class. The first was the two-ship Porpoise class built by Portsmouth Navy Yard as an improved *Cachalot*. The lead ship

THE TOP PROFILE DEPICTS an S-class boat, several of which were used for combat duties early in the war despite dating back to 1918–24. Small and fitted with primitive diesel engines, they were handicapped by their limited endurance. **THE MIDDLE PROFILE IS** cruiser-type boat *Argonaut* (formerly *V-4*). The large V-class boats were designed to operate with the main fleet, but this proved impossible since the diesel engines of the late 1920s and early 1930s didn't have sufficient power to propel submarines at the 17–22 knots required for fleet operations. The engineering and hydrodynamic trade-offs for large submarines produced boats that were slow to dive and unwieldy when submerged. **THE BOTTOM PROFILE SHOWS** *Pickerel*, a Perch-class fleet-type boat commissioned in 1936. The fleet boats combined a reliable diesel-electric power plant, a substantial torpedo load, and good endurance to allow long-range patrols. (Artwork by Tony Bryan, © Osprey Publishing)

USN Submarine Design in the 1930s

Beginning in the early 1930s, the USN made significant strides in submarine design and construction. The new classes used the lessons learned from building and operating the V class with an eye on the requirements of a submarine war that would be fought over vast distances in the Pacific. Submarine commanders wanted more speed and reliability, better habitability to increase crew endurance, more torpedoes and torpedo tubes, and larger deck guns. These desires had to be tempered with considerations of cost, manning, and the constant trade-offs of power, displacement, and size.

Progress was fostered by competition between the private shipbuilder Electric Boat Company and the government's Portsmouth Navy Yard. Each was given the general design and specifications in the four-boat FY 1934 program and then separately charged to create a detailed design. The four boats were in essence prototypes of separate classes worked up from the same set of specifications. Portsmouth built *Porpoise* and *Pike*; Electric Boat built *Shark* and *Tarpon*. This unofficial competition proved beneficial in the rapid development of the fleet submarine through the 1930s. The evolution in design during the decade prior to World War II can be seen through the differences in the Porpoise to the Tambor-class boats. This evolution culminated in the Gato- and Balao-class designs, which were the mainstay boats of the war years. Starting after the large V-boats, boats reverted to a generally common length around 300ft and a beam of 24–27ft. The major changes were in the number and location of torpedo tubes, the propulsion equipment arrangement, and the hull construction technique.

The arrangement of torpedo tubes started with four tubes forward and two aft, with two additional deck tubes located in the forward superstructure. The evolution ended with six tubes forward and four aft – all internal. Propulsion equipment was initially a combination of direct-drive diesels and diesel generators in a single engine room space, but led to four diesel generators, two each in two engine rooms, and the electrical controller cubicle and main propulsion motors in a separate compartment. Construction technique started with all-riveted hull, superstructure, and tankage and ended with welded construction throughout. The changes were reflected in a general sense by the class designations, but in reality they overlapped and specific ships in a class did vary widely in their technical specifications, except in their major characteristics. One interesting outcome of the unofficial competition between naval shipyards and civilian shipyards was the division within a single class of the characteristics of the two design groups. The Portsmouth Navy Yard had the lead in the so-called "Government" or "Portsmouth" design while Electric Boat Company had the civilian design. Construction contracts awarded to naval shipyards used the Government design and those awarded to civilian yards used the Electric Boat design. Thus, Mare Island, Portsmouth, and Boston Navy Shipyards used the Government design drawings while Electric Boat, Manitowoc, and Cramp Shipyards used the Electric Boat design drawings. A major difference was in the main diesel generators. Electric Boat units used General Motors engines, while Portsmouth designs used Fairbanks-Morse engines.

was commissioned in 1935. The boats were not considered a success with their riveted hulls, old-style berthing and messing arrangements, mediocre endurance, and unreliable all-electric propulsion plants. Both were retired early in the war and sent to training commands.

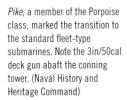

Pike, a member of the Porpoise class, marked the transition to the standard fleet-type submarines. Note the 3in/50cal deck gun abaft the conning tower. (Naval History and Heritage Command)

Porpoise Class Specifications (as built)	
Displacement	Standard 1,310 tons; submerged 1,934 tons
Dimensions	Length: 301ft; beam 24ft 11in
Propulsion	4 main generator engines generating 4,300shp for a maximum surface speed of 18.8kt; submerged speed 8kt
Operating depth	250ft
Range	11,000nm at 10kt; patrol endurance 75 days
Crew	50 (1944)

The other two boats in the FY 1934 program were two Shark-class units (*Shark* and *Tarpon*) built by Electric Boat. They were identical to the Porpoise class in armament (six tubes – four bow and two stern with a capacity of 16 torpedoes) and machinery. The propulsion system used the same one as on the Porpoise class in which high-speed electric motors powered the engines through reduction gears. This diesel-electric drive propulsion system still exhibited growing pains and was not reliable. The boats of this class were the first all-welded submarines built for the USN. An all-welded hull increased underwater survivability and reduced the amount of oil leakage.

Shark Class Specifications (as built)	
Displacement	Standard 1,316 tons; submerged 1,968 tons
Dimensions	Length: 298ft 1in; beam 25ft 1in
Propulsion	4 main generator engines generating 4,300shp for a maximum surface speed of 19.5kt; submerged speed 8kt
Operating depth	250ft
Range	11,000nm at 10kt; patrol endurance 75 days
Crew	50

The USN was so impressed with Electric Boat's Shark class that it ordered six nearly identical boats in for FY 1935. These became the Perch class. The new class carried the same propulsion system but used three different diesel engines. Those built in the government yards had such issues their diesel engines had to be replaced. The engine room was lengthened 2ft to improve access to the machinery. The armament fit was unchanged. Of the six boats, three were built by Electric Boat, two by Portsmouth, and one to Mare Island Navy Yard. The boats built in government yards were the last built with riveted hulls. The class was considered successful and saw extensive wartime action.

Perch Class Specifications (as built)	
Displacement	Standard 1,335 tons; submerged 1,997 tons
Dimensions	Length: 300ft 7in; beam 25ft 1in
Propulsion	4 main generator engines generating 4,300shp for a maximum surface speed of 20.1kt; submerged speed 8kt
Operating depth	250ft
Range	11,000nm at 10kt; patrol endurance 75 days
Crew	50

The FY 1936 submarine build consisted of six units of the Salmon class. As in the previous year, three were built by Electric Boat, two by Portsmouth Navy Yard, and the final boat at the Mare Island Navy Yard. In most regards, this was the USN's preferred fleet boat and it provided the template for future construction. The armament was increased to eight tubes – four each in the bow and stern. Twenty torpedoes were carried internally. A new propulsion system was used to increase top surface speed to over 21 knots on trials. This composite system had one engine and two motors driving each shaft while the other two generator engines were used to charge the batteries. Though cramped, this arrangement proved successful. All saw extensive war service, and none were lost. They were transferred to training duties as more modern units became available.

Salmon Class Specifications (as built)	
Displacement	Standard 1,449 tons; submerged 2,210 tons
Dimensions	Length: 308ft; beam 26ft 2in
Propulsion	2 main and 2 generator engines generating 5,500shp for a maximum surface speed of 21.4kt; submerged speed 9kt
Operating depth	250ft
Range	11,000nm at 10kt; patrol endurance 75 days
Crew	55

The six submarines funded in FY 1937 were similar to the Salmon class. The six units of the Sargo class were allocated to three yards in the manner of the two previous FYs. The new class carried the same armament and the same propulsion system. Among the refinements introduced on the Sargo-class boats were a new higher-capacity battery, 2ft extra in length to alleviate engine room crowding, and other internal alterations. *Squalus* sank on trials in March 1939 but was raised and renamed *Sailfish*. Only one boat was lost during the war.

Sargo Class Specifications (as built)	
Displacement	Standard 1,460 tons; submerged 2,350 tons
Dimensions	Length: 310ft 6in; beam 27ft 1in
Propulsion	2 main and 2 generator engines generating 5,500shp for a maximum surface speed of 20.6kt; submerged speed 8.75kt
Operating depth	250ft
Range	11,000nm at 10kt; patrol endurance 75 days
Crew	55

Only four boats were ordered for FY 1938. The four were split between Electric Boat and Portsmouth Navy Yard. The only difference from the preceding class was a reversion to an all-electric drive. Two of the four boats were war losses.

Seadragon Class Specifications (as built)	
Displacement	Standard 1,450 tons; submerged 2,350 tons
Dimensions	Length: 310ft 6in; beam 27ft 1in
Propulsion	4 main generator engines generating 5,200shp for a maximum surface speed of 20kt; submerged speed 8.75kt
Operating depth	250ft
Range	11,000nm at 10kt; patrol endurance 75 days
Crew	55

USN Submarine Weapons

World War II submarines had two major weapons: the torpedo and the deck gun. The two standard USN wartime torpedoes were the Mark 10 and Mark 14. Both fit the standard 21in torpedo tube and were just short of 22ft long. The Mark 10 was a straight-running torpedo that required the submarine to be pointed directly at the target. The fire-control system for boats that used the Mark 10 consisted of manual slide rules of various designs combined with the intelligence and experience of the submarine's skipper who had to mentally solve the relative motion problem. The Mark 10 had a 497lb warhead and ran at 36 knots to a maximum range of 3,500 yards; in practice, torpedo shots were rarely taken at ranges exceeding 1,000 yards.

Theoretically, the Mark 14 torpedo was a massive improvement. It had two speeds (31.5 knots and 46 knots) that were selected prior to firing and it could make one adjustment to a new course after firing. The speed selection and the setting of the amount of turn were performed either manually or electrically via the fire-control computer from the conning tower. The ability to turn to a new course after firing meant the submarine did not have to be maneuvered to point the torpedo as a part of the firing solution. The Mark 14 torpedo had a 660lb warhead filled with Torpex and could run out to 4,500 yards at high speed and 9,000 yards at slow speed. In practice, the torpedo was almost always used at high speed with little, if any, gyro angle.

The Mark 14 torpedo used the Mark 5 and Mark 6 exploders. The Mark 5 was a contact exploder and the Mark 6 was a magnetic influence exploder. The magnetic exploder was designed to detonate the warhead under the keel of the target, which was potentially much more deadly than a torpedo hitting the side of the ship. However, both exploders had serious design flaws and the torpedo ran as much as 10ft below the set depth. The problems with the torpedoes were exacerbated by the secrecy attached to the magnetic exploder and the initial impulse to blame the submarine skippers and the weapons personnel who maintained and prepared the torpedo. It was not until late 1943 when the contact exploder problem was fixed, the depth problem cured, and

the magnetic exploder was dispensed with that submarines were sent out on patrol with a fully effective weapon. Later in the war, an electric torpedo, designated the Mark 18, was introduced. It was the same size as the Mark 14, was slower at 30 knots, carried a lighter warhead (575lb), and possessed a maximum range of 4,000 yards. Very late in the war the Mark 23 was introduced. It could be fired from depths greater than 150ft and used a hydrophone mounted in the nose of the weapon to direct it toward the loudest noise. It only carried a 95lb warhead sufficient to hole a submarine or knock the screw or rudder off a troublesome escort.

Most USN fleet submarines entered the war with a 3in/50cal deck gun mounted aft of the conning tower. This weapon fired a 13lb projectile with a maximum range of just over 14,000 yards. A few months into the war commanding officers were authorized to have the gun remounted forward where its firing could be directly supervised from the bridge. A handful of submarines carried larger deck guns. *Argonaut*, *Nautilus*, and *Narwhal* carried the largest deck gun on any USN submarine – two 6in/53cal guns, one forward of the conning tower and one aft. Cruiser-type submarines *V-1* to *V-3* were initially fitted with 5in/51cal guns. These were removed early in their careers and ended up on four Tambor-class units during the war. By June 1944, the 4in gun in a wet mount was introduced. These could fire a 33lb shell to a maximum range of over 16,000 yards. The gun that became the standard during the latter stages of the war and which replaced the 3in and 4in guns as boats went through mid-war overhauls was the 5in/25cal. It fired a 53lb projectile to a range of over 14,000 yards. Seven boats were fitted with two 5in/25cals and a dedicated fire-control system. Only one was ready before war's end.

Submarines also carried antiaircraft guns. The initial fit of .50cal and .30cal machine guns proved ineffective and was upgraded by 20mm Oerlikon guns. These guns, either in single or twin mounts, were mounted on platforms forward or aft of the bridge and occasionally on the main deck. A single mount Bofors 40mm gun became available for submarines after mid-1944.

The 12-ship Tambor class was a final peacetime refinement on the ideal fleet boat design before mass wartime production began. The 12 boats in the class were funded six in FY 1939 and six the following year and divided among Electric Boat, Portsmouth Navy Yard, and Mare Island Navy Yard in the usual manner. The refinements incorporated were significant.

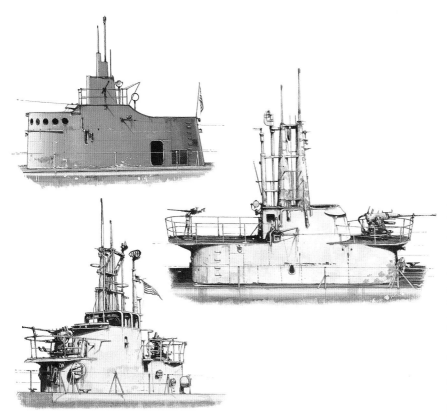

The changes in USN wartime conning towers were driven by the need to reduce their silhouette. Pre- and early-war conning towers were cut down in two phases; one was the reduction of the aft portion and the placement of an antiaircraft gun on the resulting platform. **THE TOP VIEW SHOWS** this on Tambor-class boat *Trout*. All Balao- and Tench-class boats were built with this reduced silhouette. The placement and type of deck gun depended on a combination of the commanding officer's preference, the gun type availability, and the foundation structure available. **THE MIDDLE ILLUSTRATION SHOWS** a 20mm antiaircraft gun on the aft platform and a 40mm forward on the Balao-class boat *Lionfish*. **THE BOTTOM ILLUSTRATION SHOWS** Gato-class boat *Flasher* late in the war. Gato and earlier classes received a further reduction that placed an antiaircraft gun on a forward platform and opened the periscope support structure. To retain its structural strength, the support structure was reinforced by steel beams from one side of the conning tower structure to the other. (Artwork by Tony Bryan, © Osprey Publishing)

In response to requests from submarine commanders, the number of bow tubes was increased to six, all internal; four tubes remained on the stern. The addition of the two tubes brought the overall torpedo capacity to 24. Another modification to the boats' armament was a provision for the much heavier 5in/51cal deck gun to replace the usual 3in/50cal gun decried by submarine commanders as inadequate. Other features directly affecting combat performance were a larger sail, a new type of periscope, and improved sonar and fire-control equipment. To make construction easier and faster, the hull was simplified. These boats were used heavily during the war, and seven were war losses.

Tambor Class Specifications (as built)	
Displacement	Standard 1,475 tons; submerged 2,370 tons
Dimensions	Length: 307ft 3in, beam 27ft 3in
Propulsion	4 main generator engines generating 5,400shp for a maximum surface speed of 20kt; submerged speed 8.75kt
Operating depth	250ft
Range	11,000nm at 10kt; patrol endurance 75 days
Crew	60

PART 3: THE WAR-BUILT CLASSES

The Gato class, totaling 77 boats, was the culmination of a series of incremental improvements beginning with the *Dolphin* launched in 1932. The first six units were repeats of the Tambor class ordered in the FY 1941 program. These boats were lengthened by 5ft to allow the engine room to be divided into two smaller compartments, but otherwise the boats were identical to the Tambor class. Another improvement did not require any actual changes, but rather a decision that the hulls were able to safely operate down to 300ft. After these final modifications, the class went into mass production. Electric Boat built the most boats – 41 – followed by Portsmouth and Manitowoc each with 14 and Mare Island with eight. Of the 77 completed, 20 were lost to enemy action.

The first boats arrived in the Pacific in mid-1942. Throughout the war, only evolutionary modifications were made to these boats, which was a testimony to the excellence of the basic design. The conning tower was modified to permit the addition of 20mm and 40mm guns, and the original 3in/50cal deck gun was replaced by 4in or 5in/25cal guns. The highest number of Gato-class boats available was 64 in 1944. These boats were the backbone of USN wartime submarine operations in the Pacific. Gato-class boats made 587 of the 1,635 war patrols (34 percent) in the Pacific.

Gato Class Specifications (as built)	
Displacement	Standard 1,526 tons; submerged 2,424 tons
Dimensions	Length: 311ft 9in; beam 27ft 3in
Propulsion	4 main generator engines generating 5,400shp for a maximum surface speed of 20.25kt; submerged speed 8.75kt
Operating depth	300ft
Range	11,000nm at 10kt; patrol endurance 75 days
Crew	60 (wartime 81)

The Balao class was the largest class of USN submarines ever built. A total of 256 were ordered, but the war ended before this expansive program could be completed. Only 119 were completed to the original wartime design. Portsmouth led the way with 44 boats, followed by Electric Boat with 40, Manitowoc with 14, Cramp with ten, Mare Island nine, and Boston Navy Yard with two. The Balao class was virtually identical to the preceding Gato class both externally and internally. There was a major

This photograph of Gato-class boat *Dace* was taken immediately after the war. The boat has a 40mm gun on the forward conning-tower platform, both surface and air search radars, and a 5in/25cal deck gun aft. *Dace* was one of the more successful Gatos, having sunk an IJN heavy cruiser in October 1944. (Naval History and Heritage Command)

difference, and it constituted a significant upgrade in the new boats' warfighting capabilities. The Balao class used high-tensile steel on the hulls instead of the previous mild steel. This increased their operating depth to 400ft. Any of the wartime modifications to the Gato-class boats were also incorporated in the Balao class during construction. Another enhancement halfway through the Balao construction program was an improvement in torpedo storage that brought total capacity to 28 weapons.

The fact that these boats could operate down to 400ft was never discovered by the Japanese who continued to think that USN boats were only capable of operating at comparable depths to their own boats. Japanese depth charges were not capable of attacking targets at this depth until late in the war. This, and the fact that the Balao class entered service beginning in February 1943 and most did not appear until the IJN was a shadow of its former self, held war losses to only nine boats.

Sterlet, a Balao-class boat commissioned in October 1943, was externally identical to the Gato class. The boat carries a 20mm and a 40mm gun on its conning tower and a 4in/50cal deck gun aft. The Gato-Balao-class submarine was among the USN's most important weapons of the entire war. (Artwork by Tony Bryan, © Osprey Publishing)

Balao Class Specifications (as built)	
Displacement	Standard 1,525 tons; submerged 2,415 tons
Dimensions	Length: 311ft 9in; beam 27ft 3in
Propulsion	4 main generator engines generating 5,400shp for a maximum surface speed of 20.25kt; submerged speed 8.75kt
Operating depth	400ft
Range	11,000nm at 10kt; patrol endurance 75 days
Crew	81

Archerfish was a Balao-class submarine commissioned in September 1943. On its fifth war patrol on November 28, 1944 off Tokyo Bay, *Archerfish* torpedoed and sank the IJN supercarrier *Shinano*. At 72,000 tons, *Shinano* remains the largest ship ever sunk by a submarine. This is *Archerfish* in June 1945. (Naval History and Heritage Command)

The final refinement to the fleet boat was the Tench class, which was ordered in 1943 and laid down beginning on April 1, 1944. A total of 147 were authorized, but only 80 were ordered. Of these, only 25 were completed. All but two were built in Portsmouth, with Electric Boat and Boston Navy Yard completing one apiece. Most were finished too late to see war service. Externally the boats were indistinguishable from the late Gato-class or Balao-class boats. There were several important internal differences intended to reduce the vulnerability to flooding. Wartime experience demonstrated that the noise generated by high-speed electric motors and reduction gear was a vulnerability since it could be detected by passive ASW sensors. To alleviate this potential weakness, the USN developed low-speed electric motors that used direct drive to drive the shafts. This direct drive propulsion was first trialed on a Balao-class boat and was found to greatly reduce noise.

Submarines photographed passing in review during an inspection by Commander Submarines, Pacific, off Pearl Harbor after the war in 1945. The submarine in the foreground is Tench-class boat *Sarda*, commissioned too late to see war service. The Tench class was a virtual copy of the preceding Gato and Balao classes, at least externally. *Sarda* was fitted with an experimental enlarged conning tower. The boat carries a heavy gun armament of two 5in/25cal deck guns and two single 40mm guns on the conning tower. (Naval History and Heritage Command)

Tench Class Specifications (as built)	
Displacement	Standard 1,570 tons; submerged 2,415 tons
Dimensions	Length: 311ft 8in; beam 27ft 3in
Propulsion	Diesel-electric direct drive with 4 main generator engines generating 5,400shp for a maximum surface speed of 20.25kt; submerged speed 8.75kt
Operating depth	400ft
Range	11,000nm at 10kt; patrol endurance 75 days
Crew	81

USN SUBMARINES IN WORLD WAR II – AN ANALYSIS

The USN's submarine force went from an opening dismal performance to become the most proficient and deadly component in the entire Navy. At the start of the war, things did not go well. Twenty-nine submarines were stationed in the Philippines at Cavite, the naval base near Manila. Of these, six were S-class boats, but the rest were the most modern boats available. Their mission was to help repel the expected Japanese invasion of the Philippines. Not only did they fail to impede the Japanese advance in any serious manner, they accounted for only 14 Japanese ships sunk (two destroyers and 12 merchants) even though they were operating in the middle of extensive Japanese ship concentrations in the Philippines and later in the Dutch East Indies for the next four months.

There were several reasons for this stupendous failure. At the beginning of the war the submarine force suffered from four serious problems. First, the Mark 14 torpedo with the Mark 5 and Mark 6 exploders didn't work. The next problem was the lack of aggressiveness by the individual submarine commanders. This problem was compounded by the inexperience of the skippers in tactics, ship handling, the effects of long patrols under arduous conditions, and the material conditions of the submarines. Many had engine design defects that eventually required wholesale replacement of one engine type, and the ability to quickly and accurately develop torpedo fire-control solutions in combat was proving more difficult than expected.

The third serious problem that plagued the force was the lack of a comprehensive strategy for conducting the submarine war in the Pacific. During much of the early war the force was used reactively and defensively trying to intercept convoys and task forces in a manner that wasted much valuable patrol time. The two principal submarine commands at Pearl Harbor and Fremantle in western Australia were in receipt of intelligence from code breakers who were reading significant portions of the Japanese naval code. The code breakers supplied the submarine commands with information on movements of the Japanese naval and merchant shipping. These messages and this intelligence, generally called ULTRA (after the level of classification), were used to move submarines to areas where they might find targets. This movement had a downside. The communication to and, in the early days, from the submarines gave the Japanese direction-finding information on the location of the submarines. In addition, the constant movement of the submarines wasted valuable time through their transiting from one location to another looking for targets.

The final and perhaps the most telling problem was the unfortunate choice of leaders early in the war. In a time when cooperation was vital, there were clashes between force commanders that slowed the identification and correction of the torpedo problem and the strategy problem.

The situation began to turn around when Admiral Charles Lockwood was placed in command of the submarine force at Pearl Harbor. His view of submarine strategy was focused on conducting long-range offensive patrols in Japanese-controlled waters to slow the importation of raw materials. In addition, instead of having his submarines chase Japanese merchant and warship convoys all over the place, he stationed boats at choke points where convoys would have to transit to and from Japanese home waters.

Finally in late 1943, nearly two years after the start of the war, the problems with the torpedoes were identified and corrected. The Gato- and Balao-class submarines were making their appearance in sufficient numbers

This plate shows Gato-class boat *Tang* savaging a Japanese convoy on the night of October 24–25, 1944 in the northern Taiwan Strait. The boat was under the command of Commander Richard O'Kane, the USN's most successful submarine skipper, credited with 33 Japanese ships sunk. He attacked a convoy on the night of October 23–24 and torpedoed two freighters. The following night he found another large Japanese convoy. *Tang* charged into the midst of the convoy on the surface and O'Kane emptied his six bow and two stern torpedo tubes. Two freighters were confirmed later as sunk. O'Kane returned to fire his last two torpedoes. The last torpedo *Tang* fired that night was a Mark 18 electric torpedo. It broached and made a left turn heading right for *Tang*. O'Kane attempted to avoid it, but it struck *Tang* aft only 20 seconds after being fired. The submarine sank in 180ft of water. Several men were thrown from the bridge into the water, including O'Kane, and 13 more made successful escapes from the forward torpedo room using the escape trunk and Momsen Lungs (an escape apparatus). Only nine men were rescued and imprisoned by the Japanese. All survived their harsh treatment and were liberated at the end of the war. (Artwork by Tony Bryan, © Osprey Publishing)

to relieve the older boats that had seen the brunt of the fighting. By this point most of the non-aggressive commanders had been replaced. The ability of the boat skippers to use the available equipment and the men under their command to form an effective information management team started to solve the difficulties of the torpedo fire control. The result was the virtual annihilation of the Japanese merchant force and the strangling of the Japanese empire.

At its peak, the USN's submarine force consisted of about 230 submarines and just over 17,000 men. The force's effect was far beyond its size. Submarines sank 1,178 merchant ships for a tonnage total just shy of five million tons – 55 percent of all Japanese shipping losses. The other 45 percent was sunk by all the other forces (all Allied air forces, surface forces, and mines) combined. In 1944 alone, Japanese merchant losses totaled over four million tons – a crippling toll. In addition, USN submarines sank 214 IJN ships for another half million tons. To accomplish this, 288 USN subs fired 14,748 torpedoes. The submarine force lost 52 submarines from all causes and just over 3,500 men. This toll in such a small group of men (16,500 personnel who conducted a total of 1,682 patrols) was the highest loss rate in any branch of the USN. Of the 52 boats lost, 41 were to enemy action. Of the 11 not lost to enemy action, two were sunk in friendly-fire incidents, and two by their own torpedoes.

Not only did USN submarines sink ships, but they were also important adjuncts to fleet operations. This was especially the case in 1944 when at the Battle of the Philippine Sea USN submarines provided the only tracking information available on the IJN's battle force during the early parts of the battle as it moved toward the Mariana Islands. During the battle, USN submarines sank two IJN fleet carriers, as opposed to only one by the entire Fast Carrier Task Force. Months later at the Battle of Leyte Gulf, USN submarines did much the same, tracking IJN fleet elements and accounting for four heavy cruisers sunk or damaged and another light cruiser sunk. Throughout the war, submarines performed a variety of special missions across the Japanese-held areas of the Pacific. Beginning in February 1944, they picked up another mission – rescuing downed USN aviators. Admiral Lockwood embraced this mission and quickly set up a scheme for controlling the submarines in specific areas so that he could direct them toward the locations of downed aviators. The lifeguard services resulted in the saving of 504 downed airmen.

CHAPTER 9

THE UNITED STATES NAVY IN WORLD WAR II – AN ASSESSMENT

Before the first Japanese plane appeared over Pearl Harbor, the USN had already laid the foundation for victory. This was in the form of several prewar naval construction bills that ensured the new ships required to fight a global naval war were begun well before the United States formally entered the war, not when the bombs began dropping on Pearl Harbor. In the 1920s and 1930s, the USN had lagged behind the other principal navies in even building up to its treaty limits. In March 1934, the Vinson-Trammell Act authorized the USN to build up to its treaty allowances. The so-called Second Vinson Act, officially known as the Naval Act of May 1938, made provisions for a 20 percent growth of the Navy. Among the new ships authorized were two carriers and three battleships. In the Third Vinson Act of June 1940, fleet tonnage was increased by another 11 percent, this included three more carriers, and many cruisers and submarines.

One of the iconic images of the Pacific War shows *Pennsylvania* leading one other battleship and three cruisers in Lingayen Gulf in January 1945. This was part of the operation to invade the main Philippine island of Luzon and led to a strong response by Japanese suicide aircraft which damaged battleships *Mississippi* and *New Mexico*. (Naval History and Heritage Command)

The fall of France that same month brought the potential German threat into much clearer focus. In July 1940, the Two-Ocean Navy Act increased the size of the fleet by another 70 percent. The size of the resulting fleet was far beyond that which any of the Axis powers could even come close to matching, and in fact was many times greater than their combined production during this period, with the exception of submarines. Some of the ships authorized in 1938, and all of those approved in 1940, were completed during the war. The table below indicates the enormity of this effort.

USN Naval Construction December 1941–August 1945	
Fleet aircraft carriers	17
Light aircraft carriers	9
Escort carriers	75
Battleships	8
Heavy and large cruisers	12
Light cruisers	33
Destroyers	338
Submarines	202
Destroyer escorts	417
Cargo transports	229
Personnel transports	281
Oilers	62
Liberty ships	2,661
This does not include the thousands of amphibious ships and craft that were so numerous they were not even given names.	

Building ships was easy compared to putting together their crews. In 1934, there were only 5,790 officers in service. By July 1940, with the fleet's expansion in full swing, the number of officers increased to 13,162. In total, the USN had 203,127 officers and men on the books in July 1940. This was destined to increase by many times before the end of the war. On August 31, 1945, personnel in naval service reached an astounding total of 4,064,455, including 485,833 Marines and 170,275 Coast Guardsmen.

Incorporation of the flood of new personnel was aided by several factors. New personnel relied on standardized procedures instead of the theoretical education and training favored in the much smaller prewar Navy. Despite the massive influx of new personnel, the USN proved able to incorporate new tactics and technology far faster than did any other Navy, and in

A study in seapower: Task Group 38.3 enters the fleet anchorage at Ulithi Atoll in December 1944 following operations off the Philippines. Light carrier *Langley* leads the column, followed by Essex-class carrier *Ticonderoga*, three battleships and four light cruisers. (Naval History and Heritage Command)

particular the IJN. The IJN did possess an early-war advantage in terms of tactics and training, but the USN's ability to adapt new tactics and better technology swept the initial Japanese advantages aside by 1943. The Japanese fell further behind during the war since their highly trained prewar cadre of ship crews and aviators was heavily attrited and could not be replaced. In comparison, the USN was able to expand rapidly and still maintain qualitative standards.

During the war, the USN virtually reinvented itself. But the first year of the conflict was a difficult period during which the USN displayed some reluctance to embrace new ideas and tactics. The lack of adaptability evinced in the early part of the war can be traced back to the prewar mentality of highly scripted exercises. This was most apparent in the series of night battles in 1942. Admirals relied on prewar doctrine in which gunnery was paramount and the potential of torpedoes was restrained by the refusal to use destroyers in a different manner than practiced before the war. A series of setbacks made it appear that the admirals seemed not to learn from previous battles. What seemed like an inability to learn was caused by the pace of combat that made it difficult to learn lessons and almost immediately apply them combined with the fact that there was no standardized doctrine to fall back on. On top of having to develop new doctrine, the commanders and crews had to incorporate new technology that was also evolving quickly.

Rapidly learning lessons and then applying them turned out to be a strength of the Navy's officers and men. Doctrine was created and evolved quickly under the pressures of combat. This happened across all components of the Navy. Carrier commanders and crews learned how to better incorporate radar into CAP tactics. Gunners on ships became much more proficient at shooting down Japanese aircraft with the application of better fire-control technology. From the first carrier battle in May 1942 to the Battle of Santa Cruz in October, fleet air defense steadily improved and became a factor in deciding the victor in carrier battles. This growing capability eventually gave Admiral Spruance the confidence to throw accepted doctrine to the wind in June 1944 and let the Japanese attack first. It took the arrival of better aircraft and the rectification of the Mark 13 torpedo problem, combined with more stable air groups and better training, to fully incorporate the lessons of offensive carrier warfare. From the first raids on the Marshall Islands conducted by single carrier groups on February 1, 1942, the USN progressed to the launching of thousands of sorties from two dozen carriers against targets on the Japanese home islands during the last month of the war. The power of the carriers to engage naval targets also increased exponentially. On May 4, 1942, 99 sorties by *Yorktown* against a defenseless Japanese force off Tulagi resulted in the destruction of a single destroyer. By 1944 and 1945, USN carriers were able to coordinate massive strikes that sank the two most heavily protected battleships ever constructed.

Surface combat provided another example of the USN's ability to absorb lessons. The USN's "minor" tactics for its cruisers and destroyers proved totally inadequate in the face of the well-trained IJN in a series of night actions off Guadalcanal. Even more important than doctrine and training was the importance of detecting the enemy first and getting the first blows in. Most actions were fought at close range where the effects of gunnery and torpedoes could be deadly, making surprise essential to success. Since the USN possessed radar and the IJN did not, it should have had a huge

advantage in night engagements. But this was not always the case. Early USN radars were fairly primitive, operators were not always well trained in their use, and most importantly commanders did not have a method to receive the information and then act on it. Added to these problems, in the waters off Guadalcanal radar signals bounced off the nearby four islands creating confusion and undermining confidence in the new technology.

The importance of surprise was shown in the Battle of Savo Island. Despite the presence of radar-equipped USN ships, the Japanese surprised the Allied surface force not once, but twice, and took the opportunity to inflict a terrible toll on the unprepared Americans and Australians. In the next night action, the Battle of Cape Esperance, the USN used early warning provided by radar, gained surprise, and won its first night battle of the campaign. The victory was marred by initial confusion after gaining radar contact, incidents of friendly fire, and refusal to use destroyers offensively, but a night victory against the IJN was a notable achievement. Many of

The USN took an extraordinarily long time to recognize the capabilities of IJN torpedoes. This was never more apparent than on the night of November 30, 1942 at the Battle of Tassafaronga. On a single night, four heavy cruisers were torpedoed, and one was lost. This is *New Orleans* camouflaged in Tulagi harbor after losing its bow. If a nearby sanctuary had not been available, the ship would have been lost. (Naval History and Heritage Command)

these same problems were still on display at the First Naval Battle of Guadalcanal, but the melee resulted in an American strategic victory, albeit one achieved at a terrible price. Two nights later, Halsey abandoned all doctrine and sent two battleships into a night action to thwart another Japanese bombardment attempt. Using its radar, *Washington* was able to gain surprise, destroy a Japanese battleship, and defeat the last Japanese attempt to retake the island. After a total thrashing at the Battle of Tassafaronga on the night of November 30–December 1, the USN was left to ponder the lessons of the campaign. Future battles would be fought using radar and radar-directed fire control, destroyers would be given the opportunity to execute torpedo attacks, and efforts were made to increase coordination between ships and the information flow on each ship. Instrumental to this was the development of a concept that became known as the Combat Information Center (CIC).

The concept of the CIC seems simple today, but for 1942 it was revolutionary. Prior to its introduction, the flood of sensor reports quickly overwhelmed the ship's captain who was trying to make decisions as to how to maneuver his ship and what targets his weapons would engage. These decisions were often made instantaneously with incomplete information. The CIC was established to collect and assimilate all incoming data and produce a plot showing the location and status of friendly and enemy units. Once such a plot was created, commanders were able to act more decisively. The first CICs were ad hoc affairs, but by November 1942 their value was so clear that all USN ships were ordered to form one.

Even with the advent of the CIC, the Navy still had hard lessons to learn during the Solomons campaign. The USN could not grasp the true capabilities of the IJN's remarkable Type 93 torpedo. In several actions, USN cruiser-destroyer forces came off second-best against Japanese destroyers. At the Battle of Kolombangara on July 12, 1943, all three cruisers present were hit by Type 93s. Finally, the USN gave up on using cruisers to chase destroyers at night in confined waters. Now USN destroyers took center stage. Working together in established formation to increase cohesiveness and with effective CICs, the destroyers led the way for the remainder of the campaign. A minor tactical victory at the Battle of Vella Lavella was the last IJN surface action victory of the war.

Torpedo combat was another example of USN tactical evolution. At the start of the war, USN torpedo tactics were overshadowed by gunnery tactics. Destroyers were trained to fire at slow-moving battleships in prewar exercises. Of course, the problems with the Mark 15 torpedo did not help. In comparison, the IJN developed a formidable torpedo with capabilities

OPPOSITE USN cruisers had a tough time during the Solomons campaign. This is *Honolulu* after the Battle of Kolombangara with its bow collapsed after it was hit by a torpedo. Remarkably, there were no casualties, but the cruiser was out of action for four months. Another torpedo hit the ship in the stern but failed to explode. (Naval History and Heritage Command)

not appreciated by the USN until late 1943. Use of torpedoes was at the center of Japanese night-fighting tactics. With their destroyers tethered to the cruisers, the USN fought handicapped during the Guadalcanal campaign. By the middle of 1943 during the Solomons campaign, the pieces were in place for a renaissance of USN torpedo tactics. Commanders allowed destroyers to operate independently with torpedoes as their primary weapon. Radar and a functional torpedo made American destroyers formidable weapons.

Ultimate proof of the excellence of USN night-fighting tactics was provided in the Surigao Strait on the night of October 24–25, 1944. As part of his battle plan, the American commander used his destroyer squadrons to conduct torpedo attacks on the approaching Japanese. The destroyer commanders had the benefit of accurate plots created by radar and filtered by their CICs. Using this information, they conducted a series of attacks with the benefit of surprise. Five of the seven Japanese ships were hit by torpedoes; a battleship and three destroyers sank. The three surviving ships were then subjected to a barrage of radar-directed gunnery from cruisers and battleships waiting at the head of the strait. While the Americans were fighting a controlled, set-piece battle, the Japanese acted in a confused manner throughout the battle. The USN's mastery of night combat was complete.

The Battle of Leyte provides a good example of how the USN had surpassed the IJN in all phases of naval warfare. In night combat, the USN had proven itself far superior at the Battle of Surigao Strait. In day surface action, the battle did not provide a dramatic example of USN superiority, but it did supply an example of American flexibility and determination. Off Samar, the IJN's strongest remaining surface force was fought to a standstill by a much smaller USN force with nothing larger than a destroyer. Far to the north, American cruisers and destroyers were mopping up the remnants of the Japanese carrier force. Though the battle included examples of tactical proficiency, it also provided an example of operational-level failure since the USN's formidable fast battleships were not brought into action against the IJN. Over the course of two days, the Fast Carrier Task Force mounted a series of attacks on two Japanese forces, sinking the world's largest battleship, three carriers, and a destroyer, as well as damaging several other ships. Even though they rarely trained for such a mission, the escort carriers also proved themselves proficient at attacking naval targets. Under extreme pressure, they were able to mount strikes that sank three IJN heavy cruisers. Previously, they had sunk the heavy cruiser damaged in the Surigao Strait action and another light cruiser and a destroyer. The submarine force also showed its

boldness and skills by damaging a heavy cruiser on October 23, attacking the IJN's Center Force the next day (sinking two heavy cruisers and heavily damaging a third), and on October 25 sinking a light cruiser.

With the IJN's virtual extinction after Leyte Gulf as an ocean-going navy, the final period of the war brought a new challenge to the USN. In many ways, it was the most severe the USN would face during the war. American excellence in fleet air defense forced the Japanese to adopt suicide tactics. These were about as costly as conventional air attacks and were certainly more effective. Beginning on October 25, kamikazes were the central feature of IJN operations for the final ten months of the war. It was a recognition by the Japanese that the USN had gained almost total ascendancy over the IJN. The invasion of Luzon in January 1945 was the first major use of kamikazes. A series of kamikaze attacks reached a crescendo on January 6 when 13 ships were hit, although all but one survived. After a final burst of attacks against the invasion force in Lingayen Gulf, the Japanese ran out of aircraft. The debut of the kamikaze was unsuccessful in delaying the American invasion, and the largest USN ship sunk was an escort carrier.

The three-month Okinawa campaign was the USN's toughest fight of the war. Though it lacked the excitement of dueling fleets, it was the most bitter and costly naval battle of the war. Aside from the kamikaze offensive, the most recognizable naval aspect of the campaign was the sacrificial sortie of superbattleship *Yamato*. The plan was without any prospect of success and it contributed nothing to Japanese efforts to hold the island since the ship had no chance of reaching the island and its sortie was not even coordinated with kamikaze operations. It was yet another example of poor IJN planning that made USN planning look stellar by comparison. On April 7, *Yamato* was hit by 227 aircraft some 150 miles short of its objective and was sunk by 9–12 torpedoes and seven bombs. This callous stupidity cost 2,498 men their lives and provided another example of the IJN's tendency toward self-immolation.

Okinawa witnessed the height of the kamikaze campaign. From April 6 to June 22, 1,465 suicide aircraft were launched at the USN, most in ten mass attacks. This assault sank 36 ships and damaged some 300. Personnel casualties were 4,907 killed, more than either the Army or Marines lost in the fighting ashore. Nevertheless, the kamikaze was a flawed weapon. It extracted heavy losses from the Japanese and the aircraft used were incapable of sinking large ships. The USN learned to handle the threat and never suffered any delay in its operations attributable to kamikaze operations.

The USN also proved itself the master of amphibious operations during the war. This stemmed from an uncertain beginning in August 1942 at

Guadalcanal. Fortunately, this first landing was not contested. Subsequent landings in the Central and Northern Solomons were vital in mastering the art of amphibious warfare as the USN learned how to conduct landings within range of Japanese air bases and close to significant IJN naval concentrations. Quick unloading minimized the time under an air threat and gave the IJN minimal time to respond. The use of island hopping was possible in the Solomons and on New Guinea since the Japanese could never cover all possible landing sites.

Island hopping was not always possible in the Central Pacific. To take defended Japanese positions like those on Tarawa, Saipan, and Iwo Jima, USN amphibious doctrine had to be sound. Tarawa gave the Americans a bloody nose, but USN amphibious doctrine and capabilities proved able to take even a well-defended island. After the seizure of well-defended Saipan, the Japanese realized the futility of defending against American amphibious assaults. Their new strategy abandoned any attempt to defeat an invasion and concentrated on prolonging the battle and exacting as much attrition as possible.

One of the USN's most important capabilities during the war was its ability to sustain large forces at sea for prolonged periods. As an example of this capability, between October 6, 1944 and January 26, 1945, the Fast Carrier Task Force was at sea for 13 of 16 weeks. This required a dedicated force of 34 fleet oilers. In this view, carrier *Hornet* is shown refueling from an oiler in August 1944. (Naval History and Heritage Command)

The scale of USN amphibious operations continued to grow as the Central Pacific drive accelerated. For the invasion of the Gilberts, 63 amphibious ships embarked 34,214 assault and garrison troops. The Marshalls operation just two months later took 122 ships carrying 85,201 troops. The Marianas was by far the biggest operation so far in the Pacific with 210 ships lifting 141,519 men. Leyte was a comparable operation in size; by October 25, 132,400 men and just under 200,000 tons of supplies were ashore and the invasion fleet had departed. This simple fact made the entire IJN plan at Leyte Gulf pointless. All these were dwarfed by the Okinawa operation with 458 ships embarking 193,852 men. Okinawa was the ultimate exercise in amphibious doctrine and logistics given the complexity of the movements to the island and the size of the force involved. Movement began with almost 183,000 troops and 746,850 tons of supplies loaded aboard 433 assault ships and landing ships at 11 different bases extending from Seattle to Leyte. The final expeditionary force comprised about 1,400 amphibious ships and craft. Had it occurred, the invasion of Kyushu in November 1945 would have far surpassed the size of the forces committed to Okinawa.

Underwriting victory in both theaters was logistics, and the USN far surpassed any other navy in this regard. The scope of the effort was truly spectacular. The Pacific Fleet's Base Force Train possessed 51 craft of all types in 1940. This total included one drydock that could handle up to a destroyer-sized ship, 14 oilers, two repair ships, and one hospital ship. This would have been inadequate for any War Plan Orange-like offensive. To sustain its offensive later in the war, the USN developed the concept of building mobile bases. To accomplish this, in February 1944 Service Squadron Ten was established at the newly captured Majuro Atoll in the Marshalls. This formation was responsible for providing forward support to the fleet for the remainder of the war. By July 1945, the Service Force was assigned 2,930 ships and craft of all types. This included 62 oilers, 21 repairs ships, and six hospital ships. Thirty drydocks were available, including three which could handle battleships. Total personnel assigned to this effort was one-sixth of the entire USN at its peak – 30,369 officers and 425,945 enlisted men. The American focus on logistics translated into ships and task forces being able to remain at sea for weeks and months if necessary. This allowed the pace of the advance to accelerate and undoubtedly shortened the war.

Sustained by a fully mature logistics system, in the final phase of the war the USN was able to exert strategic pressure on the Japanese. The first major strikes against the Japanese homeland were conducted on February 16–17,

1945, by the Fast Carrier Task Force that boasted nine Essex-class carriers and five light carriers. The carriers conducted 2,400 offensive sorties during this period. The largest IJN carrier strike of the war was the attack on Pearl Harbor with a comparatively meager 343 offensive sorties. In March, the fast carriers returned to strike targets on Kyushu. They closed to within 50 miles of the coast, which was not without peril. A Japanese dive-bomber hit carrier *Franklin* that created a conflagration on the flight and hangar decks. The ship came close to sinking, but the crew successfully battled the fires and saved her. The cost was extremely high since 807 of the crew died in the attack. On July 24, the USN conducted a series of strikes against the

This photograph taken at Ulithi Atoll on December 8, 1944 epitomizes the striking power of the USN's carrier force. In the front row are Essex-class carriers *Wasp*, *Yorktown*, *Hornet*, *Hancock* and *Ticonderoga*. Behind them are fleet carrier *Lexington* and two Independence-class light carriers. (Naval History and Heritage Command)

While supporting the Allied invasion of Salerno, *Savannah* was struck by a German radio-guided bomb on September 11, 1943. The bomb struck the top of Turret 3 and penetrated all the way to the magazine. This photograph shows crewmen pouring water down the hole made by the bomb. The ship survived, but this was the heaviest damage suffered by a major USN warship in the European theater. (Naval History and Heritage Command)

remnants of the IJN holed up in the Inland Sea and immobilized through lack of fuel. Since the ships posed no threat, the strikes were dubious from a military standpoint. The cost for the prestige strikes were heavy – 133 aircrew lost. But the last of the IJN was demolished – one carrier, three battleships, two heavy cruisers, and a light cruiser sunk, and another carrier damaged. The end of the war came after two atomic bombs exploded over Japanese cities in August. The surrender was fittingly signed on the deck of battleship *Missouri* with Nimitz signing for the US. To the annoyance of the American admirals, the ceremony was presided over by General MacArthur.

The USN fought a global naval war for over three years and nine months. The cost of victory was high, but perhaps not as high as it could have been against as skilled and determined a foe as the Japanese and the technologically sophisticated Germans. The table below summarizes USN losses during the war, the great majority taking place in the Pacific.

Losses of Principal USN Naval Units 1941-45	
Fleet aircraft carriers	4
Light carriers	1
Escort carriers	6
Battleships	2
Heavy cruisers	7
Light cruisers	3
Destroyers	82
Destroyer escorts	13
Submarines	52

In exchange for these losses, the IJN was virtually annihilated. Of its 20 fleet and light carriers, only four were left afloat at the end of the war. Only one of 12 battleships survived the war afloat. Of the IJN's 18 heavy cruisers, only two remained, and these were both in Singapore in a non-operational condition. Of the 22 light cruisers, one was surrendered immobile, and only the last one to be completed in November 1944 was surrendered intact. Of 34 old destroyers, seven were left afloat. The IJN used 132 modern destroyers during the war; only 32 were left at the end of the war, and the majority of these were just-completed ships which never took part in combat operations. The Japanese employed 190 submarines during war and lost 129 of them. Facing invasion at the end of the war, the IJN was reduced to a mere shadow. The total of undamaged ships left in home waters totaled one light cruiser, 27 destroyers, and some 50 submarines.

From a strategic perspective, Admiral King was not only the most important USN command figure in the war, but one of the most impactful Allied command figures of the entire war. His efforts to fight a naval war in the Pacific were immensely successful from the standpoint of the allocation of US military and naval resources. The USN's major warships were concentrated on the Pacific theater throughout the war. Amphibious forces were roughly split between the two theaters. A significant proportion of American air and ground forces were allocated to the Pacific, certainly more than those required for a defensive strategy fully coherent with the "Germany first" strategy. The impact of King's private war against the Japanese is hard to judge. It remains an open question whether the Allies were capable of and would have committed to a 1943 invasion of northern Europe had a "Germany first" strategy fully guided American resource allocation.

The backbone of Allied sea power was provided by the United States through its immense naval production capabilities and in the form of its Navy, which grew larger, more proficient, and more confident as the war progressed. It is not an exaggeration to state that the USN was the principal enabler of Allied victory in World War II. Even so, the RN's contribution to victory must also be kept in mind. The RN contributed the majority share of Allied naval forces in the North Atlantic and the Mediterranean. The RN also carried the main burden of defeating the U-boat threat. In addition, it kept the sea lanes open in the South Atlantic and Indian Oceans. It took the combined efforts of the RN and the USN to defeat the German submarine threat and keep the sea lanes to Europe open. The huge Allied armies that landed in France in June 1944 and went on to smash German forces and secure final victory were landed and supported without any major German naval challenge.

It would be an exaggeration to state that naval power, or the USN, decided the war in the Allies' favor. But without control of the seas, the Allied cause would have been lost. Control of the seas enabled Allied victory, both in the Atlantic and much more clearly so in the Pacific, where the USN played the leading role.

SELECT BIBLIOGRAPHY

Alden, John D., *The Fleet Submarines in the U.S. Navy*, Naval Institute Press, Annapolis, Maryland (1979)

Breyer, Siegfried, *Battleships and Battle Cruisers 1905–1970*, Doubleday & Company, Garden City, New York (1978)

Campbell, John, *Naval Weapons of World War Two*, Naval Institute Press, Annapolis (2002)

Chesneau, Roger, *Aircraft Carriers*, Naval Institute Press, Annapolis (1992)

Cressman, Robert J., *The Official Chronology of the U.S. Navy in World War II*, Naval Institute Press, Annapolis (2000)

Ewing, Steve, *American Cruisers of World War II*, Pictorial Histories Publishing Company, Missoula, Montana (1984)

Faltum, Andrew, *The* Essex *Aircraft Carriers*, Nautical and Aviation Publishing Company of America, Charleston, South Carolina (2000)

Faltum, Andrew, *The* Independence *Light Aircraft Carriers*, Nautical and Aviation Publishing Company of America, Charleston, South Carolina (2002)

Frank, Richard B., *Tower of Skulls*, W.W. Norton & Company (2020)

Friedman, Norman, *Battleship Design and Development 1905–1945*, Mayflower Books, New York (1978)

Friedman, Norman, *Naval Radar*, Conway Maritime Press, Greenwich (1981)

Friedman, Norman, *U.S. Aircraft Carriers*, Naval Institute Press, Annapolis (1983)

Friedman, Norman, *U.S. Cruisers*, Naval Institute Press, Annapolis (1984)

Friedman, Norman, *U.S. Battleships*, Naval Institute Press, Annapolis (1985)

Friedman, Norman, *U.S. Submarines Through 1945*, Naval Institute Press, Annapolis (1995)

Friedman, Norman, *U.S. Destroyers* (revised edition), Naval Institute Press, Annapolis (2004)

Friedman, Norman, *Naval Firepower*, Naval Institute Press, Annapolis (2008)

Gregor, Rene, *Battleships of the World*, Naval Institute Press, Annapolis (1997)

Hodges, Peter, *The Big Gun*, Naval Institute Press, Annapolis (1981)

Hone, Trent, *Learning War*, Naval Institute Press, Annapolis (2018)

Ireland, Bernard, *Jane's Battleships of the 20th Century*, HarperCollins Publishers, New York (1996)

Jordan, John, *Warships After Washington*, Naval Institute Press, Annapolis (2011)

Marriott, Leo, *Treaty Cruisers*, Pen and Sword Maritime, Barnsley (2005)

Mawdsley, Evan, *The War for the Seas*, Yale University Press, New Haven (2019)

Morison, Samuel Eliot, *History of United States Naval Operations in World War II, Volume II, Operations in North African Waters, October 1942–June 1943*, Little, Brown and Company, Boston (1975)

Morison, Samuel Eliot, *History of United States Naval Operations in World War II, Volume III, The Rising Sun in the Pacific, 1931–April 1942*, Little Brown and Company, Boston (1975)

Morison, Samuel Eliot, *History of United States Naval Operations in World War II, Volume V, The Struggle for Guadalcanal, August 1942–February 1943*, Little, Brown and Company, Boston (1975)

Morison, Samuel Eliot, *History of United States Naval Operations in World War II, Volume VI, Breaking the Bismarck's Barrier, 22 July 1942–1 May 1944*, Little Brown and Company, Boston (1975)

Morison, Samuel Eliot, *History of United States Naval Operations in World War II, Volume VII, Aleutians, Gilberts, and Marshalls, June 1942–April 1944*, Little, Brown and Company, Boston (1975)

Morison, Samuel Eliot, *History of United States Naval Operations in World War II, Volume VIII, New Guinea and the Marianas, March 1944–August 1944*, Little, Brown and Company, Boston (1975)

Morison, Samuel Eliot, *History of United States Naval Operations in World War II, Volume IX, Sicily-Salerno-Anzio, January 1943–June 1944*, Little Brown and Company, Boston (1975)

Morison, Samuel Eliot, *History of United States Naval Operations in World War II, Volume X, The Atlantic Battle Won, May 1943–May 1945*, Little, Brown and Company, Boston (1975)

Morison, Samuel Eliot, *History of United States Naval Operations in World War II, Volume XI, The Invasion of France and Germany, 1944–1945*, Little, Brown and Company, Boston (1975)

Morison, Samuel Eliot, *History of United States Naval Operations in World War II, Volume XII, Leyte, June 1944–January 1945*, Little, Brown and Company, Boston (1975)

Morison, Samuel Eliot, *History of United States Naval Operations in World War II, Volume XIII, The Liberation of the Philippines: Luzon, Mindanao, the Visayas, 1944–1945*, Little, Brown and Company, Boston (1975)

Morison, Samuel Eliot, *History of United States Naval Operations in World War II, Volume XIV, Victory in the Pacific, 1945*, Little, Brown and Company, Boston (1975)

Newhart, Max, *American Battleships*, Pictorial Histories Publishing Company, Missoula, Montana (1995)

O'Hara, Vincent, *The U.S. Navy Against the Axis*, Naval Institute Press, Annapolis (2007)

O'Hara, Vincent, Dickson, W. David, and Worth, Richard, *On Seas Contested*, Naval Institute Press, Annapolis (2010)

Reynolds, Clark, *The Fast Carriers*, Naval Institute Press, Annapolis (1968)

Robbins, Guy, *The Aircraft Carrier Story, 1908–45*, Cassell, London (2001)

Rohwer, Jurgen, *Chronology of the War at Sea 1939–1945*, Naval Institute Press, Annapolis (2005)

Sumrall, Robert F., "The Yorktown Class," *Warship 1990*, Naval Institute Press, Annapolis (1990)

Symonds, Craig L., *World War II at Sea*, Oxford University Press, New Haven (2018)

Terzibaschitsch, Stefan, *Battleships of the U.S. Navy in World War II*, Bonanza Books, New York (1977)

Terzibaschitsch, Stefan, *Escort Carriers and Aviation Support Ships of the US Navy*, Rutledge Press, New York (1981)

Terzibaschitsch, Stefan, *Cruisers of the U.S. Navy in 1922–1962*, Naval Institute Press, Annapolis (1984)

Terzibaschitsch, Stefan, *Submarines of the U.S. Navy*, Arms and Armour Press, New York (1991)

Whitley, M.J, *Destroyers of World War Two*, Naval Institute Press, Annapolis (1988)

Whitley, M.J, *Cruisers of World War Two*, Naval Institute Press, Annapolis (1995)

Whitley, M.J, *Battleships of World War Two*, Naval Institute Press, Annapolis (1998)

Y'Blood, William T., *Hunter-Killer*, Naval Institute Press, Annapolis (1983)

Y'Blood, William T., *The Little Giants,* Naval Institute Press, Annapolis (1987)

INDEX

References to images and maps are in **bold**.